LITIGATING THE SEXUAL HARASSMENT CASE

A GUIDE FOR PLAINTIFF AND DEFENSE ATTORNEYS

JUANITA B. LUIS,

EDITOR

Tort and Insurance Practice Section
American Bar Association

Cover design by Laura Jacobson for Seven Rays Inc.

Printed in the United States of America.

Library of Congress Catalog Card Number 94-72687
ISBN 1-57073-036-9

99 98 97 96 95 5 4 3 2

CONTENTS

FOREWORD

The field of sexual harassment law continues to be one of the hottest and fastest growing areas of employment discrimination and employment tort law on both the state and federal levels. Unlike other forms of employment discrimination, sexual harassment claims are often joined with related tort claims for emotional distress, assault, invasion of privacy and so forth. These claims provide for jury trials (which are now also available under Title VII) and for opportunities to recover unlimited damages, given the right set of facts. These cases, more often than not emotionally super-charged, require some of the most sophisticated skill and handling of any type of employment law trial. Thus, they provide serious challenges to all members of the employment law bar, especially those not used to trying cases in front of a jury.

As serious and important a subject as this is, the Supreme Court has only looked at this issue twice, once in 1986 and again in a decision dated November 1993. In *Meritor Savings Bank v. Vinson,* 477 U.S. 57 (1986), then-Justice Rehnquist delivered the opinion of the Court and made it clear that a plaintiff could state a claim for hostile environment sexual harassment so long as the harassment was "sufficiently severe or pervasive 'to alter the conditions of [the victim's] employment and create an abusive working environment.' " To state such a claim, a plaintiff would not have to prove a "tangible" economic-type loss as had been contended by some defendants and courts. The Court also held that the test for a sexual harassment claim was whether the sexual conduct was "unwelcome" and not its voluntariness. Finally, the Court declined to establish firm guidelines for employer liability.

In November 1993, the Supreme Court handed down its second and most recent pronouncement on the law of sexual harassment. *Harris v. Forklift Systems, Inc.,* __U.S. __, 63 FEP Cases (BNA) 225 (November 9, 1993). The Court accepted this case to resolve a split amongst the circuits as to whether a claim solely for hostile environment sexual harassment required proof of a tangible psychological injury to the employee. The Court answered in the negative. "So long as the environment would reasonably be perceived, and is perceived, as hostile or abusive, [citation omitted], there is no need for it also to be psychologically injurious." The result of this decision will be to create more cases of sexual harassment being brought forward meritoriously. Such claims are obviously fact intensive and provide added grist for the jury trial system.

This book, which focuses on sexual harassment law and trials, is meant to educate both plaintiff and defense attorneys. In addition, this book provides guidance to employees who are victims of sexual harassment and to human resource personnel concerned with maintaining a workplace environment free from sexual hostility or abusiveness. More particularly, this collective work is designed to assist lawyers and non-lawyers in dealing with the substantive and procedural intricacies of the various statutory and common law claims which protect individuals against sexual harassment in the workplace. Additionally, this resource tool provides invaluable guidance in pretrial and trial tactics from both the plaintiff and defense perspectives. In 1991 and 1992, the Employer-Employee Relations Committee of the Tort and Insurance Practice Section held two National Institutes on the subject of the "Trial of a Sexual Harassment Case." Both National Institutes were extremely successful and created a great demand for the written material published at the Institutes. This book is a compilation of that written material and has been updated to include recent developments in this evolving area of the law. Each of the papers was prepared by an individual with expertise in his or her respective field.

The papers contained herein also present diverse viewpoints on compliance and litigation issues generally. This compilation also addresses various current and socially relevant questions relating to sexual harassment issues. Since sexual harassment claims are growing significantly, it follows that there is an increasing need for education and debate regarding this subject.

I hope that this book is helpful to those who are seeking compliance with federal and state laws and also to those involved in this complex and expanding area of litigation. The goal the American Bar Association hopes to accomplish through the publication of these papers is to give guidance and education in the law of sexual harassment along with guidance on successful trial techniques associated therewith.

Peter Bennett
Portland, Maine
Chair, Employer-Employee Relations Committee

PETER BENNETT

Peter Bennett is managing partner in the Portland, Maine, law firm of Herbert H. Bennett and Associates, P.A. Mr. Bennett represents management in labor law and employment matters throughout New England and upstate New York. These matters include union campaigns, NLRB and other government agency proceedings, contract negotiations, human rights proceedings, employment litigation, arbitration hearings (against unions and individuals), and other matters. He is a frequent speaker on these and other topics which relate to his practice.

Mr. Bennett received an A.B. degree, with honors, from Harvard College, a J.D. degree, with honors, from Boston University School of Law and an M.B.A. degree from Boston University Graduate School of Management. After graduation he practiced labor law with Fulbright & Jaworski in Houston, Texas.

Mr. Bennett is Chair of the TIPS Employer-Employee Relations Committee. He serves on the Executive Committee of the American Trial Lawyers Association's Employment Rights Section. He is also a member of and is active in other Bar groups.

Mr. Bennett is also quite active in community affairs including United Way, Junior Achievement (Board of Directors), Boston University School of Law (Vice President of Maine Alumni Chapter) and Phillips Academy.

SEXUAL HARASSMENT AND RELATED EMPLOYMENT TORTS: THE EMPLOYER'S PERSPECTIVE

BRUCE S. HARRISON
AND
ALISA H. REFF
SHAWE & ROSENTHAL
BALTIMORE, MARYLAND

I. INTRODUCTION

In his book of the same title, E.B. White inquired: "Is Sex Necessary?" Many companies ask themselves the same question when faced with claims involving sexual issues. The reality is that employees have always possessed sexual feelings upon which they could choose to act. The only difference is that today their choices may involve their employers in convoluted and costly litigation. Thus, the prudent employer must become informed of the sources of its potential liability for sexual harassment and related claims, as well as various strategies to reduce the risks of such allegations.

Before reviewing some of the myriad causes of actions that have been spawned by sexual conduct/misconduct in the employment environment, one point should be stressed. While we often speak about the value of preventive lawyering, it is still tempting for lawyers, particularly litigators, to focus on the defenses to actual claims. Be that as it may, employers would be wise to concentrate their attention on claims avoidance when it comes to sexual harassment. In fact, it may be critical to the defense of such contentions that an employer show it was aware of the potential for misconduct and took reasonable steps to ward off its actual occurrence, even if those steps ultimately are proven insufficient for that purpose.

II. Sexual Harassment Defined

There is not complete consensus as to what distinguishes unlawful sexual harassment from the acceptable (at least in a legal context) expression of sexual feelings. A decade of litigation, however, has substantially narrowed the area for disputes.

The first widely promulgated view concerning what constitutes unlawful sexual harassment was contained in guidelines issued by the EEOC in 1980. They define sexual harassment as:

> . . . Unwelcome sexual advances, requests for sexual favors, and other verbal or physical conduct of a sexual nature constitute sexual harassment when (1) submission to such conduct is made either explicitly or implicitly a term or condition of an individual's employment, (2) submission to or rejection of such conduct by an individual is used as the basis for employment decisions affecting such individual, or (3) such conduct has the purpose or effect of unreasonably interfering with an individual's work performance or creating an intimidating, hostile, or offensive working environment.[1]

This general definition has been adopted by the courts, including the Supreme Court in its decision in *Meritor Savings Bank. FSB v. Vinson*,[2] discussed below.

Others have somewhat differently stated the same propositions. Thus, courts often divide sexual harassment claims into two categories: "quid pro quo" allegations and "hostile environment" contentions. An allegation of quid pro quo sexual harassment is one in which the plaintiff alleges that sexual considerations were required in return for obtaining or retaining job benefits. A hostile environment allegation is one in which the claimant contends that he or she was subjected to unwelcome conduct which may have had no economic effect but was so pervasive that it altered the conditions of employment and created an abusive working environment.[3]

In *Henson v. City of Dundee*,[4] a former police dispatcher brought a Title VII action against the city alleging, among other things, that she was the victim of sexual harassment because the chief of police created a hostile and offensive working environment for women in the police station. The court held that "under certain circumstances the creation of an offensive or hostile work environment due to sexual harassment can violate Title VII irrespective of whether the complainant suffers tangible job detriment." In reaching this conclusion, the court stated that:

> Sexual harassment which creates a hostile or offensive environment for members of one sex is every bit the arbitrary barrier to sexual equality at the work place that racial harassment is to racial equality. Surely, a requirement that a man or woman run a gauntlet of sexual abuse in return for the privilege of being allowed to work and make a living can be as demeaning and disconcerting as the harshest of racial epithets.

III. Elements Of Proof In A Sexual Harassment Case

Although the harm suffered may be different, four of the five elements of a prima facie case are the same for quid pro quo and hostile environment claims of sexual harassment. In both instances, a claimant has to prove:

1. membership in a protected class;
2. that he or she was subject to unwelcome sexual harassment;
3. that the harassment complained of was based upon sex; and
4. a basis for imposing respondeat superior liability.

Additionally, in a quid pro quo case the plaintiff has to prove that her reaction to the harassment complained of affected tangible aspects of her compensation, terms, conditions, or privileges of employment. A plaintiff alleging a hostile environment claim has to prove that the harassment was so severe and pervasive to alter the conditions of the victim's employment and create an abusive working environment.[5]

Any dispute about the viability of the hostile environment theory of sexual harassment was put to rest by the Supreme Court in its decision in *Meritor Savings Bank* and reaffirmed in its decision in *Harris*.[6] In concluding that a plaintiff may establish a violation of Title VII by proving that discrimination based on sex has created a hostile or abusive work environment, the Court relied heavily on the Guidelines issued by the EEOC.[7]

A. Membership in a Protected Class

Courts addressing situations where the alleged harasser is of the same sex as the individual being harassed, have held that they raise viable Title VII claims. In *Wright v. Methodist Youth Services, Inc.*,[8] for example, a male plaintiff alleged that he was discharged because he rejected advances made toward him by his male supervisor. The court recognized that the typical sexual harassment cases are predicated on the notion that making a demand of a female employee that would not be made of a male employee involves sex discrimination. It held, however, that the "the obverse of that coin -- an alleged demand of a male employee that would not be directed to a female," also stated a claim for sexual harassment.

A distinction should be made between homosexual sexual harassment[9] and discrimination based on an individual's sexual preference. For example, a male employee who alleged sexual harassment based on the hostile environment theory due to him being mental harassed by male co-workers who disapproved of his live-in relationship with another man, failed to establish a prima facie case of sexual harassment. There the harassment was based on sexual preference and not gender.[10]

An individual may state a claim of sexual harassment by alleging that the person has been harmed by another employee's accommodation of a supervisor's sexual requests. In *Toscano v. Nimmo*,[11] the plaintiff asserted that in order for a woman to be selected for a particular position, it was necessary that she grant a management representative sexual favors. She presented evidence that the selecting official was having an affair with the individual ultimately picked for the job. The court held that the plaintiff had stated a viable claim as there was credible evidence that the granting of sexual favors was a condition for promotion.

DeCintio v. Westchester County Medical Center[12] presented a similar fact pattern as *Toscano*, but there the court reached a different conclusion.

In *DeCintio*, the plaintiffs, male physical therapists, brought an action against their employer alleging that they were unfairly disqualified from promotion so that a woman with whom the Program Administrator was romantically engaged could be hired. Relying on the same portion of the EEOC's Guidelines as was cited by the court in *Toscano*, the Second Circuit concluded that such a claim was not cognizable. It reasoned that "submission" implies an element of coercion or harassment, which was present in *Toscano* but not *DeCintio*. The court also noted that any female employee interested in the job would have found herself in exactly the same situation as the male plaintiffs, because no one but the individual selected would have been considered for the position. It concluded that though the defendant's actions may not have been fair, they did not violate Title VII.

Since *Toscano* and *DeCintio*, the EEOC has issued a memorandum providing guidance to the Commission's field staff on the extent to which an employer should be held liable for discriminating against individuals who are qualified for a specific position because another individual submitted to sexual advances or requests. The memo states that isolated instances of favoritism towards a "paramour" are not prohibited but that favoritism based upon coerced sexual conduct may constitute quid pro quo harassment and widespread favoritism may constitute hostile environment harassment.[13]

B. Unwelcomeness

The crux of any sexual harassment claim is that the alleged sexual advances were "unwelcome." Conduct is "unwelcome in the sense that it is unsolicited or uninvited and is undesirable or offensive to the employee."[14]

The fact that the sexual conduct at issue was voluntary does not mean that it was not unwelcome. In *Meritor Savings Bank*, the district court had concluded that if an intimate or sexual relationship did exist between the plaintiff and her manager it was a voluntary one, and therefore did not constitute harassment. In affirming the appellate court's reversal, the Supreme Court discussed the difference between "voluntary" and "unwelcome". The Court stated that "[t]he gravamen of any sexual harassment claim is that the alleged sexual advances were 'unwelcome"'. The court further stated that the fact that sex-related conduct is "voluntary," in the sense that the complainant was not forced to participate against her will, is not a defense to a sexual harassment claim. The correct inquiry is whether the plaintiff by her conduct indicated that the alleged sexual advances were unwelcome, not whether the actual participation in sexual intercourse was voluntary.

C. RESPONDEAT SUPERIOR

One factor which the EEOC considers in determining welcomeness is whether the employer provided an effective means of communicating complaints of sexual harassment, and whether the alleged victim utilized it:

> When welcomeness is at issue, the investigation should determine whether the victim's conduct is consistent, or inconsistent, with her assertion that the sexual conduct is unwelcome . . . . If the victim failed to complain or delayed in complaining, the investigation must ascertain why.
>
> . . .
>
> When there is some indication of welcomeness or when the credibility of parties is at issue, the charging party's claim will be considerably strengthened if she made a contemporaneous complaint or protest.[15]

Courts and the EEOC have delineated the standards for determining an employer's liability for sexual harassment. The EEOC, in its brief in *Meritor Savings Bank*, took the position that there should be two different standards for employer liability depending on the type of sexual harassment alleged. In a quid pro quo case, the Commission urged, the employer should be held strictly liable, as it was the employer's delegation of authority that empowered the supervisor to undertake the actions at issue.[16] Under this view, the employer would be liable whether or not the employer knew, should have known, or approved of the supervisor's actions. Although it did not issue a definitive ruling on the subject, the Supreme Court in *Meritor Savings Bank* did conclude that "the Court of Appeals erred in concluding that employers are always automatically liable for sexual harassment by their supervisors . . . [and that] absence of notice to an employer does not necessarily insulate that employer from liability."

As to hostile environment claims, it is generally agreed that an employer should be held liable only if it knew or should have known of the harassment in question and failed to take prompt remedial action.[17]

As one court has stated

> An employer's response after learning of an employee's harassment may negate liability in a 'hostile environment' case, but it is not relevant under quid pro quo theory, which imposes strict liability on employers for the conduct of supervisory personnel who exercise significant control over an employee's firing, hiring, or conditions of employment.[18]

D. Hostile Environment

The EEOC considers the following factors (not to exclude others) in determining whether harassment was so severe and pervasive that it created a hostile environment:

- whether the conduct was verbal or physical, or both
- how frequently it was repeated
- whether the conduct was hostile and patently offensive
- whether the alleged harasser was a co-worker or a supervisor
- whether others joined in perpetrating the harassment
- whether the harassment was directed at more than one individual

In *Henson*, the plaintiff made out her prima facie case where she alleged the harasser subjected her and co-workers to "numerous harangues of demeaning sexual inquiries and vulgarities. . .and repeatedly requested that she have sexual relations with him" over the course of two years. A hostile environment was shown in *Paroline v. Unisys Corp.*,[19] where the employee had been subject to unwanted touching, feared coming to work, and suffered a "depressive neurosis."

IV. Common Evidentiary Issues In Sexual Harassment Cases

A. Evidence of the Accused's Involvement in Other Sexual Harassment Incidents.

An alleged victim of sexual harassment may, in certain instances, introduce evidence of the accused's involvement in other sexual harassment incidents. For example, in *Jones v. Flagship International*,[20] the Fifth Circuit held that although testimony with respect to sexually harassing incidents reported by other females may be relevant in a class action suit, it did not bear on the plaintiff's individual claim of sexual harassment in the absence of evidence that such incidents affected her psychological well-being.

On the other hand, in *Priest v. Rotary*,[21] the plaintiff established her prima facie hostile environment case, at least in part, by showing that the employer subjected other female waitresses to treatment similar to her and she was aware of those incidents. Similarly, in *Ambrose v. U.S. Steel Corp.*,[22] and *Sims v. Montgomery County Commission*,[23] the courts held that evidence tending to show harassment of women other than the plaintiff was directly relevant to whether the employer created an environment violative of Title VII. As the court in *Sims* explained, evidence of prior acts is especially important in a sexual harassment case because the issue for the court is not merely whether there was harassment, but whether the harassment was so pervasive or severe as to create an abusive working atmosphere. "Recent acts of harassment could take on a more oppressive reality when considered against a backdrop of prior harassment."

B. EVIDENCE RELATING TO ACCUSED'S PAST BEHAVIOR OR REPUTATION.

Some claimants have introduced evidence of a more generalized nature regarding the alleged harasser's past behavior or general reputation. For example, in *Jones v. Lyng*,[24] the court took into consideration the director's prior reputation as a "womanizer" in holding that an atmosphere of sexual harassment had been created.

Similarly, in *Toscano*, the court considered the accused harasser's "total inability to separate his work life from personal matters' and his own description of himself as "a life-long 'womanizer'".[25]

C. EVIDENCE RELATING TO THE ACCUSER'S PRIOR SEXUAL CONDUCT

In *Meritor Savings Bank*, the district court allowed testimony about the plaintiff's "dress and personal fantasies." The appellate court, however, stated that such evidence "had no place in this litigation". The Supreme Court disagreed. While acknowledging that consent is not a defense to a sexual harassment claim (the question being whether the activities at issue were unwelcome), it concluded that it does not follow that a complainant's sexually provocative speech or dress is irrelevant as a matter of law in determining whether he or she found particular sexual advances unwelcome. Similarly, in *EEOC v. Grinnell Corp.*,[26] the court held that an employee's participation or encouragement of certain behavior might sometimes preclude a finding that the conduct was unwelcome.

In *Rabidue v. Osceola Refining Co.*,[27] the plaintiff brought an action against her former employer alleging sexual discrimination and hostile environment sexual harassment. The court concluded that in a hostile and/or abusive work environment sexual harassment case, the trier of fact must adopt the perspective of a reasonable person's reaction to a similar environment under essentially like or similar circumstances. Thus, a proper evaluation of the case, the court held, requires consideration of such objective and subjective factors as:

> the nature of the alleged harassment, the background and experience of the plaintiff, her coworkers, and supervisors, the totality of the physical environment of the plaintiff's work area, the lexicon of obscenity that pervaded the environment of the work place both before and after the plaintiff's introduction into its environs, coupled with the reasonable expectation of the plaintiff upon voluntarily entering that environment.

Although consideration may be given to the background and experience of the plaintiff, the amount of weight they should be given is generally within the fact finder's discretion. In *Barrett v. Omaha National Bank*,[28] the plaintiff's past actions were accorded great weight by the district court when it decided not to give absolute credence to her rendition of the facts stating that "[i]t is clear that [the plaintiff] was not, in every instance, a mere bystander when it came to talk of sexual activity." On the other hand, the Fourth Circuit held that while a plaintiff's past conduct including use of foul language and sexual innuendo may be taken into consideration, such action in a consensual setting "does not waive [a plaintiff's] 'legal protections against unwelcome harassment"'.[29]

V. "Reasonable Woman" Or "Reasonable Person"

While there have been courts that have adopted the standard of a "reasonable woman"[30] as opposed to a "reasonable person", this distinction has not gained favor. The Ninth Circuit which recognized the "reasonable woman" standard in *Ellison v. Brady*, explained:

> We adopt the perspective of a reasonable woman primarily because we believe that a sex-blind reasonable person standard tends to be male-biased and tends to systematically ignore the experiences of women. The reasonable woman standard does not establish a higher level of protection for women than men (citations omitted).[31]

Similarly, in *Robinson v. Jacksonville Shipyards. Inc.*,[32] the court observed:

> The objective standard asks whether a reasonable person of Robinson's sex, that is, a reasonable woman, would perceive that an abusive working environment has been created.
>
> . . .
>
> A reasonable woman would find that the working environment at JSI was abusive. This conclusion reaches the totality of the

> circumstances, including the sexual remarks, the sexual jokes, the sexually-oriented pictures of women and the nonsexual rejection of women by coworkers . . . . The fact that some female employees did not complain of the work environment or find some behaviors objectionable does not affect this conclusion concerning the objective offensiveness of the work environment as a whole.

Most courts have not seen fit to adopt a "reasonable woman" standard. Further, while not explicitly discussing the issue, the Supreme Court's holding in *Harris*[33] suggests that it is unlikely to support such a distinction. Thus, the Court held that,

> conduct that is not severe or pervasive enough to create an objectively hostile or abusive work environment -- an environment that a reasonable person would find hostile or abusive -- is beyond Title VII purview. Likewise, if the victim does not subjectively perceive the environment to be abusive, the conduct has not actually altered the conditions of the victim's employment, and there is no Title VII violation.

The Court went on to explain that whether an environment is "hostile" or "abusive" can be determined only by looking at all the circumstances. These may include:

> the frequency of the discriminatory conduct; its severity; whether it is physically threatening or humiliating, or a mere offensive utterance; and whether it unreasonably interferes with an employee's work performance. The effect on the employee's psychological well-being is, of course, relevant to determining whether the plaintiff actually found the environment abusive. But while psychological harm, like any other relevant factor, may be taken into account, no single factor is required.

VI. Preventive Measures

As previously discussed, there are compelling reasons for taking affirmative steps to prevent valid claims of sexual harassment. For one thing, employers should not tolerate supervisor or co-worker harassment of their employees, whether such harassment is based on the individual's sex, race, national origin, or any other basis. Second, the law imposes an obligation on employers to take certain steps to prevent sexual harassment, an obligation that can be ignored only at a company's peril. Finally, efforts to prevent sexual harassment may operate as an affirmative defense to certain sexual harassment claims.

Initially, an employer should adopt and publish a policy prohibiting sexual harassment. The policy should be specific with respect to sexual harassment and not be grouped together with other forms of discrimination. The policy should also set forth a procedure to be followed by employees who believe they have been a victim of harassment. The complaint procedure should include the identification of individuals other than the employee's supervisor with whom the employee can discuss the situation. The policy should be widely disseminated to the employees and posted on company bulletin boards. The policy and procedures set forth therein should be uniformly followed and strictly enforced.

The employer should reinforce the substance of its policy against sexual harassment with its managers and supervisors and provide them with training concerning how to respond if a complaint of harassment is lodged with them and how to recognize conduct that might be subject to harassment claims.

Kotcher v. Rosa & Sullivan Appliance[34] is one of many cases that illustrates the benefits of a sound policy prohibiting sexual harassment. There, the Plaintiffs brought a claim under Title VII against their former employer alleging that they were sexually harassed by their supervisor. They asserted they had been subject to continuous episodes of sexual harassment by their supervisor, most particularly vulgar comments and gestures. The employer had an established procedure for employees to report sexual harassment. The employees acknowledged that they were aware of the procedure and they chose not to use it. Moreover, when the complaint procedure was finally utilized by these employees, the employer took immediate action. (Within twenty-four hours of receiving the complaint, an investigation was conducted which resulted in the offending manager being demoted and transferred.)

The court concluded that under these facts, even though the plaintiffs succeeded in showing that the actions of the manager were unwelcome and were of a sufficient pervasiveness to create a hostile work environment, they failed to state a claim under Title VII as they did not report the conduct to their employer in a timely manner.

Similarly, in *Saxton v. At&T,*[35] the court held that the plaintiff's claim of sexual harassment was deficient because she did not establish that AT&T "failed to take prompt and appropriate remedial action upon discovering the harassment." It was undisputed that the plaintiff's department head began an investigation the day after he was advised of the plaintiff's complaint, that he completed a detailed report two weeks later, and that the alleged harasser was transferred to another department within five weeks after the department manager learned that the plaintiff was not interested in a transfer herself. The court acknowledged that AT&T's remedial efforts may not have met the plaintiff's expectations, but they were both timely and reasonably likely to prevent the conduct underlying her complaint from recurring and that is all that Title VII requires. See also, *Swentek v. USAir, Inc.*,[36] wherein the court concluded that in taking remedial action, "USAir was obliged to investigate [the plaintiff's] charges and to present a reasonable basis for its subsequent actions. It was not, however, required to credit all of [the plaintiff's] allegations in order to escape liability."

A. Receiving a Complaint of Sexual Harassment

When a complaint of sexual harassment is lodged, the employer should obtain as much information as possible concerning the nature of the allegations. The complaining party should be encouraged to be as specific as possible in describing the harassing incidents, including the names of people who might have seen or heard of the events she alleges took place, as well as others who may have suffered similar harassment.

At the time the complaint is made, the employer should obtain the individual's consent to investigate. Consideration should be given to using written consent forms although some commentators feel that to do so would discourage individuals from making complaints. The complaining employee should be apprised of the general scope of the investigation and the employee should be allowed to set forth the particulars of the sexual harassment allegations. If a complaint form is used, it should contain language acknowledging that the company has been given permission to disclose the information contained in the complaint to third parties whom it feels must also be apprised of the facts in order that it be able to conduct a thorough investigation. If the employee refuses to authorize an investigation or objects to the release of portions of the information provided the company, she should be asked to sign a statement confirming those desires.

Of particular concern are cases where an employee raises a claim of sexual harassment, but then requests that the employer not take any action upon it, or conditions the release of information regarding the claim in such a fashion that a complete investigation cannot be conducted. In general, the appropriate response is to note such an occurrence in a writing and have that writing confirmed by the employee's signature. Where a transfer of the employee would resolve the problem, that option should be explored. Additionally, special effort should be made to again communicate the company's policy against sexual harassment to its employees. It should be noted, however, that these steps may not be sufficient, and more aggressive action may need to be contemplated. In some situations it may be necessary to investigate notwithstanding the employee's refusal to consent. In that case, the decision to proceed with the investigation should be made known to the alleged victim. This situation may arise, for example, when the alleged conduct is so egregious that, it true, the accused individual would be subject to immediate termination, and a repeat of the conduct could subject the company to civil liability for negligent retention or similar torts.

B. INVESTIGATING THE COMPLAINT

With respect to conducting the investigation of a charge of sexual harassment, the employer should exercise discretion in selecting the employees who will be interviewed. Generally, it is advisable to confine the investigation within the circle of the alleged victim's immediate co-workers. Interviewing a greater number of employees concerning their observations of alleged incidents of sexual harassment may expose the complaining employee to unnecessary embarrassment.

The objective of the interview of potential witnesses is to find out as much as possible while revealing only that information which must be disclosed in order that a fair investigation be conducted. Questions should be phrased in such a way that the answer is not suggested to the witness, such as "How do you like working with Joe?" and "How does Joe treat his employees?" instead of "Does Joe harass the women in the office?" If an open-ended approach is not successful, more specific questions should be used. The interviewer should be alert to the person's attitude and relationship towards the alleged harasser as well as towards the victim. Each witness should be reminded of the confidential nature of the investigation and of the importance of preserving that confidentiality.

Having gotten a clearer idea of the conduct that is being alleged, the next step, if it has not already been done, is to confront the alleged harasser with the fact that allegations have been made. This should be done in a non-accusing way, because at this point in the investigation, no determination has been made concerning the truth of the allegations. If the accused person is represented by a labor union, he will have the right (if he chooses) to have a representative present during any investigatory interviews that could lead to discipline.

After discussing the allegations with the alleged harasser, the individuals he identifies as having information which would disprove the allegations should be contacted.

C. Acting on the Investigation

Once all the individual believed to have relevant information have been contacted, the evidence that was gathered must be weighed and a determination made as to what happened. In that regard, it may be necessary to re-interview the alleged victim or the alleged harasser to discuss new facts that the investigation has revealed and to provide a chance to explain. In both cases, the interviewer should be alert to inconsistencies in their statements.

There will be occasions where the investigation is inconclusive, leaving the employer with a Hobson's choice. On the one hand, if it fails to discipline or discharge an alleged harasser, the victim of the alleged harassment is more likely to file a claim or lawsuit against the employer. On the other hand, if the employer takes adverse action against the alleged harasser on the basis of inconclusive facts, it may also find itself subject to a defamation or other common law claim.

A direct approach to this problem, and one that entails nominal legal risks, is to advise the alleged harasser that the investigation was inconclusive. At the same time, the Company should reaffirm to all involved individuals its policy against sexual harassment and reiterate the consequences of the failure to abide by that policy. These communications should be documented for future reference. The person alleging harassment should then be told that the claim has been resolved and informed of her right to bring complaints in the future whenever she believes they are warranted. That conversation should also be documented.

In some situations it is appropriate to transfer one of the individuals involved. In *Nasa v. Electrospace System*,[37] the court held that the employer was not liable where the director of human resources immediately began an investigation after a subordinate's complaint and then transferred the subordinate to another department, with the same pay and benefits, after being unable to corroborate allegations because the supervisor denied engaging in the harassment and co-workers had not experienced or observed him engaging offensive behavior.

Consistency in handling of cases is critical. Disciplinary guidelines should be established and adhered to in handling sexual harassment claims, because deviation from discipline in prior cases may prompt claims by either the complainant or the alleged harasser.

D. Documenting the Investigation

The company's investigation should be accurately and carefully documented. Notes should be made of conversations with witnesses, and where possible, signed statements should be obtained from them. A record of the decision made during the investigation should also be made. The documentation should be maintained in a separate file which is not generally accessible. References to the claim should not appear in personnel files unless the offender has been issued a disciplinary action after thorough investigation, or if a notation is necessary in the victim's file to explain frequent use of sick leave or excessive absenteeism during the period of harassment. The investigation file should be retained at least as long as the statute of limitations for bringing a sexual harassment claim or a tort action based on either the harassment or the company's investigation and decision.

VII. Potential Claims By The Accused Against The Company

As already alluded to, lawsuits have been brought by individuals who have been accused or "found guilty" of sexual harassment, claiming that the employer defamed them, that the sexual harassment investigation was conducted negligently, or that the investigation constituted an invasion of their privacy. For example, in *Foley v. Polaroid Corporation*,[38] the plaintiff and his wife brought malicious prosecution, false imprisonment, defamation, and outrageous conduct claims against his employer.

He sought recovery for damages that allegedly resulted from Polaroid's response to accusations that he sexually assaulted a co-worker on company premises. The jury verdict and an award of five million dollars was entered in favor of the plaintiff on all claims except for malicious prosecution.

On appeal, all of the jury's verdicts were overturned except for the false imprisonment claim which was remanded for further processing. Nonetheless, *Foley* demonstrates the need for employers to take measures to ensure that the scope of the investigation and the release of information obtained as a result of the investigation is limited only to that which is necessary.

VIII. Employment Torts Related To Claims Of Sexual Harassment

Sexual harassment claimants are not likely to limit their suits to Title VII claims. In most cases, common law tort claims are also alleged. While it is possible that the passage of the Civil Rights Act of 1991 allowing for jury trials and the recovery of compensatory and punitive damages in sexual harassment cases will induce plaintiffs not to add state tort claims to their sexual harassment actions, there still is incentive to do so. That incentive comes from the fact that in many jurisdictions, compensatory and punitive damages are not subject to the caps applicable to Title VII claims. Following is a general discussion of the most common torts alleged by victims of sexual harassment. (It should be kept in mind that the specific elements of each tort may vary from state to state.)

A. INTENTIONAL INFLICTION OF EMOTIONAL DISTRESS

Generally, the tort of intentional infliction of emotional distress requires the plaintiff to prove the following elements:

(a) outrageous conduct by the defendant;

(b) intention to cause, or conscious disregard of the probability of causing, emotional distress;

(c) severe emotional suffering; and

(d) actual and proximate causation of the emotional distress by defendant's outrageous conduct.[39]

While generally difficult to prove, the prospect of prevailing on an intentional infliction of emotional distress claim is clearly enhanced if the underlying conduct involves sexual harassment. As one court noted:[40]

> . . . given an employee's fundamental, civil right to a discrimination free work environment . . . by its very nature, sexual harassment in the work place is outrageous conduct as it exceeds all bounds of decency usually tolerated by a decent society.
>
> Accordingly, if properly pled, sexual harassment will constitute the outrageous behavior element of a cause of action for intentional infliction of emotional distress . . .

In *Ruich v. Ruff, Weidenaar & Reidy*,[41] the court held that a former law firm secretary who claimed that she was sexually harassed by a partner was allowed to pursue her claim under for intentional infliction of emotional distress. The plaintiff alleged the partner made lewd remarks and engaged in periodic sexual touching and that the law firm failed to reprimand him and that it retaliatory reduced her severance pay.

N.B. In certain jurisdictions it has been held that claims of emotional distress based on alleged sexual harassment are preempted by workers' compensation statutes.[42]

B. False Imprisonment

False imprisonment is defined as the "non-consensual, intentional confinement of a person, without lawful privilege, for an appreciable period of time, however short it may be."[43] In order to succeed with such a claim, a plaintiff must establish that she was deprived of her liberty (i.e., forced to remain where she did not wish to be, or go where she did not wish to go).

In *Priest* the court held that the plaintiff succeeded in establishing a claim of false imprisonment with respect to two situations. The first occurred when the defendant physically picked her up against her will and carried her across the room. The second occurrence was when the defendant trapped her between himself and another male employee, preventing her escape while he fondled her body.

C. Battery

A battery occurs when a person is intentionally subjected to a harmful or offensive touching which actually and proximately causes the individual to suffer injury. Again, the plaintiff in *Priest* succeeded in establishing that the defendant subjected her to repeated offensive touching, which established his liability for battery. The defendant's actions caused the plaintiff to suffer physical injury by way of physical pain, humiliation, anxiety, and sleeplessness.

D. DEFAMATION

With less frequency, alleged sexual harassment victims have asserted that they were defamed. Typically, the basis for such a claim is statements made by employer representative investigators to the effect that the complainant's allegations had no merit or statements discussing the complainant's mental health. For example, in *Coleman v. American Broadcasting Company*,[44] the court held that statements regarding plaintiff's emotional and mental health were defamatory. On the other hand, a statement that the plaintiff's "claims have been fully reviewed and we have concluded there is no merit to them" was held to be opinion and therefore, not defamatory.

IX. CONCLUSION

Claims of sexual harassment, whether of a quid pro quo nature or based on a hostile environment are not going to disappear as long as we have men and women working together in the same work place. A company's potential liability, however, can be substantially limited by the adoption and enforcement of a sound policy prohibiting sexual harassment.

End Notes

1. 29 C.F.R. § 1604.11(a).

2. 477 U.S. 57 (1986).

3. Henson v. City of Dundee, 682 F.2d 897 (11th Cir. 1982).

4. Id.

5. Harris v. Forklift Systems, Inc., ___ U.S. ___, 114 S. Ct. 367 (1993).

6. Id.

7. 29 C.F.R. § 1604.11(A)(3).

8. 511 F. Supp. 307 (N.D. Ill. 1981).

9. Joyner v. AAA Cooper Transportation, 597 F. Supp. 537 (M.D. Ala. 1983), aff'd, 749 F.2d 732 (11th Cir. 1984).

10. Carreno v. IBEW Local No. 226. 54 FEP Cases 81 (D. Kan. 1990).

11. 570 F. Supp. 1197 (D. Del. 1983).

12. 807 F.2d 304 (2d Cir. 1986), cert. denied, 484 U.S. 825, 108 S. Ct. 89 (1987).

13. EEOC: Policy Guide on Employer Liability for Sexual Favoritism under Title VII. BNA FEP Manual 405:6817.

14. Waltman v. International Paper Co., 875 F.2d 468 (5th Cir. 1989).

15. EEOC Guidance, BNA FEP MANUAL 405:6686, 6685.

16. 477 U.S. at 70 (citing the Brief for the United States and EEOC as Amici Curiae).

17. Henson, 682 F.2d at 905.

18. Gardinella v. General Electric, 63 FEP 284 (W.D. Ky. 1993).

19. 879 F.2d 100 (4th Cir. 1989), reversed in non-relevant part 900 F.2d 27 (4th Cir. 1990).

20. 793 F.2d 714, 721 n.7 (5th Cir. 1986), cert. denied 479 U.S. 1065, 107 S. Ct. 952 (1987).

21. 634 F. Supp. 571 (N.D. Cal. 1986).

22. 39 FEP Cases 30 (N.D. Cal. 1985).

23. 63 FEP 118 (M.D. Ala. 1991).

24. 669 F. Supp. 1108 (D.D.C. 1986).

25. 570 F. Supp. at 1200.

26. 63 FEP 387 (D. Kan. 1993).

27. 805 F.2d 611 (6th Cir. 1986), cert. denied, 481 U.S. 1041, 107 S. Ct. 1983 (1987).

28. 584 F. Supp. 22 (D. Neb. 1983), aff'd, 726 F.2d 424 (8th Cir. 1984).

29. Swentek v. USAir. Inc., 830 F.2d 552 (4th Cir. 1987).

30. See, e.g., Ellison v. Brady, 924 F.2d 872 (9th Cir. 1991).

31. Id.

32. 760 F. Supp. 1486 (M.D. Fla. 1991).

33. 114 S. Ct. 367.

34. 53 FEP Cases 1148 (N.D.N.Y. 1990).

35. 63 FEP 625 (7th Cir. 1993).

36. 830 F.2d 552 (4th Cir. 1987).

37. 63 FEP 765 (5th Cir. 1993).

38. 508 N.E.2d 72 (Mass. 1987).

39. Priest v. Rotary, 634 F. Supp. 571, 582 (N.D. Cal. 1986).

40. Fisher v. San Pedro Peninsula Hospital, 54 FEP Cases 584, 596 (Cal. Ct. App. 1989). But see Obendorfer v. The Gitano Group, Inc., et. al., 1993 WL 499197 (D.N.J. 1993)(comment allegedly made by defendant, while offensive, did not rise to the level of outrageousness required to support tort of intentional infliction of emotional distress. "Absent other conduct, these insults, no matter how out of touch they are with today's respect to the equality of women, are still nothing more than verbal assaults all to common in today's rude and inconsiderate social and business interactions.").

41. 63 FEP 449 (N.D. I.. 1993).

42. _See_, _e.g._, _Miller v. Lindenwood Female College_, 616 F. Supp. 860 (E.D. Mo. 1985)(college was not held liable for infliction of emotional distress caused by the conduct of its agent in allegedly making sexual overtures; if the agent acted within the scope of his employment, relief would lie under workers' compensation law).

43. _Priest_, 634 F. Supp. at 583.

44. 38 FEP 65, 72-73 (D.D.C. 1985).

BRUCE S. HARRISON

Bruce Harrison is a 1967 graduate of Case Western Reserve University, where he received his Bachelor of Arts degree and the National Law Center of George Washington University, where he obtained his Juris Doctor (1971) and Labor Law Masters degrees (1975).

From 1972 until 1976, Mr. Harrison was an attorney for the Equal Employment Opportunity Commission at its headquarters offices in Washington, D.C. In 1976, he joined the firm of Shawe & Rosenthal. As a partner of Shawe & Rosenthal, the principal focus of his work has been the prevention and defense of employment-related claims and litigation.

Mr. Harrison is a member of the American Bar Association, including the Section on Labor and Employment Law and is Co-Chair of the Equal Employment Opportunity Subcommittee of the Litigation Section's Labor Committee. He has authored or co-authored many articles and monographs concerning labor relations matters, including "Avoiding Employment Discrimination Charges," Matthew Bender, 1984. He is also the editor of Matthew Bender's Employment Law Deskbook. In addition to advising clients regarding coming into compliance with the Americans with Disabilities Act, Mr. Harrison also has been a lecturer at various labor relations bar meetings and trade association forums dealing with ADA issues.

ALISA H. REFF

Alisa Reff is an associate in the firm of Shawe & Rosenthal where her work primarily focuses on the defense of employment-related claims and litigation. She received her Juris Doctor Degree from Georgetown University Law Center and a Bachelor of Arts Degree from the American University.

Ms. Reff is a member of the District of Columbia and Maryland Bars. She is also a member of the Maryland State and American (Member, Section on Labor and Employment) Bar Associations. Ms. Reff is the Revisions Editor of "Employee Discipline and Discharge Policies," "Avoiding Employment Discrimination Charges," and "Responding to Employment Discrimination Charges," Matthew Bender; a Contributing Author of the Maryland Chamber of Commerce's "The Maryland Handbook on Labor and Employment Laws," 1990; a Contributor to the "Employment Law Deskbook," Matthew Bender, 1989; and co-author of "Sexual Harassment and Related Employment Torts -- The Employer's Perspective," published by the American Bar Association.

REPRESENTING THE ALLEGED HARASSER: PRACTICAL AND ETHICAL CONSIDERATIONS OF JOINT AND SEPARATE REPRESENTATION

Sandra R. McCandless
Sonnenschein Nath & Rosenthal
685 Market Street, 10th Floor
San Francisco, California 94105
Telephone: 415/882-2412

Lisa P. Sullivan
Graham & James
One Maritime Plaza, Suite 300
San Francisco, California 94111
Telephone: 415/954-0385

I. INTRODUCTION

A survey of Fortune 500 companies revealed that almost 90% of major U.S. companies had received at least one formal complaint of sexual harassment in a one year period. In a great many of these cases, plaintiffs sue individual supervisors as alleged harassers along with the corporate employer. The employer must then decide whether to provide legal representation for the alleged harasser. If the company chooses to provide a defense, it may provide a joint defense or may opt to indemnify the alleged harasser supervisor for separate legal representation and, possibly, any potential judgment. Counsel for the company should consider all the practical and ethical implications in determining whether to undertake a joint defense or whether each party's interests are better served if the individual harasser has separate counsel.

II. TACTICAL CONSIDERATIONS

There can be many strategic advantages to a joint defense. An employer's chances of success on the merits often rise or fall with the jury's opinion of the alleged harasser. A jury may interpret separate representation as a clear sign that the employer and alleged harasser have different, or conflicting, interests. A jury understandably may expect that if an employer believes in the alleged harasser's innocence, it would be "on his side." Furthermore, when the alleged harasser and employer are engaged in battle between themselves, the overall defense may be eroded, leaving the plaintiff in a better position to win the war.

The alleged harasser is often also the key witness in the case. It is in the company's best interest to insure that this important witness is cooperative, forthcoming and, above all, controllable. A successful defense may require that this witness' interests be aligned as much as possible with those of the company.

A joint defense may also be the most economical defense. An employer may have a contractual or statutory duty to defend or indemnify an employee or corporate officer who is sued by a third party when the employee is acting lawfully under the direct instruction of the employer.[1] A single defense will usually cost less than two defenses. A coordinated defense may also be more practical. The corporation's attorneys are generally more familiar with the company's personnel policies and practices, records, record-keeping, personalities, and internal politics. For example, the corporate attorney would know the company's history regarding sexual harassment complaints and whether certain employees should not be relied upon as defense witnesses. This familiarity saves time and money and enables counsel to most effectively defend the lawsuit.

Even if the company is under no legal obligation to defend the supervisor, it may choose to undertake a joint defense out of a sense of loyalty, either to that particular person or to its managers and employees generally. A company may especially be compelled to "stand by" an important corporate executive or a senior supervisor with many years of service.

There are also many countervailing reasons not to undertake a joint defense of the alleged harasser and employer. If the employer is considering asserting a defense which implicates the alleged harasser, or taking a position which is adverse to that of the alleged harasser, joint representation would create a conflict of interest. Such a conflict would occur if the alleged harasser has acted outside the course and scope of employment because an employer may not be liable for such acts and may wish to distinguish its defenses from those of the individual employee.

An obvious conflict of interest would exist if the company has a right of indemnification against the individual co-defendant. For example, if a jury finds the supervisor guilty of harassment but finds that he or she acted beyond the scope of employment or disobeyed the company's express policy forbidding such harassment, the employer may sue the supervisor for indemnity. In such a case, any joint counsel would be representing the employer defendant in suing his or her other client, the alleged harasser defendant.

Finally, joint representation may give rise to frustrating attorney-client privilege issues. Counsel representing the employer and alleged harasser may be privy to admissions from the individual defendant which counsel may not be able to divulge to the employer. In a worst-case scenario, if the attorney becomes aware that the alleged harasser is guilty of sexual harassment, the attorney must then grapple with the dilemma of whether to tell the corporate client of the harasser's guilt and whether to continue to represent the corporate client.

III. ANALYSIS OF THE SEXUAL HARASSMENT CLAIM

In determining whether to undertake a joint defense, counsel must first determine whether a conflict of interest exists. In this regard, counsel should analyze the facts and legal basis for the sexual harassment claim to determine whether the employer defendant could be vicariously liable for the acts of harassment committed by the supervisor, whether the supervisor could be held personally liable for his or her conduct, and whether the employer's interests would be served by taking a position adverse to that of the supervisor.

A. Understanding the Law

Title VII of the Civil Rights Act of 1964,[2] as amended in 1972, prohibits sexual harassment by employers.[3] In the past, successful Title VII claimants have had the right to recover back pay, front pay, the value of lost fringe benefits, their attorneys' fees, and injunctive relief such as reinstatement and restoration of seniority. The Civil Rights Act of 1991, the new legislative amendment to the 1964 Act, authorizes compensatory and punitive damages under certain circumstances. The Civil Rights Act of 1871[4] also prohibits sexual harassment against public employees, such as those employed by police and fire departments and public schools and hospitals, and provides for recovery of punitive and emotional distress damages. Most states also have statutes which expressly prohibit sexual harassment.[5] For example, the California

Fair Employment and Housing Act ("FEHA")[6] prohibits employment discrimination, and California Government Code section 12940 specifically makes sexual harassment an unlawful employment practice. Damages available in these cases include back pay, front pay, lost fringe benefits, emotional distress damages, and injunctive relief. Punitive damages may also be awarded by a court, although not in a Fair Employment and Housing Commission proceeding.

The federal and state regulations generally recognize two types of sexual harassment: "quid pro quo" and "hostile work environment." To evaluate an employer's and supervisor's respective potential liability and available defenses, it is important to distinguish between the two types of harassment at the outset of litigation.

1. **Quid Pro Quo Harassment.** "Quid pro quo" harassment usually involves sexual demands made in exchange for employment benefits. For example, if an employee is terminated or disciplined for refusing to date a supervisor or respond to a supervisor's sexual advances, quid pro quo harassment has occurred. Quid pro quo harassment can also occur in a "constructive discharge" situation, where an employee resigns because of intolerable, harassing work conditions.

An employer may be liable for quid pro quo harassment, whether or not the employer knew of the offending conduct, if the harassment is committed by a supervisor.[7] If an employer delegates authority to a supervisor, and the supervisor acts improperly while exercising that authority, the supervisor's actions will be imputed to the employer whose delegation of authority enabled the supervisor to take the actions.[8] In fact, employers are even at risk for supervisor harassment if the harassment occurs away from the work site, if the supervisor was using his or her authority to hire, fire or promote in order to extort sexual consideration from the employee.[9]

2. **Hostile Work Environment Harassment.** Hostile work environment harassment cases usually involve a work atmosphere which is so pervasively hostile that it alters the conditions of employment for employees of one gender. This type of harassment occurs where unwelcome sexual conduct unreasonably interferes with an individual's job performance or creates an intimidating, hostile or offensive working environment. The victim need not suffer tangible or economic job consequences.[10] An employer will be held liable for hostile work environment harassment created by either a supervisor or non-supervisory employee if the employer knew or should have known of the harassing conduct. This knowledge of the harassment may be actual, such as where an employer observes the conduct or is aware of the victim's internal complaint. The employer may be held to have "constructive" knowledge if the incidents of harassment are found pervasive or well-known among employees. Constructive knowledge can be the basis for employer liability for acts of supervisors.

However, the United States Supreme Court, in Meritor Savings Bank v. Vinson,[11] ruled that employers are not automatically liable for acts of their supervisors in hostile work environment situations. The Court stated, though, that the absence of notice to an employer does not necessarily protect the employer from liability.[12] An employer may have derivative or "imputed" liability in a hostile environment case even without actual or constructive knowledge of a supervisor's actions if those actions were within the supervisor's scope of employment or apparent authority. A supervisor's actions are deemed within the scope of employment if the supervisor's conduct is within the authority vested in him or her by the employer. It is, of course, rare for an employer to actually authorize sexual harassment. It is not as unusual, however, for an employer to become aware of work-related sexual misconduct and to do nothing to stop it or prevent it from occurring. This failure to take corrective action is sufficient "authorization" to bring the supervisor's actions within the scope of employment and impute liability to the employer.[13]

The alleged harasser may also be held personally liable for his or her own acts of sexual harassment.[14] A supervisor can also be held personally liable if he or she had personal knowledge of the harassment and failed to take immediate corrective action.[15]

B. Understanding the Facts

In light of the various legal bases for employer and supervisor liability, counsel must also analyze the facts in each case to determine whether a conflict of interest exists, thereby making a joint defense improper. If theories of vicarious liability or respondeat superior render the employer liable for an employee's acts performed within the scope of employment, the supervisor and the employer are effectively in the same position, and there is no conflict of interest. If the alleged harasser has acted outside the scope of employment and is personally liable, a conflict may arise because the employer's defense involves implicating the supervisor. Therefore, it is essential to conduct a full investigation of the facts and circumstances surrounding the alleged harassment to determine if the alleged harasser acted within the scope of employment.

The alleged harasser should be interviewed at length regarding his or her involvement in the situation. This will allow counsel to evaluate the truthfulness, and possibly the guilt, of the individual named in the suit. In a case where it appears the individual is not being honest, joint representation is inadvisable. The interview should preferably be conducted before counsel agrees to represent the alleged harasser because any conversation which occurs after formation of the attorney-client relationship will be protected by that relationship, and counsel may not be able to disclose certain information to the employer client. To guard against future claims by the employee, however, the attorney should make it clear before the interview that he or she is conducting the interview on behalf of the employer and that no attorney-client relationship yet exists between the employee and counsel.

Other employees should also be interviewed regarding the alleged harassment, the alleged harasser's conduct in general and on other occasions, and working conditions and working environment. Counsel should determine whether the employer has a policy prohibiting sexual harassment and whether the employees have been made aware of this policy. The employer can use the existence and dissemination of such a policy as evidence that it does not condone harassment and as protection against liability. The alleged harasser's personnel file should also be studied to determine whether he or she has been involved in other incidents and whether other claims of sexual harassment have been made against that individual. If other claims have been made, counsel should determine what action the employer took in these cases to remedy the problems.

If the investigation reveals that the plaintiff's allegations are exaggerated or false, the employer may choose to defend the alleged harasser and to indemnify him or her against any judgment. If, on the other hand, it appears that the plaintiff's claims are legitimate, or if the parties disagree about the employer's knowledge, authorization, or ratification of the alleged harasser's conduct, joint representation is not advisable because the defendants' defenses differ. If the employer learns during the investigation for the first time that the alleged harasser has acted wilfully in violation of the employer's policies, the employer has an obligation to discipline and possibly discharge the supervisor and should not provide a defense for such an individual.[16] The employer may also be able to protect itself from liability by taking immediate and appropriate corrective action against the supervisor. If the employer conducts a prompt investigation and discovers improper action of which it was previously unaware, disciplining the supervisor may protect the employer from vicarious liability.[17]

IV. JOINT REPRESENTATION

If, after investigation, counsel is considering representing both the employer and the supervisor, the ethical implications of discovering a conflict between the clients should be analyzed. According to the American Bar Association,

> The critical questions are the likelihood that a conflict will eventuate, and if it does, whether it will materially interfere with the lawyer's independent professional judgment in considering alternatives or foreclose courses of action that reasonably should be pursued on behalf of the client.[18]

In a sexual harassment case, there is always the possibility that, through discovery, facts will emerge which implicate the supervisor. If this happens, the employer now has knowledge of the wrongdoing and is obligated to discipline the harasser. This is always a "potential" conflict in a sexual harassment lawsuit which must be fully disclosed to both clients. Although their interests may be the same at the outset, circumstances can change and a conflict can develop. An actual conflict of interest would exist the moment counsel discovers that the alleged harasser acted outside the course and scope of employment and committed the harassment. Such a conflict would also exist if it ever becomes clear that the alleged harasser's conduct did create a hostile work environment because the employer's defense would then be strengthened if it disciplined the harasser. Counsel has a duty to disclose these possibilities and explain all other facts and circumstances which both parties must understand to make a fully-informed decision regarding representation, including the possibility of seeking independent advice.[19] It is wise, therefore, to address with the employer and individual defendants the legal basis of the sexual harassment claim and the issue of the employer's liability vis-a-vis that of the employee, and the implications of their respective liability. Such frank discussion early in the case is intended to attempt to avoid the problematic situation where a conflict of interest arises well into the litigation.[20]

Counsel representing the employer and alleged harasser should document the informed consent by having the parties sign a consent letter. An example of such a letter to the individual client is attached as Exhibit A. An informed, signed consent by the parties to joint representation does not, however, guarantee that the potential conflict of interest between employer and alleged harasser will not become actual. If an actual conflict arises, the interests of the employer and harasser instantly diverge and counsel should consider whether to withdraw from the case.[21]

Model Code of Professional Responsibility Cannon 5 requires that attorneys exercise independent professional judgment on behalf of their clients and that the interest of one client not dilute the attorney's loyalty to another client. The American Bar Association Committee on Ethics and Professional Responsibility issued an Informal Opinion which analyzes the issue of joint representation of employer and employee.[22] The Committee considered a case where a lawyer, who was retained by an insurer to represent the employer and employee, learned from the employee that the employee acted outside the scope of employment such that the employee would not be covered under the insurance policy. The Committee concluded that "the lawyer should not reveal to the insurance company the information gained by the lawyer . . . when the revelation might result in denial of insurance protection to the employee." By analogy, an attorney in a sexual harassment case who learns that his or her employee client has acted outside the scope of employment may not disclose this information to the employer client without knowingly revealing a confidence in violation of ethical canons.

The attorney's duty to protect the confidentiality of attorney-client privileged communication can clearly become an issue when a conflict exists in a joint representation situation. When the American Bar Association Committee considered this issue in the context of joint representation of employee and employer, it concluded that:

> The employer's liability to the plaintiff may be affected by scope-of-employment circumstances. The lawyer would be unable to represent the employer-client in denying the employer's legal responsibility for the employee's conduct without concurrently acting adversely to the interest of the employee-client in preserving the employee's insurance protection. Possibly, the employer-client in the insurance company would be willing to forego a scope-of-employment defense and stand with the employee, in which case the interests of the lawyer's clients would not differ. The lawyer's dilemma, however, is that in seeking this consent the lawyer must disclose the information that he should preserve in confidence. He should not do so without the employee's consent after full advice as to the possible consequences. If the matter cannot be resolved by

agreement of insurance company, employer, and employee, then the lawyer may have a duty to seek withdrawal from the litigation. . . . If the lawyer so withdraws, he should recommend to the insurance company that separate counsel be retained to represent only the employee's interests.

Of course, the lawyer also should not represent the insurance company in asserting that the employee-client is outside policy coverage.[23]

If the attorney decides it is not proper to represent the employee, the attorney should also consider whether it is proper to continue to represent the employer client whose interests conflict with those of the former employee client. Once a lawyer stops representing the employee, a lawyer may be forced to discontinue representing the employer if, in the course of the attorney-client relationship with the employee, the lawyer acquired information that will or may be used against the employee in the litigation.[24] This would no doubt be the case in a sexual harassment suit if the attorney has discovered the harasser's wrongful conduct.

V. SEPARATE REPRESENTATION

If, after considering all of the ethical and tactical implications, the employer decides not to undertake a joint defense but to pay the fees of the alleged harasser's independent counsel, other issues become relevant. Counsel for the alleged harasser in this situation must make clear at the outset that the mere fact that the employer, or its insurance company, is paying for the employee's counsel does not create an attorney-client relationship between the employer and the employee's separate counsel. Independent counsel is retained for the express purpose of protecting the alleged harasser, and the employer should not be able to breach the attorney-client privilege between the employee and independent counsel. Both the alleged harasser's counsel and the employer's counsel must always be aware of the limits of this attorney-client relationship. The individual defendant's counsel should not allow the employer's counsel to speak with the individual unless he or she is present. The alleged harasser's personal documents are also privileged and subject only to proper discovery requests. If the employer's attorney is in a position to recommend separate counsel for the alleged harasser, he or she should recommend an attorney with whom a good rapport is probable. Such rapport will facilitate each defendant's defense and make it less likely that the plaintiff will benefit from the sparring of defendants' separate counsel.

Of course, counsel for the alleged harasser should analyze the client's liability in a sexual harassment case and consider how his or her liability relates to the employer's liability. Under some legal bases for recovery, individual employees can be liable for back pay damages awarded to the plaintiff.[25] An individual defendant in a sexual harassment lawsuit may also suffer economic loss if the employer does not indemnify him or her for legal expenses or damages. An alleged harasser may even be required to reimburse the prevailing party for reasonable attorney's fees and costs in some circumstances.[26] Counsel for the alleged harasser should explore the issue of insurance coverage to determine if the employer's workers' compensation or general liability insurance will cover the alleged harasser. An individual may also be covered by his or her homeowner's policy.

The individual defendant also may suffer economic and personal loss, such as damage to reputation, as a result of any disciplinary action - up to and including termination - the employer takes against the harasser. The likelihood of this is especially significant in light of the fact that, as noted above, employers are able to avoid liability in many cases by taking immediate corrective action against a wrongdoer.

The alleged harasser may be ultimately accountable to the employer if the employer asserts a cross-claim for contribution or indemnity against him or her. If an employer is ordered to pay damages to a plaintiff because of its actions or failures to act and because of the alleged harasser's wrongdoing, it only has a right to seek contribution from the individual harasser. However, if the employer is ordered to pay damages solely based on the harasser's acts, it has a right to indemnity and, standing then in the shoes of the plaintiff, may recover the full amount of damages from the harasser.

Counsel for the alleged harasser should also be aware of potential criminal liability issues. An alleged harasser may be found liable for assault and battery in cases of physical harassment.[27] An alleged harasser may also be held liable for attempted rape. In the face of any potential criminal liability, the alleged harasser's attorney should consider whether the defendant should claim a Fifth Amendment privilege against self-incrimination.

In actual practice, most sexual harassment cases involving business and individual co-defendants are resolved by payment of most or all of a settlement by the business defendant. Nevertheless, the outcome of litigation is always uncertain. Counsel faced with real or potential conflict situations in these cases must therefore assume an eventual trial and judgment and engage in decision-making on that basis.

VI. CONCLUSION

Whether counsel undertakes joint or separate representation of an employer and alleged harasser, there are many ethical and practical issues to be analyzed. If, upon investigation, it appears that the alleged harasser acted outside the course and scope of employment, or that his or her interests differ from those of the employer on some other basis, counsel should not undertake joint representation. Even if no such conflict seems to exist at the outset of litigation, counsel should undertake joint representation only after full disclosure of the potential conflict to both clients.

EXHIBIT A

This letter is only a sample of the type of letter to be provided to an individual defendant who will be jointly represented by employer counsel. The facts of each case and applicable law should be thoroughly considered in drafting any such letter in a particular case.

ATTORNEY-CLIENT COMMUNICATION
PRIVILEGED AND CONFIDENTIAL

Dear [Prospective Employee Client]:

This letter will confirm the terms upon which we will act as counsel and perform services in connection with the lawsuit filed by [Plaintiff] against you and other parties, including [Employer]. As you are aware, we have been retained by [Employer] to represent both it and you in defending this action. In that role, we will, at [Employer]'s expense, provide you with all legal services necessary to represent your interests in this matter. Our representation of you in this case therefore will involve a complete defense on all procedural and substantive grounds and will cover all incidents of litigation, including motions, pretrial discovery, and hearings and, if necessary, trial and appeals.

In a situation like this involving multiple parties, there is a possibility that the individual parties' interests may conflict. Even when all parties' interests are initially compatible, circumstances can change and a conflict can develop. Based upon our review of the allegations made in the complaint in this action and our preliminary investigation to date of the facts relating to that complaint, we believe that in the instances of which plaintiff complains you were acting within the scope of your authority. Therefore, we do not perceive a conflict between your interests and those of [Employer] with respect to a defense of the merits of this case. We will inform both you and [Employer] immediately should a conflict appear. In such an event, we would withdraw from representing you. We would, of course, assist you in obtaining substitute counsel under such circumstances.

You should also be aware that [Employer] has informed us that by agreeing to pay your legal fees, it does not waive any right to indemnity it may otherwise have. In this regard there is a potential conflict between your interests and those of [Employer]. That conflict would become actual should [Employer] seek indemnity from you for the costs and expenses it incurs in defending you in this action. You should therefore be aware that by signing this letter and agreeing to representation by us, you are waiving any objection you may otherwise be entitled to raise to this firm representing such conflicting interests. Should you wish to retain your right to raise such an objection, or should you wish not to be represented by us due to the fact that there now exists a potential conflict, you should not sign this letter and thereby agree to our representation of you.

It is also important for you to be aware that information you provide us, or which we discover in the course of representing you, may be disclosed to the other parties whom we represent in this action. If you are aware of any information which relates to the issues in this action which you believe should be kept confidential, you should seek the advice of an independent attorney. If, during the pendency of this action, any such information comes to your attention which you do not want disclosed to the other parties we represent, we ask that you advise us in writing of that fact, without telling us what the information is, so that we can determine whether we can proceed or whether we must withdraw from our representation of you.

If the foregoing meets with your approval, please date and sign the enclosed copy of this letter where indicated and return it to this office in the enclosed, self-addressed envelope.

If you have any questions regarding any of these arrangements, please feel free to call us. We are pleased to have this opportunity to be of service to you.

Very truly yours,

[Counsel]

ACCEPTED AND AGREED ON
THIS _____ DAY OF ______________, 199___

By:____________________________

NOTES

1. For example, California Labor Code section 2802 imposes a duty on employers to indemnify an employee for "all that the employee necessarily expends or loses in direct consequence of the discharge of his duties as such, or of his obedience to the directions of the employer, even though unlawful, unless the employee, at the time of obeying such directions, believed them to be unlawful." Further, California Corporations Code section 317 provides for indemnification of officers, directors, and employees if they acted in good faith in a manner which they reasonably believed to be in the best interests of the corporation.

2. 42 U.S.C. § 2000e et seq.

3. In 1986, the United States Supreme Court ruled in Meritor Savings Bank v. Vinson, 477 U.S. 57, 106 S.Ct. 2399 (1986) that sexual harassment constitutes sex discrimination in violation of Title VII.

4. 42 U.S.C. § 1983.

5. For a text of state-by-state fair employment practice law and regulations, see Fair Employment Practices Manual, the Bureau of National Affairs, Inc., Vols. 8A and 8B, 453:1-458:9991, 1994.

6. Cal. Gov. Code § 12900, et seq.

7. Horn v. Duke Homes, 755 F.2d 599 (7th Cir. 1985); Crimm v. Missouri Pac. R.R., 750 F.2d 703, 710 (8th Cir. 1984).

8. Meritor Savings Bank v. Vinson, 477 U.S. 57, 106 S.Ct. 2399, 2407-08; EEOC Policy Guidance, N-915.035, October 25, 1988.

9. See, e.g., Schroeder v. Schock, 42 Fair Empl. Prac. Cas. 1112 (Dist. Kansas 1986).

10. 29 C.F.R. § 1604.11(a)3.

11. 477 U.S. 57, 106 S.Ct. 2399 (1986).

12. Id. at 72, 106 S.Ct. at 2408.

13. EEOC Policy Guidance, N-915.035, October 25, 1988; Title II Cal. Admin. Code §§ 7286.6(b) and 7287.6(3); see EEOC v. Hacienda Hotel, 881 F.2d 1504 (9th Cir. 1989) (employer found liable for supervisors' sexual harassment of employees, where the general manager had actual knowledge of the allegations of harassment, and the employer should have known of the harassment because of its severity and pervasiveness which seriously tainted the employees' working environment); Waltman v. International Paper Co., 875 F.2d 468 (5th Cir. 1989) (employer held liable for sexual harassment by its supervisors and employees despite its

taking remedial action against the harassers, when employer's response was not reasonably calculated to stop the harassment).

14. See Brown v. City of Miami Beach, 684 F.Supp. 1081, 1085-86 (S.D. Fla. 1988) (individuals are proper defendants if plaintiff alleges acts of personal harassment by them); Hendrix v. Fleming Companies, 650 F.Supp. 301, 303 (W.D. Okla. 1986) (individual defendants dismissed except one defendant who allegedly made rude remarks and sexual advances toward the plaintiff); Boyd v. Hayes Living Health Care Agency, 671 F.Supp. 1155, 1167 (W.D. Tenn. 1987) (manager personally liable for his acts of harassment).

15. Hall v. Gus Const. Co., 842 F.2d 1010, 1015-16 (8th. Cir. 1988) (supervisor held liable for hostile work environment created by plaintiff's male co-workers even though the supervisor was not alleged to be personally involved in the sexual harassment); Robson v. Eva's Supermarket, Inc., 538 F.Supp. 857, 863 (N.D. Ohio 1982) (supervisor may be held personally liable for employment discrimination where the employer or supervisor acquiesces or condones subordinates' unlawful acts).

16. See Kyriazi v. Western Elec. Co., 476 F. Supp. 335 (D.N.J. 1979) (employer ordered not to indemnify offending employees against whom punitive damages were assessed).

17. 2 Cal. Admin. Code § 7287.6(b)(3); Dornhecker v. Malibu Grand Prix Corp., 828 F.2d 307 (5th Cir. 1987) (employer not liable to employee who complained about co-worker's alleged sexual harassment because employer was prompt in responding to employee in telling her within 12 hours that she would not have to work with the co-worker after the project had ended in one and a half days); Steele v. Offshore Shipbuilding, 867 F.2d 1311, reh. and reh. en banc den. (11th Cir. 1989) (parent company not liable for sexually hostile work environment of subsidiary company because when the parent learned of the harassment it took immediate and successful remedial action).

18. Model Rules of Professional Conduct Rule 1.7 Comment (1983).

19. Klemm v. Superior Court, 75 Cal.App. 3d 893, 898, 142 Cal.Rptr. 509 (1977).

20. See Shadid v. Jackson, 521 F.Supp. 85, 89 (E.D. Tex. 1981) (joint representation was improper because the potential defense that the employee acted outside the scope of employment represented a serious potential conflict which, if actualized, would require the attorney's later withdrawal and create a tremendous hardship on the court and parties).

21. Model Code of Professional Responsibility DR 5-105 (1981).

22. American Bar Association Committee on Ethics and Professional Responsibility, Informal Opinion 1476 Duty of Lawyer to Preserve Confidences and Secrets of Client in Multiple Representation from Co-Clients, August 11 1981.

23. Id.

24. American Bar Association Committee on Ethics and Professional Responsibility, Informal Opinion 1441, Lawyer Representing Both Manufacturer and Dealer in Defending Products Liability Action, July 5, 1979.

25. Kyriazi v. Western Elec. Co., 476 F.Supp. 335 (D.N. J. 1979) (supervisor personally liable when the supervisor was aware of abusive treatment and ignored it).

26. 42 U.S.C. § 2000e-5(k) Compston v. Borden, Inc., 424 F.Supp. 157, 163 (S.D. Ohio 1976).

27. Garcia v. Williams, 704 F.Supp. 984 (N.D. Cal. 1988).

SANDRA R. McCANDLESS

Sandra R. McCandless is a partner of Sonnenschein Nath & Rosenthal and the head of its employment law practice in San Francisco. She advises and represents management in all aspects of employment law.

Ms. McCandless received her undergraduate degree at Harvard College and her J.D. from Georgetown University Law Center. She is an active member of the Tort and Insurance Practice Section and Labor Section of the American Bar Associations, the former Chair of the Committee on Employer-Employee Relations of the Tort and Insurance Practice Section, and a frequent moderator and lecturer for business and legal groups on employment law topics. Her numerous publications include articles published in The Brief (Tort and Insurance Practice Section) on international employment law, the examination of expert psychotherapists, and workplace defamation.

LISA P. SULLIVAN

Lisa P. Sullivan is an associate in the San Francisco office of Graham & James, a graduate of Georgetown University and the University of Santa Clara School of Law, and a member of the American Bar Association. She also specializes in the representation of employers in the area of labor and employment and has spoken to employer and management groups on employment-law issues.

INSURANCE COVERAGE OF EMPLOYEE CLAIMS AGAINST EMPLOYERS

David B. Ritter
Marcia E. Goodman
Mayer, Brown & Platt
190 South LaSalle Street
Chicago, IL 60603-3441
312/782-0600

I. INTRODUCTION

Employers are subjected to a variety of claims by former employees. In addition to discrimination actions under Title VII of the Civil Rights Act of 1964 (as amended by the Civil Rights Act of 1991) ("Title VII"),[1] the Age Discrimination in Employment Act ("ADEA"),[2] the Equal Pay Act,[3] the Americans with Disabilities Act ("ADA")[4] and state discrimination laws,[5] state law tort suits have increased markedly in recent years. Such tort suits raise claims such as wrongful discharge, retaliatory discharge, breach of oral, written or implied contracts, breach of a covenant of good faith and fair dealing, defamation, intentional or negligent infliction of emotional distress and negligent hiring, retention or supervision of employees.

Traditionally, employers have simply referred such lawsuits to their labor counsel and pursued them to eventual trial or settlement. Sometimes an employer will defend against the employee's claim and then decide to settle the case after incurring large legal fees. However, employers have increasingly been willing to consider another alternative: determining whether the employer's general liability, directors and officers, or other insurance policy covers such employee claims. In fact, some insurance companies are now offering policies specifically designed to cover employment-related litigation. If the employment-related claim is covered, whether by design or otherwise, the employer may be able to shift the obligation to provide a legal defense and perhaps damages to the insurance carrier.

Section II of this paper discusses general and well-settled insurance law concepts regarding an insurance company's duty to defend the insured and what happens if a conflict of interest arises between the insured and insurer. Also discussed is the insured's duty to cooperate with the insurer. Section III addresses the circumstances in which an employer may be able to invoke the obligation of the insurance company to defend as a response to employee claims of employment discrimination, wrongful termination, and other tort-based causes of action.

II. THE INSURER'S DUTY TO DEFEND

A. *In General*

Most jurisdictions have held that the insurer's duty to defend is much broader than the duty to indemnify.[6] The insurer's duty to defend is contractual, and the insurer has a duty to provide a defense for claims asserted against its insured if the insurance policy has a duty-to-defend provision and if the claims against the insured are encompassed by the insurance policy.[7]

Moreover, an insurer may even have a duty to defend where the insurance policy language gives the insured a "reasonable expectation" that the insurer will provide a defense or where the complaint alleges facts which are potentially within the policy's coverage.[8] If the complaint alleges some facts which are within the policy's coverage, the insurer is obligated to defend, even if the allegations are vague, ambiguous, groundless, false or fraudulent, or if other allegations are clearly outside the scope of coverage.[9] Furthermore, an insurer may even be obligated to defend an insured even though the action is not in fact covered under the policy.[10]

The claims stated in the complaint must be analyzed to determine whether a duty to defend exists. For example, in *Danek v. Hommer,*[11] the court stated that:

> [T]he complaint should be laid alongside the policy and a determination made as to whether, if the allegations are sustained, the insurer will be required to pay the resulting judgment, and in reaching a conclusion, doubts should be resolved in favor of the insured.

Similarly, in *Seaboard Surety Co. v. Gillette Co.,*[12] the court noted:

> Though policy coverage is often denominated as "liability insurance," where the insurer has made promises to defend "it is clear that [the coverage] is, in fact, 'litigation insurance' as well. . . ." As such, "[s]o long as the claims [asserted against the insured] may rationally be said to fall within policy coverage, whatever may later prove to be the limits of the insurer's responsibility to pay, there is no doubt that it is obligated to defend."[13]

Moreover, the duty to defend cannot be circumvented by an inartfully drafted complaint.

> [A] policy protects against poorly or incompletely pleaded cases as well as those artfully drafted. Thus the question is not whether the complaint can withstand a motion to dismiss for failure to state a cause of action. Nor is the insured's ultimate liability a consideration. If, liberally construed, the claim is within the embrace of the policy, the insurer must come forward to defend its insured no matter how groundless, false or baseless the suit may be.[14]

An insurer must defend the entire action even if only one claim in a multiple claim complaint falls within the policy coverage.[15] However, if the cost of the defense can be readily apportioned between covered and noncovered occurrences, the insurer may owe the employer a partial defense from the employee claims.[16]

If an insurer fails to provide an insured with a defense against a complaint which contains any allegations potentially covered by the policy, it may be liable to the insured for breach of contract.[17] In addition, if the insurer wrongfully refuses to defend, it may be estopped from later raising policy defenses in any subsequent actions brought by or against it.[18] In some jurisdictions, an insured may also bring an action for "bad faith" where an insurer wrongfully refuses to defend.

B. *Conflicts of Interest and the Duty to Defend*

Where a "serious" conflict of interest between insured and insurer exists, a narrow exception exists to the general rule that an insurer must step in and defend the insured or seek a declaratory judgment as to coverage.[19] In such cases, the insurer must decline to participate in any defense, but instead, "must pay the costs of independent counsel for the insured."[20] The exception to the general rule was created in order to avoid the serious ethical problems presented when an insurer and insured have different interests in the conduct of the insured's defense.[21]

A "serious" conflict of interest between an insurer and the insurer may arise where the underlying action asserts some causes of action that are covered by the policy and others that are not covered.[22] In determining whether a departure from the general rule is necessary, courts compare the allegations of the complaint to the policy terms and consider whether the interest of the insurer would be furthered by providing a "less than vigorous" defense to those allegations.[23] Therefore, "serious" conflicts of interest which trigger the exception arise where the insurer hopes to establish one set of facts that will put the claim outside of the coverage of the policy, while the insured's interest is directly opposed.[24]

The interest of the insurer in negating coverage, however, does not alone create a sufficient conflict of interest to preclude the insurer from assuming the defense of its insured.[25] Rather, the insurer and insured must be "diametrically opposed" in their approach to the defense of the particular theory of liability in order for the court to find that the insurer was prevented from controlling the defense of the case.[26]

For example, in *Burlington Northern R.R. v. Illinois Emcasco Insurance Co.*,[27] the estate of a woman hit by a freight train while boarding a passenger train sued Burlington for, among other things, negligence in its duty to operate both the train and railroad station to avoid causing "damages or injuries to persons boarding or departing the train."[28] Burlington brought a declaratory judgment action against its insurer, seeking a declaration that the insurer had a duty to defend the suit. The insurer argued that it had no duty to defend because its policy specifically excluded coverage for accidents happening on the railroad tracks.

The appellate court, in reversing the trial court, held that the insurer had a duty to defend because the allegation that the railroad improperly operated the railroad station, although extremely vague, potentially fell within the scope of the policy. The court noted that even though the allegations of the complaint could be construed to mean that the railroad was negligent in operating the track and train, a situation not covered by the policy, the duty to defend was triggered by the presence of "just one claim [which] falls within the ambit of coverage."[29]

However, the court also found that because the complaint contained allegations which triggered coverage and others which did not, a conflict of interest occurred between the insurer and the insured. The court stated that "in such a situation, the insurer is absolved from providing a defense but must underwrite the cost of the defense."[30] Furthermore, the court stated that if the insurer wrongfully refuses to underwrite the defense, it "remains liable for the costs of the insured's defense and must reimburse him in the event that an adverse result occurs in the underlying action."[31]

C. *Insurer's Options When a Conflict of Interest Arises*

Generally, an insurer has three options when its insured has requested it to defend against an action that the insurer believes to be outside the scope of coverage. First, the insurer can seek a declaratory judgment regarding its obligations before or pending trial of the underlying action. Second, the insurer can defend the insured under a reservation of rights; and third, the insurer can refuse either to defend or seek a declaratory judgment, running the risk that might be found to have breached its duty to defend.[32]

1. Declaratory Judgment Action

When an insurer believes that a claim against its insured is not covered by the policy, it will normally seek a declaratory judgment to clarify its obligation to defend the action.[33] The insurer's options become more limited when there is a conflict of interest between the insurer and the insured. Where such a conflict of interest arises, courts may consider a declaratory judgment action prior to trial premature and therefore, in some instances, may not permit such an action.[34]

The reason behind this exception is based on the doctrine of collateral estoppel. "[D]eciding the question of coverage in a collateral proceeding prejudices no party" when the issues in the declaratory judgment action and in the underlying suit are different.[35] However, where the declaratory judgment action in a conflict of interest action presents issues substantially the same as those that will be presented at trial, the doctrine of collateral estoppel applies, and consequently, the result of the declaratory judgment controls in the underlying suit.[36]

Courts also disfavor declaratory judgments where there is a conflict of interest because such actions may prejudice both the insurer and the plaintiff in the underlying action.[37] In a declaratory judgment action, the insurer bears the burden of proof on issues which are integral to the plaintiff's case.[38] Consequently, the plaintiff loses the right to control the presentation of its case and also is bound by the doctrine of collateral estoppel to the results of the declaratory judgment.[39]

In certain circumstances, however, it may be prudent for the insurer to institute a declaratory judgment action at the onset of litigation even in light of a potential conflict of interest between insurer and insured. The purpose of bringing a declaratory judgment action in such a situation is to discover whether an actual conflict of interest exists. One court has stated that "the existence of a conflict of interest should be identified early in the proceeding so that it can be treated yeffectively before prejudice occurs to either party."[40]

Where a potential conflict of interest exists and the issues in a declaratory judgment are identical to those in the underlying action, the court may determine that the declaratory judgment is premature and decline to rule on those issues.[41] However, if the court finds that there is no conflict of interest, it may rule on the coverage issue and eliminate the need for the insurer to participate further in the lawsuit. The insurer, therefore, may protect itself from being estopped in claiming noncoverage if no conflict of interest exists by bringing a declaratory judgment action at the onset of litigation.[42]

2. Reservation of Rights

Alternatively, the insurer may decide to defend the underlying claim if it can reserve the right later to deny coverage or seek indemnification.[43] The insurer must notify the insured that it is undertaking the defense, subject to a reservation of rights within a reasonably prompt time after the potential coverage conflict has been discovered. An insured prejudiced by an unreasonable delay may seek legal redress.[44]

Equally important, the rights letter must specifically outline the exact nature of the coverage conflict.[45] In *St. Paul Mercury Ins. Co. v. Ralee Engineering Co.*,[46] the insurer sought a declaratory judgment that it had no duty to defend the employer's intentional act of wrongful discharge and that it was entitled to reimbursement for litigation costs previously expended in defending the employer. The court concluded that the claim was indeed not covered by the policy, but that the insurer was not allowed to recover money previously expended in conducting the employer's defense because the reservation of rights letter only stated that the insurer might "refuse to defend . . . *further* at any time."[47]

A California appellate court ruled in *San Diego Navy Federal Credit Union v. Cumis Ins. Soc'y*[48] that a conflict of interest exists *whenever* the insurer reserves its right to deny coverage at a later date. The *Cumis* rule was later limited to apply only where the reservation of rights is "based on the nature of the insured's conduct, which as developed at trial would affect the determination of coverage."[49]

3. Refusal to Defend

If an insurer chooses the third option and simply refuses to defend, it runs the risk of being estopped from later raising policy defenses to the coverage.[50] The insurer also could be held liable for the award against the insured and the costs of the suit because the duty to defend is broader than the duty to indemnify.[51]

D. *Insured's Duty to Cooperate*

The insured has a general duty to cooperate with the insurer. For example, the insured must notify the insurer of the occurrence in order to give rise to the insurer's duty to defend. Liability policies frequently contain a clause providing that the insured will, among other things, cooperate with the insurer by attending hearings and trials, assisting in the settlement of the suit, or securing and giving evidence. The purpose of the clause is to prevent collusion between the insured and plaintiff in the underlying action.[52]

The insurer may satisfy its burden of proving that the insured breached its duty of cooperation by establishing that the insured failed to disclose material information, intentionally provided false statements, or refused to testify at trial.[53] Upon such a showing, the insurer will have a defense to liability under the policy.[54]

E. *The Duty to Settle*

In the course of defending an insured, the insurer also has a duty to settle a claim when it is appropriate to do so. Generally, the insurer must take into account the interests of the insured and accord it at least as much consideration as its own interests.[55] As a practical matter, the insurer must evaluate the possibility that a judgment might be entered against the insured in excess of the policy limits. If such an event is a reasonable possibility, the insurer must attempt to settle the case within the policy limits.[56]

Additional problems arise if the insurer believes that the subject matter of the underlying suit is not covered by the policy. The insurer's belief that the policy does cover the underlying claim, however, is not a basis on which it may refuse to settle where appropriate.[57] A good faith doubt regarding coverage does not excuse the insurer's failure to settle within the policy limits.[58] In such a situation, the insurer should either attempt to stay the underlying action against the insured and file a declaratory judgment action or settle the action against the insured subject to a reservation of rights to seek indemnification from the insured.[59]

III. THE INSURER'S DUTY TO DEFEND EMPLOYEE CLAIMS AGAINST EMPLOYERS

A. *Employment Discrimination*

There are two general theories of employment discrimination under Title VII, ADEA and state discrimination laws: disparate treatment and disparate impact.

> Disparate treatment . . . is the most easily understood type of discrimination. The employer simply treats some people less favorably than others because of their race, color, religion, sex or national origin . . . .
>
> Claims of disparate treatment may be distinguished from claims that stress "disparate impact." The latter involve employment practices that are facially neutral in their treatment of different groups but that in fact fall more harshly on one group than another and cannot be justified by business necessity . . . .[60]

Simply stated, the theory of disparate treatment involves *intentional* discrimination. In contrast, because disparate impact discrimination involves a determination of whether a facially neutral employment policy (e.g., height or weight requirement) impacts upon one group of individuals in a disproportionate manner, such discrimination is generally considered *unintentional*. Whether an insurer has a duty to defend may depend in part on whether the plaintiff has alleged the theory of disparate treatment or disparate impact.

1. Disparate Treatment

It is well-settled that disparate treatment employment discrimination claims will be held not to be covered under the typical general liability policy definition of "occurrence" because such discrimination is viewed as an intentional act.[61] The case of *American Guarantee & Liability Ins. Co. v. Vista Medical Supply*[62] provides an example of the analysis typically followed by the courts.

There, the insurer (American) sought a declaratory judgment that it was not obligated to defend or indemnify its insured (Vista) against a variety of claims alleged by an employee (Wilson) discharged by Vista. Wilson alleged, among other claims,[63] that Vista intentionally discriminated based on sex with respect to pay and committed sexual harassment.

The insurance policy between Vista and American covered "bodily injury or property damage . . . caused by an occurrence."[64] Occurrence was defined as "an *accident*, including continuous or repeated exposure to conditions, which results in bodily injury or property damage neither expected nor intended from the standpoint of the insured."[65] Under the policy, American had the duty to defend "any suit against the insured [Vista] seeking damages on account of such bodily injury or property damage, even if any of the allegations of the suit are groundless, false or fraudulent."[66]

In deciding whether American had a duty under the policy to defend Vista, the court "laid the complaint alongside the policy"[67] and determined that American was not obligated to defend Vista against claims of intentional conduct or "purposeful acts."[68] This holding was based, in large part, on the court's definition of an "accident" as "arising from extrinsic causes . . . occurring unexpectedly or by chance . . . [or] happening without intent or through carelessness."[69] Applying its interpretation of the policy to the facts of the case, the court thereafter found that Wilson's allegations of sex discrimination and sexual harassment were intentional acts not covered by the insurance policy.

Sexual harassment claims are one type of employment discrimination as to which coverage continues to be debated. In *Continental Ins. Co. v. McDaniel*,[70] the plaintiff (McDaniel) alleged various claims including sexual harassment by her employer (Handgis). The insurer (Continental) defended the insured (Handgis) under a reservation of rights because the complaint alleged various intentional acts not covered by the policy. Continental thereafter brought a declaratory judgment action seeking a ruling that Handgis' conduct was not covered by the insurance policy.

The policy between Continental and Handgis insured against legal obligations caused by an occurrence which was defined as "an accident, including continuous or repeated exposure to conditions, which results in bodily injury or property damage neither expected nor intended from the standpoint of the insured."[71] The sexually harassing acts complained of were committed by Handgis against McDaniel for approximately one year and included talking in a vulgar manner as well as unwelcome physical advances.[72]

The court had little difficulty concluding that the actions of Handgis were "intentional," "wrongful under the law of torts and public policy," and not subject to a duty to defend by Continental. According to the court, "[i]n the context of insurance coverage . . . the intentional torts alleged here are 'torts that ought to be compensable only at the expense of the wrongdoer. . . .'"[73]

Some courts have gone so far as to hold that the intentional and repugnant nature of the act is so pervasive that it vitiates coverage for other associated torts which might normally be covered. In *Commercial Union Ins. Cos. v. Sky, Inc.*,[74] the court stated:

> [E]ach and every allegation made by [plaintiff] arises out of the alleged acts of sexual harassment. Her allegations are not mutually exclusive; they are related and interdependent. Without the underlying sexual harassment claim there would have been no alleged "personal injury" and no basis for a suit against [the employer] for imprisonment, defamation, outrage or negligent supervision.

Other courts, however, have found coverage for the employer in suits alleging a variety of claims relating to sexual harassment because the intentional act was that of the employee, rather than the corporation. According to the reasoning of such cases, the corporation is merely negligent for failing to observe or put a stop to the sexual harassment.[75] Therefore, coverage must be provided. In *Seminole Point Hospital Corp. v. Aetna Casualty & Surety Co.*,[76] the plaintiff's complaint alleged that the hospital's president and executive director engaged in sexual harassment by requesting sexual favors and otherwise engaging in verbal and physical conduct of a sexual nature. Although the executive director was listed as an insured on the policy, the insurer had no duty to defend because his actions of sexual harassment were not covered by the policy which excluded coverage for discriminatory and intentional acts.

The hospital was insured under the same policy as the executive director. The court recognized that the actions of the executive director were outside the scope of his employment, but reasoned that the hospital may be held liable in any event "for its own negligent supervision and failure to undertake an investigation" into this matter.[77] The insurer was required to defend the hospital because the "policy's intentional acts exclusion [did] not preclude coverage for a negligent insured."[78]

In *Omark Industries v. Safeco Ins. Co. of America*,[79] the plaintiffs alleged sex discrimination in violation of Title VII, the Equal Pay Act, and various Oregon state statutes. The plaintiffs alleged that Omark: (1) denied jobs and promotions to females based on sex; (2) paid lower wages to females than males for similar jobs based on sex; (3) retaliated against females for complaints of sex discrimination; (4) denied females training granted to males; and (5) otherwise treated females less favorably than males regarding terms and conditions of employment.

The insured (Omark) tendered defense of the claims to its insurer (Safeco), but Safeco refused the tender on the ground that the insurance policy did not provide coverage for the plaintiffs' claims. The case settled and Omark sought reimbursement from Safeco for the cost of settlement in the amount of $60,000 plus attorney fees.

The court correctly stated that the "primary question [is] whether the claims alleged in the . . . complaint [came] within the coverage extended by the Safeco general liability insurance policy."[80] Under Oregon law, the "duty to defend arises whenever there is a possibility that the policy provides coverage for the claim made."[81]

Coverage A under the Safeco insurance policy "insured all sums which the insured shall be legally obligated to pay for damages because of bodily injury or property damage . . . caused by an occurrence."[82] Bodily injury was defined as "sickness or disease" and occurrence was defined as "an event including continuous or repeated exposure to conditions, which results in bodily injury or property damage neither expected nor intended from the standpoint of the insured."[83]

Coverage A also contained an exclusion stating that coverage "does not apply to bodily injury to any employee of the insured *arising out of and in the course of his employment by the insured. . . .*"[84] Even though the court preliminarily concluded that severe emotional distress resulting from sex discrimination in employment such as that alleged by the plaintiffs was included under Coverage A, Exclusion (c) removed such claims from coverage and Safeco was under no duty to defend these claims.[85]

2. Disparate Impact

In *Castle & Cooke, Inc. v. Great American Ins. Co.*,[86] the insured (Castle) filed a declaratory judgment action seeking reimbursement for legal fees in excess of $350,000 after the insurer (Great American) refused to defend a class action discrimination suit brought against Castle. The underlying action was filed in federal district court and alleged discrimination with respect to nonwhites on a classwide basis. As relief, the plaintiffs requested lost wages and damages for physical suffering, arbitrary termination, and mental anguish. The Great American policy insured against "damages because of personal injury." Personal injury was defined to expressly include "racial discrimination not committed by or at the direction of the insured."[87] The policy also contained an exclusion for mental anguish or bodily injury to any employee arising out of and in the course of employment.

The court found that although there was no duty to defend the employees' claims for bodily injury or mental anguish, there was a duty to defend "nonintentional employment race discrimination claims which allege damage for lost wages and arbitrary termination."[88] Great American did not dispute that under the policy it had a duty to defend claims of unintentional or disparate impact discrimination. Great American instead argued that the complaint only stated a claim for disparate treatment discrimination and consequently there was no coverage or duty to defend. The court responded that "[t]his argument is difficult to sustain in view of the complexity of employment discrimination law and in view of the fact that the case was actually tried on both disparate impact and disparate treatment theories."[89]

Castle & Cooke is significant in one important respect. The complaint filed by the plaintiffs was an example of notice pleading under the Federal Rules of Civil Procedure.[90] Terms such as disparate treatment, disparate impact, intentional or unintentional discrimination were not used in the complaint. The complaint generally alleged that certain employment policies resulted in racial discrimination. The allegations in the complaint supported both the theories of disparate impact and disparate treatment.[91] The court refused to permit Great American to deny coverage solely on the basis of the complaint. Great American had an obligation to investigate in order to determine whether a duty to defend existed. "Because the . . . case was pled and tried, at least in part, on a disparate impact theory Great American had a duty to defend Castle & Cooke."[92]

The interplay between the theories of disparate treatment and disparate impact discrimination was also addressed in *Solo Cup Co. v. Federal Ins. Co.*[93] A complaint filed against the employer (Solo Cup) by the Equal Employment Opportunity Commission (EEOC) alleged sex discrimination on a classwide basis and in the failure to promote an individual female employee. Solo Cup and the EEOC entered into a consent decree and the employee was paid $25,000 to settle all claims. Solo Cup thereafter sought indemnification for the settlement and legal fees from its insurer (Federal).

The Complaint stated that Solo Cup "*intentionally* engaged in unlawful employment practices . . . in violation . . . of Title VII."[94] The violations included failing and refusing to promote women based on sex; compensating women at a lower rate than men for substantially the same work; maintaining job classifications segregated on the basis of sex; having different terms and conditions of employment for women based on sex; and discharging women in retaliation for exercising protected rights under Title VII.[95]

The insurance policy covered an occurrence which was defined as "an accident or happening or event or a continuous or repeated exposure to conditions which *unexpectedly* and *unintentionally* results in personal injury."[96] Personal injury was broadly defined and expressly included "discrimination."[97] The insurer

(Federal) was also obligated to pay for "salaries, wages, compensation, fees, charges and law costs, . . . expenses for . . . lawyers . . . and for litigation, settlement, adjustment and investigation of claims and suits."[98]

Federal argued that it had no duty to defend or indemnify Solo Cup because the complaint stated that Solo Cup "intentionally" discriminated in violation of Title VII. The Seventh Circuit adopted a different view. Although the underlying complaint was filed by a single employee based on a failure to promotion claim, it included class allegations of sex discrimination with respect to compensation, promotion, job placement, and other terms and conditions of employment. The court concluded that the insurance policy did not cover disparate treatment discrimination, but that Federal had a duty to defend claims of disparate impact discrimination. Solo Cup was entitled to damages in the amount of costs and fees in defending and settling the claims minus the policy deductible.[99]

The courts in California have pioneered a different view of disparate impact employment discrimination. In *American Guarantee*,[100] the plaintiff (Wilson) alleged both disparate treatment and disparate impact sex discrimination with respect to wages. Wilson argued that her claim of disparate impact discrimination was not excluded from coverage under the policy because neither intent to discriminate nor any purposeful act was alleged. The court disagreed and "focused not on whether the claim requires proof of intent . . . but rather . . . whether the alleged act giving rise to damages [was] purposeful."[101] The court held that the act of setting an employment policy that allegedly caused the discrimination was an intentional act and therefore not an occurrence under the policy. Under the holding in *American Guarantee*, it would be unlikely that any claims of disparate impact discrimination would invoke a duty to defend.[102]

3. The American With Disabilities Act

The employment provisions of the ADA, which first took effect on July 26, 1992, contain some unique features. These unique features carry with them the possibility that the courts will analyze coverage of such claims differently than they have analyzed coverage of traditional employment discrimination claims. Unlike Title VII, the ADEA and the Equal Pay Act, the ADA requires employers not only to refrain from discrimination, but to take affirmative action by providing "reasonable accommodation" to individuals with disabilities. The standard for what is "reasonably" required of employers is not well-established. Under these circumstances, employers may well argue that their failure to make a reasonable accommodation or to properly determine what type of accommodation is reasonable is not an intentional act. Therefore, they might argue, coverage should be provided under certain policies for some types of claims under the ADA.

4. Administrative Proceedings

As a prerequisite to filing a discrimination action under either federal or state law, the parties must generally exhaust applicable administrative procedures. For example, under Title VII, ADEA, and the Equal Pay Act a charge of discrimination must be filed with and investigated by the EEOC.[103]

In *Solo Cup*,[104] the employer sought reimbursement for legal fees and costs related to an administrative compliance review conducted under Executive Order 11246 investigating allegations of sex discrimination.[105] The court ruled that under the facts of the case there was no duty to defend or indemnify on the part of the insurer because no formal claim or liability as defined under the policy had yet occurred.

The Seventh Circuit implied, however, that the insurer's duty to defend was not limited to judicial proceedings.

> [The] duty to defend in Endorsement 1 [of the policy] obligates the insurer to "defend any *suit* against the insured." The indemnity provisions of the policy, by contrast, obligate the insurer to indemnify Solo for all

sums paid by reason of liability imposed "by law." In light of this language in the indemnity provisions, we think that the duty to defend "suits" might in some circumstances be triggered by adjudicatory proceedings before an administrative body.[106]

B. *Wrongful Discharge*

It seems clear that "the *actual* discharge of an employee cannot be an accidental event and that there is no coverage for such a discharge where the policy contains an exclusion for intentional acts."[107] For example, in *American Guarantee*,[108] the plaintiff Wilson alleged a variety of causes of action including wrongful discharge. The insurance policy at issue did not cover "purposeful acts."[109] The court ruled that the discharge of an employee was an intentional or purposeful act and that American had no duty to defend the insured against a claim of wrongful discharge.[110]

In *St. Paul Mercury Ins. Co. v. Ralee Engineering Co.*,[111] a former employee (Torres) filed an action against his former employer (Ralee) alleging wrongful discharge and intentional infliction of emotional distress. Ralee was insured under a policy issued by St. Paul and requested that St. Paul defend it in the Torres action. St. Paul agreed under a reservation of right to assert noncoverage at a later time because the policy did not cover intentional acts or punitive damages. In holding that no duty to defend existed, the court rejected Ralee's argument that despite the plain language of Torres' complaint alleging "intentional and deliberate conduct," there was a "potential for damages based upon negligence which may invoke an obligation to defend."[112]

In *St. Paul Mercury Ins. Co. v. Medical Lab. Network*,[113] the court considered a different question: whether a *constructive discharge* was an accidental or intentional occurrence under the insurance policy. The plaintiff alleged in her complaint that she resigned after she was demoted and that the employer's conduct was a constructive discharge.[114]

The insured (Network) argued that in contrast to a discharge, a constructive discharge "is by definition an accidental event, . . . neither intended nor foreseen."[115] The court disagreed, concluding that because Network had "knowledge of the intolerable actions and conditions and of their impact on the employee," it was presumed that the employer "intended" that the employee resign.[116] Accordingly, the plaintiff's resignation or constructive discharge was not "accidental" under the policy and the insurer was under no duty to defend.[117]

A similar conclusion was reached by the Montana Supreme Court in *Daly Ditches Irrigation Dist. v. National Surety*

Corp.[118] There, a former employee alleged that his termination breached the covenant of good faith and fair dealing and was also in violation of the public policy of Montana. Daly (the employer and insured) commenced a suit to establish that the plaintiff's action and any accompanying damages were covered by its insurance policy. The policy covered "bodily injury or property damage" and defined occurrence as an "accident, including continuous or repeated exposure to conditions, which results in bodily injury or property damage neither expected nor intended from the standpoint of the insured."[119] The court agreed with the position of the insurer that "persuasive authority holds that discharge from employment is not an accident under the policy language at issue here."[120]

In *Falkenstein's Meat Co. v. Maryland Casualty Co.,*[121] instead of alleging a wrongful discharge or a constructive discharge, the underlying complaint was that the employer engaged in retaliatory conduct because the employee complained about unsafe working conditions.[122] The plaintiff sought damages for "emotional distress, impaired personal dignity and loss of wages."[123] The court held that the insurer did not have a duty to defend the claim because it alleged an intentional act not covered by the policy's definition of occurrence and because "retaliatory . . . conduct . . . [consists of] acts from which an intention to cause harm must necessarily be inferred."[124] The court also failed to accept the employer's argument that the complaint could be read to allege "negligent conduct" which may invoke a duty to defend because no facts in the complaint indicated that negligence was involved.[125]

C. *Retaliatory Discharge*

A claim for retaliatory discharge may be brought if an employee claims he was terminated in violation of a public policy. The most common type of wrongful discharge claim is that an employee was discharged for exercising his rights under the state worker's compensation laws. As expected, the courts have disagreed over whether such claims are covered.

In *United States Fire Ins. Co. v. Beltmann North American Co.*,[126] the Seventh Circuit held that a plaintiff that proves his discharge was in retaliation for exercising a protected right has *de facto* proven actual malice. As a result, insurance policies that deny coverage for personal injuries arising from offenses committed with actual malice automatically exclude claims for retaliatory discharge.

A different result occurred in *Dixon Distributing Co. v. Hanover Ins. Co.*[127] There, the employer (Dixon) argued that the claim of retaliatory discharge was covered under its umbrella insurance policy. The Illinois court of appeals rejected the *Beltmann*[128] approach that "actual malice exists in every retaliatory discharge case" and that a trier of fact should determine that issue. Because the policy could have potentially covered this claim, the insurer breached its duty to defend.

D. *Breach of Written or Oral Employment Contracts*

A frequent claim of a discharged employee is that the discharge violated a written or oral employment contract. Written employment contracts are sometimes created by virtue of statements made an employee handbook or personnel manual distributed by an employer to its employees.[129] Oral statements or other actions by an employer may create an oral or implied employment contract.[130]

Typically, contractual claims are not covered under general liability policies. For example, in *American Guarantee,*[131] the plaintiff alleged that her termination breached an oral employment contract. Under the insurance policy, American's liability was limited to legal obligations "because of bodily injury or property damage."[132] American argued that under California law, such language covered tort, but not contractual liability.[133] The court agreed and American was under no duty to defend the insured.

A different result was achieved in *Interco Inc. v. Mission Ins. Co.*[134] There the employer and the insured (Interco) discharged one of its vice presidents (Egol). Egol thereafter filed suit alleging breach of contract. The suit was ultimately settled for $105,000 and Interco sought reimbursement of the settlement amount plus attorney fees from its two insurance carriers, Mission Insurance Company and Hartford Fire Insurance Company.

Interco successfully argued that Mission was under a duty to defend. The policy at issue defined occurrence as an "accident or a happening or event . . . which unexpectedly and unintentionally results in personal injury."[135] Under Missouri law "reckless acts are included in the term of unexpected happenings or accidents."[136] Although Egol's discharge was not unexpected or unintended, the complaint's allegations of "reckless acts" brought the action "potentially or arguably within the coverage of Mission's policy."[137]

E. *Defamation*

Defamation claims are increasingly brought against employers when an employee is discharged for poor performance or misconduct. Most general liability policies provide coverage for defamation claims. However, some policies exclude defamation arising out of employment.

In *American Guarantee*,[138] the plaintiff alleged that her employer repeatedly and falsely accused her of dereliction of duties including problems associated with the computer system and excessive spending on supplies and building renovations. The plaintiff also alleged that on a number of occasions she was "humiliated" in front of the staff. The insurance policy defined "personal injury" to include "a publication or utterance . . . of a libel or slander or other defamatory or disparaging material."[139] The court ruled that such statements could give rise to a claim of defamation under the policy and, therefore, American had a duty to defend against the claim.

Similarly, in *United States Fire Ins. Co. v. St. Paul Fire & Marine Ins. Co.*,[140] two former employees commenced an action against the employer alleging, among other claims, that the employer made "false and defamatory remarks" concerning their "morals and character."[141] The insurer had a duty to defend because the policy at issue included coverage for employment related claims for libel, slander, and invasion of privacy.

In *Omark Industries*,[142] the insured, Omark, alleged that the plaintiffs' allegations constituted a cause of action for defamation and as a result the insurer, Safeco, had a duty to defend under the policy's Coverage P. Coverage P insured Omark for the "publication or utterance of a libel or slander or of other defamatory or disparaging materials" if such offenses were committed in the course of Omark's business.[143] Omark contended that the plaintiffs' allegations that Omark "engaged , and continues to do so, in the practice of degrading females by insisting that good-looking blondes with good legs be hired for secretarial positions" could invoke liability under Coverage P.[144]

The court concluded that Coverage P was not applicable for two reasons. First, the basis of the plaintiffs' complaint was sex discrimination, not for defamation, and the plaintiffs did not allege a cause of action for defamation or damages flowing from such statements. Second, such statements were not made to or concerning any of the plaintiffs. Accordingly, Coverage P did not invoke a duty to defend on the part of Safeco.

F. *Infliction of Emotional Distress*

A plaintiff filing an action against his or her former employer will often include a claim for intentional or negligent infliction of emotional distress or similar damages. Such claims are most common when the plaintiff's underlying cause of action is for wrongful termination, breach of the covenant of good faith and fair dealing, or similar state law tort claims.

Employers have generally been unsuccessful in obtaining coverage for such claims under their general liability insurance policy. Courts have accepted the insurer's position that claims for emotional distress resulting from an intentional discharge are a derivative injury and also considered intentional and thereby not subject to policy coverage or a duty to defend. In *Network*,[145] the employee's underlying claim was one for constructive discharge. The plaintiff's additional claim for negligent infliction of emotional distress was considered "an integral part of the assertedly wrongful discharge" and an intentional act "not within the policy's coverage."[146]

In *Daly Ditches*,[147] the Montana Supreme Court held that "the alleged intentional conduct of Daly could be expected to cause the injury claims by the employee. . . . Damages for emotional mental suffering may be expected to flow directly as injuries from such a discharge."[148] The court relied on and adopted the reasoning of *Mary & Alice Ford Nursing Home v. Fireman's Ins. Co.*,[149] where an employee claimed she was discharged because of her disability. In holding that the employee's claims for emotional injury in *Ford Nursing Home* were not covered by the insurance policy, the court stated that:

> If, in fact, [the employee was] discharged . . . from her employment because of her disability, it cannot be said that the mental and emotional injuries alleged by [the employee] as flowing directly from [the employer's] intentional discriminatory practice were

> unexpected and unforeseen by . . . the insured. While "it is not legally impossible to find accidental results flowing from intentional causes, *i.e.*, that the resulting damage was unintended although the original act or acts leading to the damage were intentional" [citation omitted], such is not the case here, for the damages alleged in the [employee's] complaint are the intended result which flows directly and immediately from [the employer's] intentional act, rather than arising out of a claim of unintended though foreseeable events that occurred after the intentional act. . . .[150]

However, the court in *Mutual Service Casualty Ins. Co. v. Co-Op Supply Inc.*,[151] interpreted the definition of "occurrence" broadly and concluded that the plaintiff's claims of "emotional trauma" and "unintended bodily injury" fell within the policy definition even though such claims resulted from the employer's intentional termination of the plaintiff.

G. *Negligent Hiring*

One of the newest sources of potential employer liability is from claims of negligence: negligent hiring, negligent supervision and negligent retention. Most often these claims are brought by third parties who have been injured by an employee.

In *USF&G v. Open Sesame Child Care Center,*[152] the underlying action involved a claim of negligent hiring of a child care worker who molested a child at the day care center. The court considered whether the hiring of an employee was an intentional or a negligent act. The court determined that the allegation of negligent hiring was an "occurrence", despite the allegations of intentional conduct against the employee. Thus, there was coverage.

Claims of negligent hiring, supervision and retention are also sometimes brought by employees injured by co-workers or supervisors. While the outcome in such cases will depend on the wording of the particular policy and the facts being alleged, there is the opportunity for the employer to seek coverage, under an analogy to coverage of third-party claims.[153]

H. *Claims under ERISA*

Plaintiffs in employment related litigation often join claims under ERISA to claims of employment discrimination or employment torts. ERISA claims in such situations may take a variety of forms. Often a claim that a pension or medical benefit has been improperly reduced by a discharge or demotion accompanies a claim of wrongful discharge. Another common claim is that an employee was discharged to deprive him of a pension.

Claims for severance pay allegedly due on discharge are also brought under ERISA.

Where an ERISA claim alleges a breach of fiduciary duty, such claims are typically covered by fiduciary liability policies. In some cases, the policy carries a duty to defend, but does not cover the cost of any additional benefits which may be due. When a count relating to employee benefits appears in a complaint, the employer should investigate whether coverage is provided under such a policy.

IV. CONCLUSION

There are few certainties concerning an insurer's duty to defend employee claims against employers. Although the insurance law concepts discussed above are well-settled, their application in the world of employment litigation has not met with uniform results.

For example, though courts have generally held that intentional conduct is beyond the coverage of a great many policies, several courts have ruled to the contrary. Moreover, coverage, in some cases, may also be dependent on the type of discrimination alleged: disparate impact or disparate treatment. Finally, even though causes of action for defamation are more likely to be covered by insurance policies than other employment law causes of action, not all courts have held that the insurer has a duty to defend such claims.

What lessons can an employer learn from this discourse? First, that policies should be reviewed to determine whether and to what extent the different types of claims discussed may be covered. Such a review may lead an employer to obtain protection from such claims. Second, after receiving a claim from a former employee, the employer should, in the appropriate instance and when supported by the terms of the policy, notify the insurer and request that the insurer defend and indemnify regarding the claim. Though it would be inappropriate to demand coverage if not provided for under the policy, the employer should not fail to take advantage of valid insurance it has purchased and that may be applicable. In this way, the employer will have another line of defense in controlling the rising costs of employment litigation.

[1] 42 U.S.C. § 2000e-2000e-17 (1981). Title VII prohibits discrimination in employment based on race, color, religion, sex or national origin.

[2] 29 U.S.C. § 621-634 (1985). ADEA prohibits discrimination in employment based on age.

[3] 29 U.S.C. § 2006(d)(1)-206(d)(4) (1978). The Equal Pay Act prohibits discrimination based on sex with respect to wages.

[4] 42 U.S.C. § 1201 *et seq.* (1990).

[5] All fifty states, the District of Columbia, and Puerto Rico have statutes prohibiting discrimination in employment. These statutes, in general, prohibit discrimination in employment on bases similar to Title VII, ADEA, and the Equal Pay Act. The type of discrimination prohibited varies from state to state.

[6] *Enserch Corp. v. Shand Morahan & Co.*, 952 F.2d 1485, 1493 (5th Cir. 1992); *Conway v. Country Cas. Ins. Co.*, 92 Ill. 2d 388, 442 N.E.2d 245 (1982); *Montrose Chemical Corp. of California v. Canadian Universal Ins. Co.*, 6 Cal. 4th 287, 24 Cal. Rptr. 2d 467, 861 P.2d 1153 (1993); *Nandorf, Inc. v. CNA Ins. Cos.*, 134 Ill. App. 3d 134, 479 N.E.2d 988, 991 (1st Dist. 1985). See generally B. Ostrager & T. Newman, *Handbook on Insurance Coverage Disputes* § 5.01 (1988), and A. Windt, *Insurance Claims and Disputes* § 4.01 (2d ed. 1988).

[7] *Farrell Lines, Inc. v. Insurance Co. of N. America*, 789 F.2d 300, 304 (5th Cir. 1986).

[8] See, e.g., *Western World Ins. Co. v. Harford Mut. Ins. Co.*, 784 F.2d 558, 562 (4th Cir. 1986); *St. Paul Fire & Marine Ins. Co. v. Weiner*, 606 F.2d 864 (9th Cir. 1979); *Ohio Cas. Ins. Co. v. Bazzi Constr. Co.,* 648 F. Supp. 1056, 1059 (N.D. Ill. 1986), aff'd, 815 F.2d 1146 (7th Cir. 1987); *Montrose Chemical Corp. of California v. Canadian Universal Ins. Co.*, 6 Cal. 4th 287, 24 Cal. Rptr. 2d 467, 861 P.2d 1153 (1993); *Maryland Cas. Co. v. Peppers*, 64 Ill. 2d 187, 355 N.E.2d 24 (1976).

[9] *Interco Inc. v. Mission Ins. Co.*, 808 F.2d 682, 685 (8th Cir. 1987); *Trizec Properties v. Biltmore Constr. Co.*, 767 F.2d 810, 812 (11th Cir. 1985); *Thornton v. Paul*, 74 Ill. 2d 132, 384 N.E.2d 335, 339 (1978).

[10] *Nandorf*, 479 N.E.2d at 991; cf. *Brooklyn Law School v. Aetna Cas. & Sur. Co.*, 849 F.2d 788 (2d Cir. 1988) (court will read complaint liberally, but will not "imagine" allegations to find liability under the policy).

[11] 28 N.J. Super. 68, 77, 100 A.2d 198, 202 (App. Div. 1953), aff'd per curiam, 15 N.J. 573, 105 A.2d 677 (1954).

[12] 64 N.Y.2d 304, 310-11, 476 N.E.2d 272, 275, 486 N.Y.S.2d 873, 876 (1984) (citation omitted).

[13] See also *Outboard Marine Corp. v. Liberty Mut. Ins. Co.*, 154 Ill. 2d 90, 107-08, 607 N.E.2d 1204 (1992); *Waste Management of Carolinas, Inc. v. Peerless Ins. Co.*, 315 N.C. 688, 340 S.E.2d 374 (1986); *Cal-Farm Ins. Co. v. TAC Exterminators*, 172 Cal. App. 3d 564, 218 Cal. Rptr. 407 (2d Dist. 1985).

[14] *Ruder & Finn Inc. v. Seaboard Sur. Co.*, 52 N.Y.2d 663, 422 N.E.2d 518, 521, 439 N.Y.S.2d 858, 861 (1981). See also *Brooklyn Law School*, 849 F.2d at 789 (insurer has "duty to defend its insured against lawsuits, regardless of how poorly the complaint is worded").

[15] *Foreman v. Continental Cas. Co.*, 770 F.2d 487, 489 (5th Cir. 1985); *Trizec Properties, Inc. v. Biltmore Constr. Co.*, 767 F.2d 810, 811 (11th Cir. 1985); *Previews, Inc. v. California Union Ins. Co.*, 640 F.2d 1026 (9th Cir. 1981).

[16] *Harborside Refrigerated Services v. IARW Ins. Co.*, 759 F.2d 829 (11th Cir. 1985); *American Contract Bridge League v. Nationwide Mut. Fire Ins. Co.*, 752 F.2d 71 (3d Cir. 1985).

[17] *Green v. J.C. Penney Auto Ins. Co.*, 806 F.2d 759 (7th Cir. 1986); *Triple U Enterprises, Inc. v. New Hampshire Ins. Co.*, 766 F.2d 1278 (8th Cir. 1985); *San Jose Production Credit Ass'n v. Old Republic Life Ins. Co.*, 723 F.2d 700 (9th Cir. 1984); *Thornton v. Paul*, 74 Ill. 2d 132, 384 N.E.2d 335, 340 (1978).

[18] *Rhodes v. Chicago Ins. Co.*, 719 F.2d 116 (5th Cir. 1983); *Maneikis v. St. Paul Ins. Co.*, 655 F.2d 818 (7th Cir. 1981); but see *Enserch Corp. v. Shand Morahan & Co.*, 952 F.2d 1485 (5th Cir. 1992).

[19] E.g., *Thornton*, 384 N.E.2d at 335; *Nandorf, Inc. v. CNA Ins. Cos.*, 134 Ill. App. 3d 134, 479 N.E.2d 988, 991-92 (1st Dist. 1985). See generally *Insurance Claims, supra* note 6, at § 4.18.

[20] *Murphy v. Urso*, 88 Ill. 2d 444, 430 N.E.2d 1079, 1082 (1981). See also *Howard v. Russell Stover Candies, Inc.*, 649 F.2d 620 (8th Cir. 1981); *Parker v. Agricultural Ins. Co.*, 109 Misc. 2d 678, 440 N.Y.S.2d 964, 967 (Sup. Ct. 1981); *Executive Aviation, Inc. v. National Ins. Underwriters*, 16 Cal. App. 3d 799, 94 Cal. Rptr. 347 (1st Dist. 1971).

[21] See *Murphy*, 430 N.E.2d at 1084.

[22] *Nandorf*, 479 N.E.2d at 991. See also *Thornton*, 384 N.E.2d at 343.

[23] *Nandorf*, 479 N.E.2d at 992; *O'Bannon v. Northern Petrochemical Co.*, 113 Ill. App. 3d 734, 738-39, 447 N.E.2d 985 (1st Dist. 1983).

[24] See generally Ingram, *Conflicts of Interest in the Insurer's Duty to Defend in Illinois*, 17 J. Marshall L. Rev. 379, 381 (1984).

[25] *Nandorf*, 479 N.E.2d at 991.

[26] *Murphy*, 430 N.E.2d at 1083.

[27] 158 Ill. App. 3d 783, 511 N.E.2d 776 (1st Dist. 1987).

[28] *Id.*, 511 N.E.2d at 778.

[29] *Id.*

[30] *Id.*

[31] *Id.*

[32] See *Tews Funeral Home, Inc. v. Ohio Cas. Ins. Co.*, 832 F.2d 1037, 1042 (7th Cir. 1987).

[33] *St. Paul Mercury Ins. Co. v. Ralee Engineering Co.*, 804 F.2d 520 (9th Cir. 1986); *Playboy Enterprises, Inc. v. St. Paul Fire & Marine Ins. Co.*, 769 F.2d 425 (7th Cir. 1985); *Village Management Inc. v. Hartford Accident & Indem. Co.*, 662 F. Supp. 1366 (N.D. Ill. 1987).

[34] See *Thornton*, 384 N.E.2d at 335.

[35] *Murphy*, 430 N.E.2d at 1084.

[36] *Id.*

[37] *Id.*

[38] *Id.* at 1084-85.

[39] *Id.*; see also *Thornton*, 384 N.E.2d at 343.

[40] *Nandorf*, 479 N.E.2d at 993.

[41] See *Murphy*, 430 N.E.2d at 1029.

[42] See, e.g., *Nandorf*, 479 N.E.2d at 993.

[43] See, e.g., *St. Paul Mercury Ins. Co.,* 804 F.2d at 522; *Solo Cup Co. v. Federal Ins. Co.*, 619 F.2d 1178 (7th Cir.), cert. denied, 449 U.S. 1033 (1980). See also *Handbook, supra* note 6, at § 2.01.

[44] See, e.g., *Salerno v. Western Cas. & Sur. Co.,* 336 F.2d 14 (8th Cir. 1964) (ten-month delay unreasonable); *Allen v. Atlantic Nat'l Ins. Co.*, 350 Mass. 181, 214 N.E.2d 28 (1966) (rights letter should be issued before trial in underlying action begins).

[45] See also *Duke v. Hoch*, 468 F.2d 973 (5th Cir. 1972).

[46] See *supra* note 33.

[47] *St. Paul Mercury*, 804 F.2d at 522-523 (emphasis in original).

[48] 162 Cal. App. 3d 358, 208 Cal. Rptr. 494 (4th Dist. 1984).

[49] *McGee v. Superior Court,* 176 Cal. App. 3d 221, 221 Cal. Rptr. 421, 423-424 (4th Dist. 1985). See also *Native Sun Inv. Group v. Ticor Title Ins. Co.*, 189 Cal. App. 3d 1265, 235 Cal. Rptr. 34 (4th Dist. 1987).

[50] *Rhodes v. Chicago Ins. Co.*, 719 F.2d 116 (5th Cir. 1983); *Murphy*, 430 N.E.2d at 1082; but see *Enserch Corp. v. Shand Morahan & Co.*, 952 F.2d 1485 (5th Cir. 1992).

[51] *Rhodes*, 719 F.2d at 120; *Murphy*, 430 N.E.2d at 1082; see also *Village Management Inc. v. Hartford Accident & Indem. Co.*, 662 F. Supp. 1366 (N.D. Ill. 1987); *Texas United Ins. Co. v. Burt Ford Enterprises*, 703 S.W.2d 828 (Tex. App. 1986). See also *Handbook, supra* note 6, at § 5.05.

[52] See, e.g., *Board of Educ. v. CNA Ins. Co.*, 647 F. Supp. 1495 (S.D.N.Y. 1986), *aff'd*, 839 F.2d 14 (2d Cir. 1988). See also *Insurance Claims, supra* note 6, at § 3.02.

[53] See *Yale v. National Indem. Co.,* 664 F.2d 406 (4th Cir. 1981); *Transport Indem. Co. v. Home Indem. Co.,* 535 F.2d 232 (3d Cir. 1976).

[54] *Diversified Mortg. Investors v. U.S. Life Title Ins. Co.,* 544 F.2d 571 (2d Cir. 1976); *Hodges v. State Farm Mut. Auto. Ins. Co.,* 488 F. Supp. 1057 (D.S.C. 1980); *Rustia v. Prudential Property & Cas. Ins. Co.,* 440 So. 2d 1316 (Fla. App. 1983), review denied, 450 So. 2d 488 (Fla. 1984).

[55] See generally *Insurance Claims*, *supra* note 6, at § 5.01. See also *Baton v. Transamerica Ins. Co.,* 584 F.2d 907, 912 (9th Cir. 1978); *Commercial Union Assurance Cos. v. Safeway Stores, Inc.,* 26 Cal. 3d 912, 164 Cal. Rptr. 709, 712, 610 P.2d 1038 (1980). Cf. *Domangue v. Henry*, 394 So. 2d 638, 640 (La. App. 1980) (insurer must "consider the interest of the insured as paramount when an offer to settle is made"), cert. denied, 399 So. 2d 602 (La. 1981).

[56] See, e.g., *Larraburu Bros. v. Royal Indem. Co.,* 604 F.2d 1208, 1211 (9th Cir. 1979); *Boston Old Colony Ins. Co. v. Gutierrez*, 386 So. 2d 783, 785 (Fla. 1980) (insurer must settle, if possible, where a reasonably prudent person, faced with the prospect of paying the total recovery, would do so), cert. denied, 450 U.S. 922 (1981).

[57] See, e.g., *State Farm Auto. Ins. Co. v. Civil Service Employees Ins. Co.*, 19 Ariz. App. 594, 509 P.2d 725, 733 (1973) ("The mere fact that an insurer has erroneously concluded that there is no coverage...cannot excuse subsequent breaches by the insurer of other provisions of the contract, including the implied obligations pertaining to settlement. To hold otherwise would result in penalizing the more prudent insurer who initially correctly recognizes [that there is coverage]. . ., but subsequently wrongfully refuses a settlement offer").

[58] *Western Cas. & Sur. Co. v. Herman*, 405 F.2d 121 (8th Cir. 1968).

[59] See *Central Armature Works, Inc. v. American Motorists Ins. Co.,* 520 F. Supp. 283 (D.D.C. 1980); *Casualty Reciprocal Exch. v. Thomas,* 7 Kan. App. 2d 718, 647 P.2d 1361 (1982).

[60] *International Bhd. of Teamsters v. United States*, 431 U.S. 324, 335-36 n.15 (1977). See generally B. Schlei & P. Grossman, *Employment Discrimination Law* (2d ed. 1983 & Supp. 1991).

[61] See, e.g., *Lindsey v. Admiral Ins. Co.*, 804 F. Supp. 47 (N.D. Cal. 1992); *Jackson County Hosp. v. Alabama Hosp. Ass'n*, 619 So. 2d 1369 (Ala. 1993); *Sage Co. v. Insurance Co. of North America*, 480 N.W.2d 695 (Minn. App. 1992).

[62] 699 F. Supp. 787 (N.D. Cal. 1988).

[63] Wilson's other causes of action included wrongful discharge, breach of the covenant of good faith and fair dealing, intentional misrepresentation and negligent misrepresentation.

[64] Insurance contracts generally cover either "occurrences" or "claims made." Under an occurrence policy the insured is indemnified for acts or occurrences which take place within the policy period. Under a claims made policy, the insured is indemnified for claims made during the policy period regardless of when the acts giving rise to those claims occurred. See *St. Paul Fire & Marine Ins. Co. v. Barry*, 438 U.S. 531, 535 n.3 (1978); *Appalachian Ins. Co. v. Liberty Mut. Ins. Co.*, 676 F.2d 56 (3d Cir. 1982). The definitions of "occurrence" and "claim" will significantly impact on the insurer's duty to defend.

[65] *American Guarantee*, 699 F. Supp. at 789 (emphasis added).

[66] *Id.*

[67] *Danek*, 100 A.2d at 202.

[68] *American Guarantee*, 699 F. Supp. at 790.

[69] *Id.* (quoting *St. Paul Fire & Marine Ins. Co. v. Superior Court*, 161 Cal. App. 3d 1199, 1202, 208 Cal. Rptr. 5, 7 (3d Dist. 1984)). The court rejected Vista's argument that American was relieved of liability for intentional acts only if the act was committed with a "preconceived design to inflict injury." *American Guarantee*, 699 F. Supp. at 789-90. See also *Commercial Union Ins. Co. v. Superior Court*, 196 Cal. App. 3d 1205, 242 Cal. Rptr. 454 (1st Dist. 1987); *Royal Globe Ins. Co. v. Whitaker*, 181 Cal. App. 3d 532, 226 Cal. Rptr. 435 (3d Dist. 1986).

[70] 160 Ariz. 183, 772 P.2d 6 (Ariz. Ct. App. 1988).

[71] *Continental Ins.*, 772 P.2d at 7.

[72] *Id.*

[73] *Id.* at 9 (quoting *Ford v. Revlon, Inc.*, 153 Ariz. 38, 734 P.2d 580 (1987)); see also *Reliable Springs Co. v. St. Paul Fire & Marine Ins. Co.*, 869 F.2d 993, 995 (6th Cir. 1989) (No duty to defend against ADEA and state discrimination laws where policy did not include "any offense related to determination of unfair employment practices").

[74] 810 F. Supp. 249 (W.D. Ark. 1992). See also *Old Republic Ins. Co. v. Comprehensive Health Care Assocs.*, 786 F. Supp. 629 (N.D. Tex. 1992), *aff'd*, 2 F.3d 105 (5th Cir. 1993); *Coit Drapery Cleaners, Inc. v. Sequoia Ins. Co.*, 14 Cal. App. 4th 1595, 18 Cal. Rptr. 2d 692 (1 Dist. 1993).

[75] See *USF&G v. Open Sesame Child Care Center*, 819 F. Supp. 756 (N.D. Ill. 1993).

[76] 675 F. Supp. 44 (D.N.H. 1987).

[77] *Id.* at 47.

[78] *Id.* See also *Coit Drapery Cleaners, supra* note 74 (sexual harassment by president was ratified by company and therefore became company policy).

[79] 590 F. Supp. 114 (D. Or. 1984).

[80] *Id.* at 116.

[81] *Id.* (quoting *School Dist. No. 1 v. Mission Ins. Co.*, 58 Or. App. 692, 650 P.2d 929 (1982), review denied, 294 Or. 682, 666 P.2d 725 (1983)).

[82] *Omark Indus.,* 590 F. Supp. at 117.

[83] *Id.*

[84] *Id.* (Exclusion (c); emphasis added).

[85] See also *Steve Spicer Motors v. Federated Mut. Ins. Co.*, 758 S.W.2d 191 (Mo. Ct. App. 1988) (insurer not obligated to defend insured against suit by former employee alleging age discrimination because injuries alleged were neither bodily nor personal injuries as defined in the policy); *National Ben Franklin Ins. Co. v. Harris*, 161 Mich. App. 86, 409 N.W.2d 733 (1987) (insurer not required to defend against employee claim of handicap discrimination where only injury alleged was covered by workers' compensation and policy excluded claims covered by workers' compensation).

[86] 42 Wash. App. 508, 711 P.2d 1108, review denied, 105 Wash. 2d 1021 (1986).

[87] *Castle & Cooke*, 711 P.2d at 1110.

[88] *Id.*

[89] *Id.* at 1111.

[90] See Fed. R. Civ. P. 8.

[91] For other cases where allegations in the complaint supported theories of disparate impact and disparate treatment, see *Solo Cup Co. v. Federal Ins. Co.*, 619 F.2d 1178 (7th Cir.),

cert. denied, 449 U.S. 1033 (1980); *Mission Ins. Co.*, 58 Or. App. at 692, 650 P.2d at 929.

[92] *Castle & Cooke*, 711 P.2d at 1113.

[93] 619 F.2d at 1178.

[94] *Id.* at 1184 (emphasis added).

[95] *Id.*

[96] *Id.* at 1181 (emphasis added).

[97] *Id.* at 1182. Personal injury also included "bodily injury, mental injury, mental anguish, shock, sickness, disease, disability, false arrest, false imprisonment, wrongful evictions, detention, malicious prosecution . . . humiliation . . . libel, slander or defamation of character or invasion of rights of privacy." *Id.*

[98] *Id.*

[99] Accord *E-Z Loader Boat Trailers, Inc. v. Travelers Indem. Co.*, 106 Wash. 2d 901, 726 P.2d 439, 444 (1986) (although claim of disparate treatment sex and age discrimination not covered by policy, Washington Supreme Court stated that a "duty to defend might arise under some policies when disparate impact has been caused by the negligence of an employer"); *Mission Ins.*, 58 Or. App. at 692, 650 P.2d at 936 (relying on the decision in *Solo Cup*, court held that although claims of disparate treatment were not covered by the policy, "claims of discrimination based on disparate impact, which do not require a showing of discriminatory intent . . . [were] potentially within the coverage of policy").

[100] See *supra* note 62.

[101] *American Guarantee*, 699 F. Supp. at 791.

[102] See also *Loyola Marymount University v. Hartford Accident & Indem. Co.*, 219 Cal. App. 3d 1217, 271 Cal. Rptr. 528 (2d Dist. 1990).

[103] 42 U.S.C. § 2000e-5; 29 C.F.R. § 1601.

[104] See *supra* note 93.

[105] Exec. Order No. 11246, 3 C.F.R. § 339 (1964-1965), reprinted in 42 U.S.C. § 2000e, requires that nonexempt federal government contracts contain provisions that impose upon

contractors and subcontractors the obligations not to discriminate against employees or applicants for hire because of race, color, religion, sex, or national origin and to take affirmative action to insure that employees and applicants are treated without regard to such factors. See also Exec. Order No. 11375, 3 C.F.R. § 684 (1966-1970), 32 Fed. Reg. 14303 (1967) (amending 11246 to prohibit sex discrimination). Regulations of the Office of Federal Contract Compliance Programs of the U.S. Department of Labor implementing Exec. Order No. 11246 are codified at 41 C.F.R. § 60-1.

[106] *Solo Cup*, 619 F.2d at 1188 n.7 (emphasis in original).

[107] *St. Paul Mercury Ins. Co. v. Medical Lab. Network, Inc.*, 690 F. Supp. 901 (C.D. Cal. 1988).

[108] See *supra* note 62.

[109] *American Guarantee*, 699 F. Supp. at 789.

[110] See also *Commercial Union,* 196 Cal. App. 3d at 1205, 242 Cal. Rptr. at 456 ("an intentional termination is not an 'occurrence' under the policy because it is not an accident. The definition of 'accident' halts any argument that [the employer] intended his act but not the resulting harm"); *St. Paul Fire*, 161 Cal. App. 3d at 1202, 208 Cal. Rptr. at 7 (insurer was not obligated to defend its insured in any action for intentional, wrongful termination of employment, where the policy extended coverage only for claims "resulting from an accidental event").

[111] 804 F.2d 520 (9th Cir. 1986).

[112] *Id.* at 522.

[113] 690 F. Supp. at 901.

[114] See *Brady v. Elixir Industries*, 196 Cal. App. 3d 1299, 242 Cal. Rpt. 324 (4th Dist. 1987) (recognizing that an employee may be tortiously discharged without actually being terminated by an employer).

[115] *Network*, 690 F. Supp. at 903.

[116] *Id.* at 904.

[117] See also *Ralee*, 804 F.2d at 521 (employee claim that employer "made him work long hours in an attempt to cause him to resign" was not covered by a policy excluding liability for intentional acts).

[118] 234 Mont. 537, 764 P.2d 1276 (1988).

[119] *Id.* at 1277.

[120] *Id.*

[121] 91 Or. App. 276, 754 P.2d 621 (1988).

[122] The employee was a truck driver and after he complained that his vehicle was unsafe to operate, his work hours were reduced on average from 45 to 22 per week.

[123] *Falkenstein*, 754 P.2d at 622.

[124] Id. at 623. Compare *Wojciak v. Northern Package Corp.*, 310 N.W.2d 675 (Minn. 1981) (Minnesota Supreme Court held that insurer had a duty to defend and indemnify an employer in connection with an employee's claim of retaliatory discharge for filing a worker's compensation claim) with *Arundale, Inc. v. Commercial Union Ins. Co.*, 572 F. Supp. 474 (E.D. Mo. 1983) (settlement amount related to employee claim of intentional retaliatory discharge for exercising rights under state worker's compensation statute not covered by insurance policy).

[125] Under Oregon law, "a duty to defend may arise under a complaint which alleges intentional conduct when the allegations could include the lesser conduct of negligence." *Falkenstein*, 754 P.2d at 623 n.2 (citing *Ferguson v. Birmingham Fire Ins. Co.*, 254 Or. 496, 460 P.2d 342 (1969).

[126] 883 F.2d 564 (7th Cir. 1989).

[127] 244 Ill. App. 3d 837, 612 N.E.2d 846 (5th Dist.), appeal granted, 152 Ill. 2d 557, 622 N.E.2d 1203 (1993).

[128] 244 Ill. App. 3d at 845, 612 N.E.2d at 852.

[129] See, e.g., *Duldulao v. St. Mary of Nazareth Hosp.*, 115 Ill. 2d 482, 505 N.E.2d 314 (1987); *Walker v. Northern San Diego County Hosp. Dist.*, 135 Cal. App. 3d 896, 185 Cal. Rptr. 617 (4th Dist. 1982); *Toussaint v. Blue Cross & Blue Shield*, 408 Mich. 579, 292 N.W.2d 880 (1980).

[130] See, e.g., *Rulon-Miller v. International Bus. Mach. Corp.*, 162 Cal. App. 3d 241, 208 Cal. Rptr. 524 (1st Dist. 1984) (letter distributed by corporation established a "right of privacy" against discipline for off duty behavior); *Pugh v. See's Candies, Inc.*, 116 Cal. App. 3d 311, 171 Cal. Rptr. 917 (1st Dist. 1981) (employee's 32 years of service constituted an implied promise that the employer would not act arbitrarily in dealing with the employee); *Rabago-Alvarez v. Dart Industries, Inc.*, 55 Cal. App. 3d 91, 127 Cal. Rptr. 222 (1st Dist. 1976) (an

employer that at time of hire stated that new employee may only be terminated for cause is not employee at-will).

131 See *supra* note 62.

132 *American Guarantee*, 699 F. Supp. at 792.

133 See *Insurance Co. of the West v. Haralambos Bev. Co.*, 195 Cal. App. 3d 1308, 1317, 241 Cal. Rptr. 427, 430 (2d Dist. 1987).

134 808 F.2d 682 (8th Cir. 1987).

135 *Id.* at 685.

136 *Id.* (*citing Angelina Cas. Co. v. Pattonville-Bridgeton Terr.*, 706 S.W.2d 483 (Mo. App. 1986)).

137 808 F.2d at 685, 686.

138 699 F. Supp. at 793.

139 *Id.*

140 31 Ohio App. 3d 270, 511 N.E.2d 127 (1986).

141 511 N.E.2d at 128-129.

142 See *supra* note 79.

143 *Omark Indus.*, 590 Supp. at 120.

144 *Id.*

145 See *supra* note 107.

146 *Network*, 690 F. Supp. at 904 n.2.

147 See *supra* note 118.

148 *Daly Ditches*, 764 P.2d at 1278.

149 86 A.D.2d 736, 446 N.Y.S.2d 599 (3d Dept.), aff'd, 57 N.Y.2d 656, 454 N.Y.S.2d 74, 439 N.E.2d 883 (1982).

150 86 A.D.2d at 738, 446 N.Y.S.2d at 601.

151 699 F. Supp. 1438 (D. Mont. 1988).

152 819 F. Supp. 756 (N.D. Ill. 1993).

[153] *Cf. Old Republic Ins. Co. v. Comprehensive Health Care Assocs.*, 2 F.3d 105 (5th Cir. 1993).

DAVID B. RITTER

David B. Ritter is a partner at Mayer, Brown & Platt specializing in labor and employment law and litigation. He is a frequent lecturer and author on a variety of employment law topics including AIDS in the workplace, employment discrimination, collective bargaining, and employee benefits. Mr. Ritter has also been a contributing editor to *The Developing Labor Law,* published by the American Bar Association's Section of Labor and Employment Law, and the *AIDS and Public Policy Journal,* published by the University Publishing Group.

MARCIA E. GOODMAN

Marcia E. Goodman is Of Counsel with the firm of Mayer, Brown & Platt in Chicago. She specializes in labor and employment law and litigation, including litigation related to employee benefits. She has acted as defense counsel for insured claims related to employment matters and claims under ERISA. Ms. Goodman counsels corporations in a variety of industries, including a number of foreign-owned entities. She has lectured extensively on issues in labor and employment law, both in the U.S. and abroad.

INVESTIGATING SEXUAL HARASSMENT COMPLAINTS: GUIDELINES FOR EMPLOYERS

Jared H. Jossem
Torkildson, Katz, Jossem, Fonseca, Jaffe, Moore & Hetherington
Amfac Building
15th floor
700 Bishop Street
Honolulu, HI 96813
808/521-1051

INTRODUCTION

The Supreme Court and Equal Employment Opportunity Commission encourage employers to adopt procedures calculated to encourage victims of harassment to come forward. *Meritor Savings Bank v. Vinson*, 477 U.S. 57, 73, 106 S.Ct. 2399, 2408, 91 L.Ed.2d 49, (1986) 29 CFR 1604.11. The employer cannot rely upon a general policy against discrimination and a general grievance procedure in this regard. When they do come forward, the employer must take prompt and effective remedial action based upon its investigations. *Id.*

Although following *Vinson*, the Anita Hill - Clarence Thomas controversy broadened awareness of the right to complain about sexual harassment, there is little that has been written about the standard for a reasonable investigation. Cf. *Lawson v. Boeing Co.*, 58 Wash. App. 261, 265-266, 792 P.2d 545, 548 (1990), *rev. denied* 116 Wash. 2d 1021, 811 P.2d 219 (1991). Indeed, it may not be possible to define such a standard due to the variables an employer must consider in resolving these matters. This paper provides general guidelines which should be considered by human resource professionals and management labor counsel conducting a sexual harassment investigation. Readers are, of course, encouraged not only to review the cited cases but to check with competent local labor counsel familiar with current state and local policies and enforcement trends, before acting in a given factual situation.

Nevertheless, it seems clear in 1994 that an employer conducting an investigation must exercise a degree of care to avoid the Scylla of a litigable claim for defamation, wrongful termination, or other torts from the accused harasser or co-worker, and the Charybdis of Title VII and emotional distress claims from the EEOC and the victim. The employer embarking on a required investigation of a sexual harassment claim is thus between a policy rock and a legal hard place. But clearly, all the circumstances must be examined. *Harris v. Forklift Systems Inc.*, ___ U.S. ___, 114 S. Ct. 367, 63 FEP Cases 225 (1993).

I. THE EMPLOYER'S DUTY TO INVESTIGATE

The sex discrimination of the EEOC encourage prompt and effective action, and depending on the circumstances, impose strict liability for the acts of supervisors. 29 CFR 1614.11. To the extent its own investigations provide as an example, the EEOC's published *Policy Guidance on Current Issues of Sexual Harassment*, E-3, Daily Labor Report No. 60 (March 28, 1990) states:

> "The Commission recognizes that sexual conduct may be private and unacknowledged, with no eyewitnesses. Even sexual conduct that occurs openly in the workplace may appear to be consensual. Thus the resolution of a sexual harassment claim often depends on the credibility of the parties. The investigator should question the charging party and the alleged harasser in detail. The Commission's investigation should also search thoroughly for corroborative evidence of any nature. Supervisory and managerial employees, as well as co-workers, should be asked about their knowledge of the alleged harassment."

Case law, however, provides the most compelling reason to fully investigate. The judicial view is that "An employer becomes liable for sexual harassment only if it knew or should have known of the harassment and failed to take prompt remedial action." 793. E.2d 714, 719-20 (5th Cir. 1986), cert. denied, 479 U.S. 1065 (1987). In *Nash v. Electrospace System, Inc.*, —- F. 2d ——, 63 FEP Cases 765 (5th Cir. 1993), the employer's investigation within one week of the complaint "reflected a prudent response to an unpleasant situation." Summary judgment was granted to the employer whose affidavit established "a model of prompt, sensitive employer handling of these very traumatic cases." Had no investigation been timely performed, the risks of a costly trial would have been much greater.

Consistent enforcement of company policy is also required by federal law. *Valdez v. Church's Fried Chicken, Inc.*, 683 F.Supp. 596, 47 FEP 1155 (W.D. Tex 1988) (Discharge of admitted harasser violated Title VII where accusations of harassment by non-Mexicans were not usually investigated.)

Regulations in most states are modeled after federal law, but some are not specific. For example, Hawaii's DLIR Regulation § 12-46-109 (1990) resembles those of the EEOC. California regulations are less clear. FEHC Regulation § 7187.6(b)(3).

Several states recognize a common law duty of reasonable care imposed upon employers in the supervision of their employees. Cf. *Spencer v. General Electric Co.*, 894 F.2d 651, 51 FEP 1725, 1729 (4th Cir. 1990) (Dismissal of Virginia law claim of negligent supervision sustained; employer transferred employee away from accused harasser and immediately launched investigation leading to his termination.)

Company policies bearing on the investigation may be implied or express contracts. A policy setting out the prospect of specific treatment in specific circumstances may bind the employer. *Touissant v. Blue Cross & Blue Shield*, 408 Mich. 579, 292 N.W.2d 880 (1980); In *Kestenbaum v. Pennzoil Company*, 108 N.M. 20, 766 P.2d 280 (1989) *cert. denied* 490 U.S. 1109, 109 S.Ct. 3163, 104 L.Ed. 2d 1026, (1989), the employer's oral statements and a policy of termination only for cause supported a contract claim for failure to properly investigate.

The adequacy of the employer's investigation may also raise doubts about the employer's good faith, *French v. Mead Corp*, 33 FEP 830, (S.D. Ohio), aff'd 758 F.2d 652, *cert. denied* 474 U.S. 820, 106 S.Ct. 68, 88 L.Ed.2d 56 (1985) and may assist a plaintiff in asserting an unlawful harassment claim under common law or as part of a constructive termination case. *Rogers v. Leows L'Enfant Plaza Hotel*, 526 F.Supp. 523 (DDC 1981).

In sum, a prompt and thorough investigation is vital, both to build a legal defense and to resolve the workplace behaviors which prompted the complaint.

II. THE VICTIM'S INTERESTS IN THE INVESTIGATION

Employees giving evidence of discrimination and/or harassment generally are broadly protected against retaliation. Section 704(a) of Title VII prohibits retaliatory action against any individual who has opposed an unlawful practice, even if the complaint is only made within the company.

The investigation must respect the victim's interest in freedom from retaliation. Employees making complaints about working conditions generally are protected under section 8 of the Labor Management Relations Act, 29 USC §158, against retaliation for engaging in "protected concerted activities" including investigating or gathering facts relating to Sexual Harassment problems on the job. *YMCA of Pikes Peak v. NLRB*, 914 F.2d 1442, 135 LRRM 2553 (10th Cir, 1990), *cert. denied*, ____ U.S. ____, 111 S.Ct. 1681, 114 L.Ed.2d 77 (1991).

While the accuser has a clear right to be heard and to be listened to without retaliation, a "victim" who lies in the investigation can be fired for lying. *Vasconcelos v. Meese*, 907 F.2d 111 (9th Cir. 1990).

The investigation must also respect the interest of the victim in privacy. The victim may be reluctant to fully reveal intimate personal details. Difficult questions about the extent of the investigation and the propriety of inferences to be drawn from the victim's silence or lack of cooperation will arise. Care should be taken to avoid aggravating the situation with an insensitive investigation.

However, the victim's lack of cooperation does not relieve the employer who is aware of the harassment complaint of its duty to investigate. *Waltman v. International Paper Co.*, 875 F.2d 468, 50 FEP 179 (5th Cir. 1989). Where there is an issue as to whether conduct was "unwelcome" *Meritor* makes evidence of the plaintiff's workplace conduct relevant, and may even make relevant the plaintiff's non-work character, habits, and motives. Cf., *Priest v. Rotary*, 98 F.R.D. 755, 32 FEP 1064 (N.D. Cal. 1983) (Court excluded evidence which invaded plaintiff's privacy and would discourage others from complaining) and *Highlander v. K.F.C. National Management Co.*, 805 F.2d 644, 42 FEP 654 (6th Cir. 1986) (Plaintiff's prior consensual sexual relationships and meetings with accused harasser at bar after work held relevant in *quid pro quo* case.)

The investigator's duty is to advance the employer's interest in maintaining employment conditions free from discrimination and harassment. The victim's economic claims may be far less significant than the risks of unchecked misconduct. Therefore, it is critical that investigators recognize that their obligation on the part of the employer is to <u>get the facts straight</u>, not to build a technical case or a defense, either for the employer or the victim. The employer's failure to take prompt and effective action may be viewed as serving to perpetuate acts of harassment, and may delay hearings on the merits while backpay accrues. *See, e.g.*, *Stocke v. Marsh*, 912 F.2d 381, 53 FEP 1329 (9th Cir. 1990) (Question as to whether October 1988 letter was a "complaint" under Army regulations decided against Army in 1990; remanded for hearing on the merits.)

In fairness, the victim should also be given information about the right to independent counsel during investigation, upon request. Moreover, the victim's interest in bodily security should be safeguarded. *Priest v. Rotary, supra*; *Gilardi v. Schoroeder*, 833 F.2d 1226, 45 FEP 346 (7th Cir. 1987); *O'Reilly v. Executone of Albany, Inc.*, 121 A.D. 2d 772, 503 NYS 2d 185 (N.Y.A.D. 3 Dept., 1986).

As for the victim's access to company records, prior to filing suit, the victim will have a right to see the employer's investigative files provided to the EEOC, and such records will generally be discoverable. *EEOC v. Associated Dry Goods Corp.*, 449 U.S. 590, 596, 66 L.Ed.2d 762, 768, 101 S.C. 817, 821 (1981). However, the employer may, before suit, maintain the confidentiality of its records absent judicial process, and should preserve the attorney-client privilege.

III. THE ACCUSED HARASSER'S RIGHTS AND CLAIMS

Whether the accused harasser should have separate counsel is, at times, a different issue. The harasser is likely to be a separate defendant in litigation. A company attorney investigating the case should clearly disclose that she/he represents the company and that the interests of the accused may vary. However, separate counsel can substantially compound both litigation and settlement — for example by threatening to counterclaim for defamation, and/or insisting on trying a case the employer wants to settle. Whether the employer can discipline or discharge an accused because he or she wants to publicly clear his or her name in court is an interesting question in states where the "public policy" exception to the at-will rule applies.

Defamation claims by harassers have generally been unsuccessful in the face of the qualified privilege defense. *Garziano v. E.I. DuPont de Nemours & Co.*, 818 F.2d 380, 43 FEP 1790 (5th Cir. 1987) (Dissemination of memo why unnamed person was discharged held privileged); *DeSilva v. Polaroid Corp*, 45 FEP 639 (Mass. 1985) (conditional privilege in investigation and arguably absolute privilege in dissemination of information necessary to comply with Title VII); *Lawson v. Boeing Co.*, 58 Wash. App. 261, 792 P.2d 545 (1990), *Rev. denied*, 116 Wash.2d 1021, 811 P.2d 219 (1991) (Action against employer, complaining employees and investigators dismissed; standard of reasonable investigation not established.) Cf. *Kestenbaum v. Pennzoil*, 108 N.M. 20, 766 P.2d 280 (1990), *cert. denied* 490 U.S. 1109, 109 S.Ct. 3163, 104 L.Ed.2d 1026 (1989).

A harasser who works under a collective bargaining agreement, and is disciplined or discharged, may file a grievance contending the lack of just cause, claiming an inadequate or biased investigation, or asserting a lack of progressive discipline. In *Newsday v. L.I. Typographical Union*, 915 F.2d 840, 54 FEP 24, (2nd Cir. 1990) *cert. denied* 499 U.S. 922, 111 S.Ct. 1314, L.Ed.2d 247 (1991), the Second Circuit affirmed an order vacating an arbitrator's award reinstating the harasser on grounds of lack of progressive discipline. The Court found that reinstatement of the harasser would frustrate the federal and state policy against sexual harassment.

Generally, harassers have not fared well in the reported cases.

IV. CONDUCTING THE INVESTIGATION: SOME PRACTICAL POINTERS

The investigation should start, promptly.

As noted, the EEOC's regulations only encourage "immediate and appropriate corrective action." 29 CFR §1604.11(d). There appears to be an affirmative duty under Title VII to act immediately. *Robson v. Eva's Super Market Inc.*, 538 F.Supp. 857, 30 FEP 1212 (ND Ohio, 1982) *Munford v. James T. Barnes & Co.*, 441 F.Supp. 459, 17 FEP Cases 107 (ED Mich. 1977) (failure to investigate is evidence of tacit approval of harassment.)

Moreover, prompt and serious responses are of great help in disposing of claims. (*Hirschfield v. N.M. Corrections Dept.*, 916 F.2d 572, 54 FEP Cases 268 (10th Cir. 1990) (Interviews of the accused and the complainant recorded on day of incident; accused demoted) *Steele v. Offshore Shipbuilding Inc.*, 867 F.2d at 1316 (11th Cir. 1989) (Corporate employer sent a senior manager to interview employees; brought accused from Saudi Arabia to New York for a personal reprimand; promptly assured employees the harassment would stop.) *Nash v. Electrospace System, supra.*

In contrast, an incomplete investigation under Title VII will not relieve the employer of liability in a hostile work environment situation if only a fraction of the incidents which come to its attention are investigated, or where a specific incident is overlooked. *Snell v. Suffolk County*, 782 F.2d 1094 (2d Cir. 1986) (racial case).

Not only should the employer's response to a complaint be prompt and immediate, *Tomkins v. Public Service Electric & Gas Co.*, 568 F.2d 1044 (3d Cir. 1977), 29 CFR §1604.11(d), 1604.11(e), but the promptness will be evaluated in hindsight against the severity of the harassment eventually discovered. Delay of over a day after plaintiff advises management of the complaint has resulted in imputing liability to the employer on the "actual knowledge" theory, *Taylor v. Faculty Student Assoc. of State University College*, 40 FEP 1292 (WD NY 1986), while failure to investigate a hostile work environment involving non-supervisory co-workers may not trigger employer liability until there is something the employer "should have known" about. Thus, a lack of discovered pervasiveness or severity may lessen the employer's exposure due investigation delays where there was "no reason to know."

Usually, an employer's failure to investigate and take appropriate action[1] will almost certainly carry great weight in fixing liability on an employer. *Craig v. Y&Y Snacks*, 721 F.2d 77 (3rd Cir. 1983). *Katz v. Dole*, 709 F.2d 251, 31 FEP 1521 (4th Cir. 1983). Accordingly, the employer seeking to avoid liability must act promptly and effectively. The "ostrich defense" just does not work. *Robson v. Eva's Super Market Inc.*, 538 F. Supp 857, 30 FEP 1212 (ND Ohio, 1982). *Munford v. James T. Barnes & Co.*, 441 F.Supp. 459, 17 FEP 107 (ED Mich 1977) (failure to investigate is evidence of tacit approval of harassment).

The investigator should first review background materials before scheduling interviews. The investigator should probably begin with a review of:

1. Victim's Personnel File and Job Description;
2. Harasser's Personnel File and Job Description;
3. Organization chart or roster of employees;
4. Affirmative action logs and records;
5. Other reports of investigations;
6. Company policies on discipline and sexual harassment
7. Charges, complaints and grievances involving the victim;
8. Charges, complaints and grievances involving the harasser;
9. Attendance patterns and transfer requests.

In preparing for interviews, the investigator should consider the use of a standard form advising witnesses of their rights and enlisting their cooperation such as:

> "I am ______________________________, attorney for the ____________ Company. As you may know, the Company is an affirmative action/equal opportunity employer with a policy regarding sexual harassment. I am investigating an alleged violation of that policy, and it is my job to investigate the matter promptly and fairly. I ask for your cooperation. If you do not object, I would like to tape record our discussion. [If you wish, I will gladly provide you with a copy of the tape to keep or use as you wish. - Optional]
>
> You should understand that you or others may have claims against the company which you may want to assert after this investigation is finished. You have a right to do so through a private attorney, the EEOC or the State FEP agency. My present duty is to get the facts straight and your voluntary cooperation will assist the company in doing so. Of course, you have the right to terminate this interview whenever you wish. Are you willing to continue with this investigation interview voluntarily?

After the initial disclosures are given, then proceed to establish foundation of the witness's competency.

If the investigation is by or with counsel for the company, consider lawful means of protecting the work product and attorney client privilege.

After thorough preparation, the victim should be interviewed early in the investigation. The victim should be asked to provide a full account of the facts. However, as noted above, the victim's lack of cooperation does not relieve the employer of its duty to investigate. *Waltman v. International Paper Co.*, 875 F.2d 468, 50 FEP 179 (5th Cir. 1989). In this interview, as all others, strive to conduct a full, fair and impartial investigation. Examples of inadequate investigations abound: *Heelan v. Johns-Manville Corp.*, 451 F.Supp. 1382, 1389, 20 FEP 251 (D.Co. 1978) (Calling the accused to get a denial inadequate). Cf. EEOC Decision No. 72-0779 (CCH EEOC Decisions #6321) (racial harassment investigation which ended as soon as Caucasian denied using epithet found evidence of violation). An incomplete investigation will not relieve the employer of liability in a hostile work environment situation if only a fraction of the incidents which come to its attention are investigated, or where a specific incident is overlooked. *Snell v. Suffolk County*, (2d Cir. 1986) 782 F.2d 1094, 39 FEP 1590 (racial incidents not fully investigated).

- What happened?
- Where?
- When?
- General circumstances?
- How did you know?
- What did you say and do? What did (s)he say and do?
- Who else might have seen or heard what happened?
- What did you do then?
- What did you do for the rest of the day?
- How did you react?
- Did you discuss what happened with anyone else?
- What is the company policy on this sort of thing?
- Has this, or other offensive conduct, happened before?
- How do you know? What happened then? Was it reported?
- What was done about it?

Notice that these questions do not "name names" and are broad. The objective is to pull out all possible leads without defaming anyone.

Once the general facts are established, it will usually be necessary to explore more closely factors which will aid in resolving credibility issues. For example:

- Who specifically are the other persons who will provide information that supports your position?
- Has anyone else there discussed the accused's conduct with you? When?
- How often? What else was said? What else happened? What else did you see or hear?
- When did anyone first complain about this sort of problem?

  (Is there any reason for a long delay? Did anything bad ever happen to anyone who raised the issue?)

- What notes or records do you have of what happened? Can I review them and get a copy?
- How do (did) you feel? Have you consulted (the company) (a) doctor or nurse?
- Have you or anyone else lost work time because of this?
- What do you think the company should do about the situation?

Other employees should always be interviewed if they were in a position to observe the alleged misconduct or its effects. After reviewing the victim's report, proceed to other possible witnesses. Begin with the same introduction and form. Other employees probably should be interviewed before the accused, however, to give the investigator more information for the interview of the harasser, and to explore fully credibility questions and possible rebuttal at that time.

The number or proportion of non-complaining witnesses interviewed has been critical in many cases. In *Trautvetter v. Quick*, 916 F.2d 1140, 54 FEP 109 (7th Cir. 1990), top management, in conjunction with the school board's legal counsel, interviewed a *majority* of the school staff to determine if *any* of them had noticed any acts of harassment on the part of the accused. The general response was that the relationship was consensual, and that the victim actively pursued the relationship. Result: summary judgment for the employer. In contrast, in *Kestenbaum v. Pennzoil Co.*, 766 P.2d 280 (N.M. 1989) *cert. denied* 490 U.S. 1109, 109 S.Ct. 3163, 104 L.Ed.2d 1026 (1989), the investigator admitted in her deposition, on cross examination, that her summary of the interviews was not intended to stand alone, that it failed to differentiate between first hand knowledge, attributed hearsay, gossip and rumor; no attempt was made to evaluate credibility. Few neutral employees were contacted. Result: damage award to accused harasser sustained.

In searching for corroboration or probing credibility, the following are examples of useful questions:

- Has there been any conduct or speech you have observed that makes people at work uncomfortable?
- Has any of it involved sexual or ethnic matters? Who was involved?
- What have you noticed that might be related to this? Anything else?
- Would you mind calling or dropping me a note if you think of anything else?
- You mentioned Mr.__*x*__. Describe his usual method of operation or actions towards other employees or protected group members.
- Is anyone here vulgar or offensive to members of both sexes? Give examples.
- Is the conduct limited to one sex? Or one person? Why do you think that is so?
- Are there any people here (in their department) that you consider chronic complainers?

- Are any people in this department trying to get someone fired for an ulterior reason?
- Do you think some people are treated differently from others for reasons that are not job or work related? Explain.
- Are there any personality conflicts you have noticed? Please describe them.
- In your opinion, have any employees received the benefit of favoritism for reasons other than work performance? Explain.
- How do various people react when the accused "does his thing"?
- What does the victim wear to work? Does she/he ever tell dirty jokes? Has she/he made the conduct of concern welcome?
- How has this series of events affected the workplace? Has anyone's work performance been impacted? How long after the incidents did conditions here change?
- Who participates in important decisions about promotions, raises and work assignments? Has that person been involved in any of the conduct under investigation?
- When do you think management should have learned (or knew) about what is going on?
- How many actual incidents have there been?
- Over what time frame?
- In what context did each occur?

Take your time and, of course, write a summary of the interview for prompt adoption, and signature.

After you are informed of the views of the victim and others proceed to the accused. Use the same introduction and open-ended questions. Be sure to include:

- Are you aware of the company policy regarding sexual harassment? When did you first learn of it?
- Have you ever spoken with any employees about a (social relationship with you? (date? (lunch?) Which employees?
- Have you ever made reference to any employee by race or sex? What references have you made?
- Have you ever joked with anyone at work referring to anyone's race or sex in an unoffensive, welcomed sort of way? Describe the incidents. Why was that conduct welcome?
- Describe in detail why you believe that conduct was acceptable to other person.

- Are there circumstances which make it unlikely that you would have done it? For example, explore the presence of witnesses, the time of day, alibi, prior warning or training.

To the extent practical, ask the same series of questions as you asked the others witnesses, and give the accused a full opportunity to respond and explain his or her answers. Some investigators may give the accused a fair and clear chance to reflect for a few days and to supplement the responses given, to avoid any appearance of coercion. In some cases, the chance for reflection leads to a clarification of the facts.

V. REPORT RESOLVING CREDIBILITY ISSUES

Return to prior witnesses to explore any inconsistencies and obtain corroboration where possible. Of course, you should never attempt to induce or coerce a witness to lie or to obstruct a government investigation.

The investigator should then prepare a "privileged and confidential" report to decision-making management, setting forth impressions on credibility and pointing out what additional information might be necessary to resolve credibility issues.

VI. DETERMINATION

Management, preferably by a mixed gender committee (not including the accused), should then seek to determine:

1. Objectively, what is the likely or plausible version of the facts?
2. What action should be taken consistent with the results of the investigation and company practices?

The report, investigative materials and decision must be preserved, since whatever action is taken, the employer may be required to demonstrate when and how it took prompt and effective action.

VII. FOLLOW-UP BEYOND THE DISPOSITION

Whether or not the complaint is not sustained, it is prudent to assure that the complainant and all witnesses suffer no retaliation. An uncomfortable victim even maybe offered a transfer in a "no cause" case to reduce workplace friction.

The accused's next performance review might well explore how the situation was handled. Document the follow up in both the employee's file and in the affirmative action officer's diary or records, for future reference.

VIII. CONCLUSION

In *Nash v. Electrospace System*, ___F 2d ___, 63 FEP Cases 765 (5th Cir. 1993) we can see the benefits of a prompt and complete investigation and immediate remedial action. In *Nash*, a supervisor subjected his female secretary to a barrage of questions about her personal life, and during the same period she received several anonymous sexual calls on her home telephone. After Nash's complaint to the personnel department, personnel interviewed the accused harasser and Nash's female co-workers. The harasser admitted some personal discussion, contending they were not intended to be offensive, and personnel promptly transferred Nash to another department, where her career advanced. She admitted in her deposition that the transfer was not "retaliatory."

Such a case, in which summary judgment was granted by the District Court and affirmed on appeal shows us not only the rewards for the employer that acts promptly, but also reflects the benefits of a prompt investigation, apparently under the guidance of skilled legal counsel, for the employee whose career was continued in a new environment immediately after a full investigation was completed.

Footnote

1. The appropriateness of the employer's response as a result of the action is beyond the scope of this paper. But see, e.g., *Yates v. Avco Corp.* 819 F.2d 630 (6th Cir. 1987).

SOCIAL AND PSYCHOLOGICAL FACTORS IN SEXUAL HARASSMENT

A MODEL FOR PREVENTION

Mary H. Fox, Ph.D., Lynn Litow, and Michael Boyes

INTRODUCTION

Recent publicity concerning sexual harassment has resulted in an explosion of claims and a substantially accelerated interest in prevention and training programs in American business. Nearly every American worker has developed a new awareness of behaviors which can be interpreted as sex discrimination in the workplace. Increased awareness of sexual harassment appears to be representative of new normative values in American business. Over the past twenty years, humanistic and participatory management practices have increasingly become expected by employees (Lawler, 1990), and behaviors previously tolerated under more autocratic structures have lead to rapid responses --complaints, litigation, or other worker reactions. If for no other reason, the fiscal implications of sexual discrimination due to low morale, lost productivity, turnover, and litigation, have escalated the consequences and motivated companies to work seriously toward effective prevention and intervention. The Civil Rights Act (1991) defined new standards for sex discrimination and has re-focused employers' efforts toward a more proactive role in helping employees understand their rights and responsibilities, in promoting equal employment opportunity, and in protecting the psychological welfare of employees.

The first step in the process of programmatic prevention and education is to recognize that "sexual harassment" is not a unitary concept nor does it provide us with a clear-cut list of unacceptable behaviors (Konrad & Gutek, 1986; Fain & Anderson, 1987). The term "sexual harassment" can be defined legally, psychologically, socially, and from a practical business standpoint. In fact, the term has come to refer to such a wide array of complex behaviors and incidents that's it's difficult for companies to know how to handle the obviously disparate values and needs of all of their workers. Even experts have difficulty agreeing on what defines harassment, and various types of experts stray out of their own areas and into others during their work. Judges make decisions in the psychological realm, psychologists interpret legal ramifications of their client's actions, managers decide both legal and psychological decisions. One notable recent example involved the 1993 Supreme Court decision (Harris vs. Forklift Systems) that psychological "distress" is not the criteria we use to determine the existence or magnitude of a harassing incident. In cases such as this, judges are forced to rule on the psychological reality of complainants and defendants. Psychologists, in turn, contribute to legal decisions with expert testimony, articles and amicus briefs prepared in association with legal professionals, and by collaborating with legislative actions to develop guidelines for employers.

What common ground do these various interpretations and definitions share? From the legal realm, we start with the observation that sexual harassment is considered to be a form of gender discrimination. Typically, two levels of harassment are identified, quid pro quo incidents whereby economic benefit is granted in return for sexual favors or is required as a condition of employment, and "hostile work environment," usually more subtle, which usually involves conditions where a worker must tolerate repeated unwelcome verbal or nonverbal incidents of a subtle sexual nature. In the 1986 Vinson case, the Supreme Court noted that sexual harassment does not necessarily involve sexual relations. In fact, the vast majority of complaints in organizations has always involved hostile work environment claims, or as it is sometimes called, subtle sexual harassment.

Causal Factors to Sexual Harassment

Some psychological theorists have argued that quid pro quo incidents can be compared to rape; as a result, some psychological research has borrowed heavily from research literature on rape to explain why people use sexual means to overpower or influence others. Many theorists believe that sexual harassment, again especially in quid pro quo cases, is an expression of personal power (Gutek & Morasch, 1982). Most mainstream psychological theories may not make such a strong case for power issues, but all would postulate that learned social norms are critical factors in why people behave in ways others would consider to be sexual harassment. Each potentially harassing incident is an interpersonal interaction and needs to be understood in the context of an ongoing relationship or the culture surrounding the participants. Victims may find they have a hard time explaining an offense because the harasser's behaviors are borderline socially acceptable (Cooper, 1985; Konrad & Gutek, 1986). The harasser's comments are often vague, leaving room for multiple interpretations. Managers' inability to get clear evidence can ultimately protect the harasser from rejection and sanction. In other words, both the expression and interpretation of social-sexual interactions in the work place may be influenced by social factors, organizational status, roles of the parties, personal response orientations and any of dozens of other psychological and social influences.

History shows we've been tough on victims of harassment. Some research shows that up through the mid-80's, victims of harassment often quit, attempt to quit or transfer from their jobs rather than to complain about the incidents. In one study, Gutek et al (1983) found that 9% of harassed women vs. 1% of men quit their jobs as a result of harassment; 75% of the females quit without filing any kind of complaint. Another 5% of harassed women vs. 1% of harassed men transferred jobs to escape the situation.

Because of the enormous potential for clashing values, misunderstandings, and perceived objectionable behaviors, successfully preventing and resolving incidents which could involve potential sexual harassment requires that any policy description of what is and is not sexually harassing be defined in such a way to serve as a guideline or standard for resolving incidents on a case by case basis. It is for this reason that he courts have come to use the "reasonable man, reasonable woman" (Ellison vs. Brady, 1990) standard as a means to resolve those cases where it's not clear whose perspective is normative, or whose psychological reality should take precedent in determining whether a comment is objectionable or not.

Let's look at some specific examples: the person who makes offensive sexual jokes is not necessarily likely to be the same person to push for unwanted dates. Likewise, one victim may experience self blame, sadness, and generalized anxiety (Jensen & Gutek, 1982), while another may experience anger or disgust to the same incident.

Consider the following vignettes describing some social interactions in the work place. Are they sexual? Are they harassment?

Case One

The president of a small company contemplates admonishing Randy for his latest binge of the employee's all-too frequent social pastime, cornering a co-worker to recount some glorious fish story. The president has always been aware of Randy's annoying habit and tolerated it for the most part. But now things are a little different. Over the past few months the company has hired several young women into the predominantly male firm. To everyone's dismay, each young woman has been subjected to an especially heavy dose of Randy's attention. The extra attention and frequent complements have made the women feel uncomfortable and distracted from their work. Is this a personal or a management problem? How does this affect productivity? Is this hostile work environment or worse yet, quid pro quo harassment?

Case Two

Leaning over his desk, the female Information Systems Manager coyly tells Mark that she "is always ready to help him any way she can." From past experience Paula predicts Mark's response. He squirms and tells her to cut it out. "What, don't you want me to help you with your accounting program?" Paula asks while gazing into his eyes. Mark laughs nervously; Paula leaves.

Case Three

Nick and Tanya kindle a romantic relationship on a two-week trip on the road together. Nick, her boss, hoping for this to happen, has arranged to work with Tanya on several upcoming projects, including this one. When they get back home, Tanya regrets cheating on her boyfriend with her boss and tells him so. The choice assignments end shortly after Tanya tells Nick that she no longer wants to see him. Tanya blames herself for her indiscretion, but continues to wonder, "am I being treated fairly; were my colleagues treated unfairly when I was given the choice assignments?"

How do we determine which of these incidents constitutes sexual harassment, which are quid pro quo? Is it based on how the victims feel? This is extremely difficult if not impossible to objectively assess, even if different victims have similar behavioral reactions. Similarly, we can never really know the harassers' intentions -- in some cases the harasser himself may not know what he intended. While the feeling of the victim and the intention of the harasser are critical determinants of whether a complaint of sexual harassment is filed, the range of motives and reactions can lead us to quite different conclusions and remedies. To truly understand and control harassment, corporate policy makers need to become skilled at identifying different types of sexual harassment. They need to understand the differences in personal orientation that underlie many sexual harassment complaints and the social influences which contribute to complaints.

Types of Sexual Harassment

Based on hundreds of interviews with victims and their managers, Cooper (1985) categorized six types of behaviors constituting harassment: Aesthetic Appreciation; Active Mental Groping; Social Touching; Foreplay Harassment; Sexual Abuse; Ultimate Threat. The Merit Systems Protection Board Survey (1981), a springboard for much research, breaks harassment into seven similar categories. In order of their incidence they are: 1) unwanted sexual jokes, teasing and remarks; 2) unwanted suggestive looks or gestures; 3) unwanted deliberate touching or cornering; 4) unwanted pressure for dates; 5) unwanted pressure for sexual favors; 6) unwanted phone calls and other communications; and 7) actual attempted rape or assault (Fain & Anderson, 1987). These categories and those used by other authors can be roughly grouped into three types of sexual harassment: 1.) visual glares (ogling), 2.) verbal comments, and 3.) touch. Even these groupings, however, leave much potentially undefined. What if one employee tells an off-color joke to another, which they both find amusing, but a third party who hears the joke is offended? What if an employee hangs nude photos in his desk area or locker? While not all incidents and exemplars can be covered in policy-setting, some form of listing is a necessary starting point for any training program.

When attempting to define a list of unacceptable behaviors, it's also important to consider that although most on-the-job sexual contacts are clearly unwanted, some types are more likely to be experienced as harassment. In a study on sexual harassment of airline employees, Bishop et al. (1982) found that flight attendants reacted differently to incidents based on the level of their work relationships. Serious incidents of sexual harassment, i.e. comments and touching, were interpreted differently, based on the instigator's social strata in the airline. Higher level employees, e.g. pilots, but not supervisory employees, were allowed more intimate contact with the attendants without their behaviors being considered offensive.

Almost universally, intimate contact from supervisors, and especially physical contact, is likely to be regarded as inappropriate and insulting (Gutek, Morasch and Cohen, 1983). For the purpose of program planning, then, it is important to help employees develop the ability to recognize the implications of quid pro quo versus other types of sexual harassment. Employers, too, will need to develop an empathetic understanding of the different reactions that people will experience to situations.

Differences in Personal Orientation

Male - female differences in personal orientation are often an important underlying factor in many sexual harassment complaints (Konrad & Gutek, 1986). Males and females interpret social exchanges differently. Males, for example, are more likely to interpret the presence of sexuality in the conversations and actions of women than the women intend. In one study investigating sexual harassment, a male participant reported having his foot stepped on as an example of sexual touch on the job. Men are also more likely to consider sexual comments, jokes, ogling, and touch as an acceptable, even normal, part of the day. Even if they experience sexual encounters which are clearly not a normal part of the day, most men consider the incidents less anxiety provoking than do women. Psychologists believe that men are more likely to have been socialized to be sexually aggressive, to be proud of their sexuality, and consequently to feel less guilty and more positive about sexual encounters, (Abbey, 1982; Jones, et al. 1987). Gutek, Morasch & Cohen, (1983) found that 67% of the men in their survey said they would feel flattered by sexual overtures in the work place. This is in contrast to 17% of women who said they would feel flattered; most women reported they would feel insulted by these same incidents.

To complicate matters, while men may be unaware that their behavior is sexually offensive, women may be too subtle in their attempts to communicate that a behavior is offensive. Some are inclined to avoid the harasser rather than report or inform him. Terpestra (1986) finds that many victims say that confronting the harasser will at best accomplish nothing and at worst lead to reprisal.

To summarize, sexual harassment can be a self reinforcing system. Men behave in ways that offend women, women respond passively or send subtle unclear messages, men miss the messages and continue behaving "normally." Women are less likely to joke or make verbal comments than are men and more likely to be insulted by the comments than men may realize.

Social Influences

Is it possible to identify who is more likely to become the victim of sexual harassment? Researchers have investigated whether or not an individual's social status, organizational status, i.e., his or her position in the corporation, can predict sexual harassment on the job. Fain & Anderson's (1982) work suggests that social status variables are more powerful predictors of sexual harassment than either organizational status variables or personality. For example, unmarried women, young workers (ages 16 to 30) and minorities in the Merit studies were harassed more than any other groups of workers.

Investigators have also conducted survey research to test the hypothesis that women in traditionally male dominated jobs and women in traditionally female dominated jobs will be more likely to experience sexual harassment than those in jobs that are equally associated with men and women (Gutek & Morasch, 1982). Their "role spillover theory" suggests that gender roles, like social status, are carried into the employment context. They did find some evidence to support the idea that women in jobs that are traditionally male or traditionally female are more likely to be harassed. While further research is necessary, these findings suggest that corporate policy makers need to be aware of role variables that might increase the occurrence or the reporting of sexual harassment.

Types of sexual harassment, differences in personal orientation that contribute to its incidence, and social influences which identify the potential victims of harassment represent the myriad of social phenomena related to this troublesome workplace occurrence. In that these phenomena can be summarized as socialized attitudes that are deeply rooted in a person's way of thinking and behaving, corporate policy makers are presented with the dilemma of developing programs that will challenge employees 1) to question their beliefs and values and, 2) to act differently.

It follows then that companies must develop and practice a strong commitment to egalitarian practices. With a policy statement as a foundation, organizations are ready to turn their attention to developing and implementing an effective sexual harassment prevention program. Sexual harassment training is often a critical element in an organization's follow-through to help employees understand their roles, rights, and responsibilities in avoiding workplace sex discrimination.

A MODEL SEXUAL HARASSMENT PROGRAM

An effective Sexual Harassment Program will include the following elements: 1) a strong policy statement; 2) structures to support the policy statement; 3) procedures to train, treat, and follow-up any potential incidents.

1. **Policy Statement**

The starting point for an effective prevention program is creation of a strong policy statement prohibiting sexual harassment and indicating consequences for harassers. The policy statement is a necessary element in a company's stance on sexual harassment for multiple reasons. First, it communicates the philosophy of the company, telling people how they are expected to behave. Second, through the wording and stated consequences of policy violation, the company communicates how strongly it is dedicated to the cause. Third, it notifies employees in advance of the consequences of policy violation. Advance notification is a crucial element in terms of behavioral control and in terms of perceived fairness. The policy statement should include, at a minimum, several elements: 1) definition of the terms and behaviors discussed in the statement, 2) descriptions of acceptable and unacceptable behavior 3) an explanation of the reasons for the policy, i.e. the negative consequences of sexual harassment on the victim and the organization) and, 4) discussion of the consequences for unacceptable behavior.

While a policy statement with these elements can be an important communication device, it must be backed by consistent management action. Negative consequences for policy violations must be firmly established and communicated, and then must be enforced consistently for all employees in proportion to the offense.

Where possible, norms should be established for remedial action to guide managers' decisions once incidents occur. This is a difficult task because the nature of the offenses is interpreted depending on past history. Because organizations tend to be more lenient toward top executives and higher-level employees because of their "importance" to the organization, predefinition of violations and consequences should be outlined as specifically as possible. This sends the message that equality is an important goal, and that it will be uniformly applied. With a strong policy statement and credible procedures in place to back it up, employees will be less inclined to believe that any incidents which do occur have been condoned by management.

2. **Support Structures**

Despite the existence of a strong policy statement and consistent management support, some organizations will continue to experience sexual harassment. Therefore an effective sexual harassment program must have a support structure in place to handle harassment complaints. Typically, this will involve a means to disseminate, both formally and informally, the policy of the organization to all workers. It should also involve training of supervisors, and of all employees where possible, in how to receive, interpret and handle incidents and complaints.

Informal Grievance Procedures

Most reported cases of sexual harassment are actually cases of subtle sexual harassment or hostile work environment cases rather than quid pro quo (Bureau of National Affairs, 1992). Most victims of such cases are interested in putting a stop to the offensive behaviors and restoring good relations (Terpestra, 1986), therefore informal remedies are often identified and implemented. Very few victims of subtle sexual harassment, and in fact of quid pro quo cases, want the harasser to get into trouble.

The goal of every investigation is to end the harassment through appropriate corrective action. Even informal interventions should involve training for the victim to understand their rights, to identify potentially harassing actions, to assertively confront harassers if necessary, and to get help as needed from the organization. At a minimum, the harasser must be informed that the behavior in question will not be tolerated. Ideally, all parties will learn methods to resolve situations which do not seem to warrant formal organizational interventions or sanctions.

Formal Grievance procedures

Employees should be encouraged to use the company's formal grievance procedure either in quid pro quo cases, or in less grievous cases of subtle harassment where parties have unsuccessfully attempted to resolve the situation. A formal grievance system should encourage an employee to file a written complaint to an appointed grievance officer, always someone other than the employee's supervisor or the alleged harasser. It is preferable to have at least one female grievance officer in an organization since most victims are women and most harassers are men. The first order of business for a grievance officer when s/he receives a complaint is to listen to the complainant with an open mind and an empathetic heart. Depending on the severity of the complaint, the officer next determines if it's possible to work the problem out with the alleged harasser. The officer may try to have the involved parties meet to work out the issue to the complainant's satisfaction. During this coaching period, it is important for the officer to communicate that s/he takes the complaint seriously. This will minimize hostility and resentment for both parties, as well as support the victims' ability to express their concerns.

Serious harassment such as sexual touching or repeated offenses call for more dramatic action. In these latter cases, it is best for the officer to move right into the second step of the grievance procedure, formal investigation.

Grievance officers have a tough job because it is difficult to remain objective when investigating highly personal and potentially damaging allegations. Therefore, employees in these positions should be trained to recognize their personal biases. For example, a person's first reaction upon hearing the allegation may be to blame either the harasser or victim. Following any sexual harassment incident, both the victim and observers engage in a responsibility-attribution process (Jensen & Gutek, 1982) which often involves blame. Blame behavior is a normal occurrence as people try to make sense of discomfort in their relationships. In a harassment incident, observer blame helps people restore feelings of control. Victims, too, engage in blame strategies to cope with their feelings. If the victim is one who is self-blaming as well, the results can be devastating. The observer may discourage the victim's report and may prevent accurate investigation because of the victim's (realistic) fear of being stigmatized by the incident. They might even continue to live with the harassment and the potentially maladaptive self blame. Whether a victim blames herself or the harasser, a male grievance officer's first inclination is to believe a woman victim's analysis of the situation. Both male and female officers are also likely to feel conflict when they identify with the victim. All those trends must be interrupted and the officer must instead adopt an impartial stance in order to protect all parties' rights.

Any employee involved in the investigation must be taught to keep information as confidential as possible, involving only the relevant parties at first. Other parties with direct knowledge should be interviewed only when necessary. Following the investigation, a finding of sexual harassment should always lead to a disciplinary action in proportion to the offense and in accordance with company policy. It may be possible to find nondisciplinary remedies, e.g. to separate the parties either by transfer or reassignment to prevent contact between the parties if necessary. Where the working relationship between the parties remains intact, some type of mediation or reconciliation process can be arranged by the grievance officer. This type of mediation is likely to be necessary whenever the working relationship remains intact, despite the findings of the investigation.

The stronger the harassment, the more severe the remedy or disciplinary action must be. Usually, an employer will use as a reference point other actions which have taken place in the company, or lacking that reference point, will determine what are the most reasonable remedies or disciplines in order to preserve the rights of all involved parties.

In severe offenses, e.g. assault or long term quid pro quo harassment, the officer should be prepared to refer the victim to a support group or counselor. It's important that whatever corrective action is taken, the remedy be based on the seriousness of the behavior, not what the victim thinks is an appropriate remedy. To make certain the corrective action is appropriate, it's always best to refer to a central department or person who reviews all actions. Follow-up is always needed to make certain that the remedy or corrective action took place as specified, that there were no further incidents, and that no reprisals against either the victim or harasser have taken place.

3. <u>Equal Opportunity Hiring and Promotion</u>

Many women function in a work environment still dominated by male values and traditions which view women as subservient to men. From there it is a small jump to the belief that women should have different roles than men in a work setting. As women increasingly populate the workplace, this will help to change attitudes in two ways. First, research shows that stereotypes are dispelled mostly through experience with the target group. Therefore, organizations with greater gender integration will experience less harassment because women will become increasingly regarded as employees with work roles rather than women with gender roles (Gutek & Jensen, 1982). Second, because of greater integration, the actual roles and values of organizations will slowly change to be more gender shared or gender neutral.

4. <u>Training</u>

Educational programs are probably the most visible and obvious attitude change programs. When they work, training programs are essential in creating a self-aware, conscientious work force. Training programs that don't work have the opposite impact and can discredit the goals which they are meant to achieve. Employers can undermine their training efforts by failing to support the program and the practices taught.

Policy makers, managers, and employees must all be in close accord for training to be an effective tool. Once they develop a shared understanding of program objectives and activities, managers are better able to control and monitor program success. They are also able to predict each others' reactions to employee harassment problems. While managers <u>must</u> be trained; all employees should receive some level of sexual harassment training.

Training Content

As a general rule, training should provide the participants with personal insights into their own behavior and some genuinely new knowledge. Experiential exercises, e.g. role playing, coed group discussion, and behavioral modeling are examples of techniques that help employees challenge their knowledge and skills. For example, if a behavioral modeling strategy is used: 1) employees are told that they will be observing a model perform a skill (coping or counseling); 2) employees observe a model perform the skill; 3) employees practice the skill (role play) and 4) the employee receives feedback about how well he/she demonstrated the skill. Exercises like these often give the participants insight into self and others. When training doesn't provide personally relevant learning, the participants are likely to dismiss its value, believing "everybody knows this stuff." Therefore, training must go beyond descriptions of quid pro quo harassment, beyond the policy statement, and beyond simple didactic techniques. Below is a description of a sample training program.

Phase One

Training can actually be considered to begin during a new employee's initial orientation to the company, either formal or informal. During that orientation, employees should be given a copy of the employee handbook containing a policy statement regarding important issues such as equal opportunity work conditions and sexual harassment. Ideally, orientation should include the first phase of training since many small employers simply do not have the budget to go beyond this phase. Video training packages offered by several companies provide a relatively inexpensive alternative to more complete training and can be included as part of the orientation.

Large employers, employers with large numbers of traditionally male jobs, and employers with a history of complaints should continue on with Phase Two.

Phase Two

A logical starting point for this next step in training is a discussion of the various definitions and forms of harassment covered in the company's policy on harassment. Although people's conceptions of harassment often match the EEOC definition (York, 1989) most people have not considered the many forms of harassment and therefore are not prepared to deal with it when it actually occurs. Distinctions between assault, harassment, mutual attraction and friendly behavior should be discussed (Licata & Popovich, 1987). Experiential exercises such as coed group discussions, role plays or behavioral modeling can help employees explore the different forms harassment can take.

Phase Three

Common myths about the way people interact should be dispelled in phase three. For example, one common belief is that people normally realize the impact of their behavior upon others, but in reality many people do not. Myths such as "only young attractive females are harassed," and "men who are accused of harassment are bad or sex hungry" should be dispelled. Perceptual differences should be explored with the aim of heightening self-awareness and sensitivity for others. Phase three might begin with a self-awareness quiz and progress into observation and discussion of videotaped vignettes of social-sexual encounters. This method is an excellent way for employees to discover and explore their knowledge level and perceptual biases.

Phase Four

Statistics in various surveys suggest that approximately 42% - 90% of women workers are victimized by sexual harassment at some point in their lives (U.S. Merit Systems Protection Board, 1981). Many more will witness it directly or through the testimony of their friends. Therefore, it is important that people learn coping strategies and that potential witnesses learn support skills toward the victims.

Because most employees are potential witnesses as well, each needs to know the part s/he should play in a complaint investigation. For example, they should know that harassers can be of either sex, that the victim can be a "third party," that all parties need to be guarded against any form of retaliation. They must learn how to support victims rather than blame them, to be sensitive to all sides of a situation. Sophisticated counseling skills are not required; good listening skills, objectivity, and a knowledge of proper procedures are the basic tools needed.

To review, the most important preventive actions am employer can take are:

- write an effective policy statement which delineates the company's commitment to a work place free from sex discrimination
- develop and implement meaningful, practical procedures to disseminate the policy in the work place
- provide guidelines for investigating complaints
- educate supervisors and employees concerning their rights and responsibilities
- develop appropriate corrective actions which take into account both accused and accuser needs
- follow-up every complaint investigation to make certain the situation has been resolved

SUMMARY AND CONCLUSION

Psychological research in the area of sexual harassment indicates that the concept is multi-faceted in both its expression and its interpretation. Harassment incidents are influenced by a complexity of factors including status, male/female differences in personal orientation, and gender relevant social history of individuals. Most importantly, research finds that corporations, in their development of harassment prevention policies and their response to such incidents, play a critical role in reducing harassment incidents. In this paper, we have outlined a program for corporate policy to develop preventive strategies for their organizations. First, we have delimited some of the major differences in social and psychological variables that can lead to harassment incidents. Second, we have recommended the development of a sexual harassment program which includes a strong policy statement, supporting corporate structures to help managers enact this policy, and a training program aimed at managers and all employees. This program should attempt to educate all workers and also to model acceptable behaviors in the workplace. The training program should be a direct reflection of management's strong commitment to egalitarian work practices and should emphasize their position on what is effective business practice in dealing with harassment incidents.

REFERENCES

1. **Abbey, A.**, (1982) Sex Differences in Attributions for Friendly Behavior: Do Males Misperceive Female's Friendliness? Journal of Personality and Social Psychology, **42** (5), pp. 830-838.

2. **Beauvais, K.**, (1986) Workshops to Combat Sexual Harassment: A Case Study of Changing Attitudes. Signs, **12** (1), pp. 131 - 140.

3. **Bingham, S.G. & B.R. Burleson**, (1989), Multiple Effects of Messages with Multiple Goals: Some Perceived Outcomes of Responses to Sexual Harassment. Human Communication Research, **16** (2), pp. 184-216.

4. **Bishop, S.L., D.S. Feller, & R.E. Opaluch**, (1982) Sexual Harassment in the Workplace as a Function of Initiator's Status: The Case of Airline Personnel; Journal of Social Issues, **38** (4), pp. 137-148.

5. **Bulman, R.J.**, (1982) Esteem & Control Bases of Blame: "Adaptive" strategies for Victims versus Observers. Journal of Personality, **50** (2).

6. **BNA Communications, Inc.**, (1992) Sexual harassment: Addressing the new realities of the 1990's, Rockville, Md.

7. **Coleman, L., Jussim, L. & Lerch, L.**,(1987) The Nature of Stereotypes: A Comparison and Integration of Three Theories. Journal of Personality and Social Psychology **52**,(3), pp. 536-546.

8. **Cooper, K.**, (1985) Recognizing Sexual Harassment. Management Review, August, **54**.

9. **Equal Employment Opportunity Commission**, (1980) Interpretive Guidelines on Sexual Harassment. Federal Register, **45** (219), pp. 74-77.

10. **Fain, T.C. & D.L. Anderson**, (1987) Sexual Harassment: Organizational Context and Diffuse Status. Sex Roles, **5/6**, pp. 291-311.

11. **Farley, L.**, (1978) Sexual Shake Down: The Sexual Harassments of Work on the Job. New York: Warner Bros.

12. **Garvey, M.S.**, (1986) The High Costs of Sexual Harassment Suits. Personnel Journal, January, 75-80.

13. **Gutek, B. & B. Morasch**, (1982) Sex Ratios, Sex-Role Spillover, & Sexual Harassment of Women at Work. Journal of Social Issues, **38** (4), pp. 55-74.

14. **Gutek, B.A., B. Morasch, & A.G. Cohen**, (1983) Interpreting Social-Sexual Behavior in a Work Setting. Journal of Vocational Behavior, **22**, 30-48.

15. **Konrad, A.M. & B.A. Gutek**, (1986) Impact of Work Experiences on Attitudes Toward Sexual Harassment. Administrative Science Quarterly, **31**, pp. 422-38.

16. **Huckle, P.**, A Decade's Difference: Mid Level Managers and Affirmative Action. Public Personnel Management Journal, **249**.

17. **Jensen, I.W.**, (1982) Attributions For Assignments of Responsibility in Sexual Harassment. Journal of Social Issues, **38** (4), pp. 121-136.

18. **Jones, T.S. M.S. Remland, & C.C. Brunner**, (1987) Effects of Employment Relationship, Response of Recipient & Sex of rater on Perceptions of Sexual Harassment. Perceptual & Motor Skills, **65**, pp. 55-63.

19. **Kandel, William**, (1988), Sexual Harassment: Persistent, Prevalent, but Preventable. Employee Relations Law Journal, **14** (3).

20. **Konrad, A.M., & Gutek, B.A.**, (1986) Impact of Work Experience on Attitudes Toward Sexual Harassment. Administrative Science Quarterly, **31**, pp. 422-438.

21. **Lafontaine, E. & L. Tredeam**, (1986) The Frequency, Sources and Correlates of Sexual Harassment Among Women in Traditional Male Occupations. Sex Roles, 15 (7/8), pp. 433-442.

22. **Lawler, E.L.**, (1990) The New Plant Revolution Revisited. Organizational Dynamics, **19** (2), pp. 4 -14.

23. **Licata, B. & Popovich P.**, (1987) Preventing Sexual Harassment: A Proactive Approach. Training & Development Journal, May, p. 34.

24. **Moskal, B.S.**, (1989) Sexual Harassment '80s-style: more subtle now-and more costly. Industry Week, July 3, pp. 57-60.

25. **Quinn, R.E.**, (1986) Coping with Cupid: The Formation, Impact, & Management of Romantic Relationships in Organizations. Administrative Science Quarterly **22**, pp. 30-45.

26. **Robinson, R.K., D.J. Kirk, & J.D. Powell**, (1987) Sexual Harassment: New Approaches for a Changed Environment. Advanced Management Journal, Autumn, **52**, pp. 15-18.

27. **Tangri, S.S., M.R. Burt, & L.B. Johnson,** (1982) Sexual Harassment at Work: Three Explanatory Models. Journal of Social Issues, **38** (4), pp. 33-54.

28. **Terpestra D.E.**, (1986) Organizational Costs of Sexual Harassment. Journal of Employment Counseling, September 1986, pp. 12-19.

29. **Valentine-French, S. & H.L. Radtke**, (1989) Attributions of Responsibilities for an Incident of Sexual Harassment in a University Setting. Sex Roles, **21** (7/8), pp. 545-554.

30. **Werner, P., LaRussa, G.**, 1983) Persistence and Change in Sex Role Stereotypes. Sex Roles, **12**, pp. 9-10.

31. **York, K. M.**, (1989) Defining Sexual Harassment in Work Places: A Policy Capturing Approach. Academy of Management Journal, **32,** (4), pp. 830-850.

A Sexual Harassment Quiz for Employees

T/F

___ 1. Unwanted sexual attention will usually stop if no one pays attention to it.

___ 2. It isn't sexual harassment if I don't mean to impose on another worker.

___ 3. Some people won't complain about another person's behavior even though it bothers her/him just so the other person won't get in trouble.

___ 4. Most healthy people will usually tell you that you said or did something that bothers her/him.

___ 5. To avoid sexually harassing a woman worker in a traditionally male work place, men should simply not haze her.

___ 6. A sexual harasser may be told by a court to pay part of a settlement to the employee he/she harassed.

___ 7. My Company has a policy which says that employees who sexually harass other employees can be fired.

___ 8. A sexually harassed man does not have the same legal rights as a harassed woman.

___ 9. Men who offend women coworkers usually know that their comments/attention is not welcome.

___ 10. Men are more likely than women to be flattered by sexual comments and overtures.

___ 11. About 90% of all sexual harassment is done by males to females.

___ 12. Telling a person to stop his/her unwanted sexual behavior usually doesn't do any good.

___ 13. Mature men and women interpret social signals such as complements and touching in the same way.

___ 14. Most cases of sexual harassment involve a supervisor requesting sexual favors in exchange for preferential treatment.

___ 15. A person who has been harassed usually could have done something to prevent the incident.

1)F 2)F 3)T 4)F 5)T 6)T 7)? 8)F 9)F 10)T 11)T 12)F 13)F 14)F 15)F
(Questionnaire modified from Moskal, 1989)

A Sexual Harassment Quiz for Supervisors

T/F

___ 1. Men in male-dominated work places usually have to change their behavior when a woman begins working there.

___ 2. An employer is not liable for the sexual harassment committed by one of his/her employees unless that employee loses specific job benefits or is fired.

___ 3. A sexual harasser may be told by a court to pay part of a settlement to the employee he/she harassed.

___ 4. An employer is not liable for the harassment of one of its employees unless it knows about the incident.

___ 5. A supervisor can be held liable for the sexual harassment committed by one of his employees against another.

___ 6. A policy forbidding sexual harassment protects an employer from liability for incidents of which it is unaware.

___ 7. Supervisors should be direct when discussing allegations of sexual harassment with a complainant when the complaint is against the supervisor.

___ 8. Sexually suggestive visuals or objects in a work place don't create liability unless an employee complains about them and management doesn't remove them.

___ 9. It is appropriate for a supervisor, when initially receiving a sexual harassment complaint, to determine if the alleged recipient overreacted or misunderstood the alleged harasser.

___ 10. The lack of complaints is a good indication that sexual harassment is not occurring.

___ 11. The intent of a person's behavior is more important than the impact of the behavior on another person.

___ 12. Men who offend women coworkers usually know that their comments/attention is not welcome.

___ 13. Most cases of sexual harassment involve a supervisor requesting sexual favors in exchange for preferential treatment.

___ 14. Some people won't complain about another person's behavior even though it bothers her/him just so the other person won't get in trouble.

___ 15. Mature men and women interpret social signals such as complements and touching in the same way.

1)F 2)F 3)T 4)F 5)T 6)F 7)T 8)F 9)F 10)F 11)F 12)F 13)F 14)T 15)F

(Questionnaire modified from Moskal, 1989)

BIOGRAPHICAL SKETCH

Dr. Mary H. Fox is President of The Marlin Group, Inc., an organizational consulting firm based in Baltimore, Maryland.

Dr. Fox has an extensive background in designing programs for handling human resource issues. Typical work in client companies includes conducting psychological evaluations and management development with applicants and employees in clerical, managerial, and executive occupations. She has developed numerous training programs in a wide variety of client companies for example U.S. Steel, Bally's Health & Fitness Clubs, Baltimore Gas & Electric Company and Johns Hopkins University, among many others. Programs include sexual harassment prevention, cultural diversity, performance appraisal training, and supervisory skills training. She has provided expert witness testimony on interviewing, testing, and general selection methods in private industry and government.

Dr. Fox has published several articles in the field of selection, career development, sexual harassment, and work force diversity. She teaches courses in selection and training in the department of psychology at the University of Maryland.

Lynn Litow is Executive Vice President of The Marlin Group, Inc., an organizational consulting firm based in Baltimore, Maryland.

Ms. Litow has provided and managed the delivery of a wide array of organizational development and human resource planning services to small and large businesses and organizations. Her services include organizational restructuring, cultural diversity interventions, interview attitude surveys, and team building. She works closely with clients in upper management analyzing human resource needs and developing and implementing solutions to problems in these areas. To address human resource planning and development problems, Ms. Litow has installed salary administration programs, designed incentive compensation systems to motivate employees and increase productivity, and has provided ongoing management development consultation. Typical training programs include cultural diversity, supervisory skills, change management, and team building.

She has provided extensive training to client companies and has co-authored several articles in the area of sexual harassment.

SUGGESTED VOIR DIRE FOR PLAINTIFFS IN A SEXUAL HARASSMENT CASE

Mark S. Rudy
Rudy & Zieff
San Francisco, California

In any trial, voir dire is without question one of the most pivotal phases of trial. In employment litigation, especially in sexual harassment matters, voir dire is crucial. The reason is that all jurors have either been employers or employees during their careers and have, therefore, established views, beliefs and opinions about all phases of the employer-employee relationship. In light of the Clarence Thomas confirmation proceedings, the subject of sexual harassment more than likely has evoked strong personal feelings in many people related to their attitudes about sex discrimination, sexual harassment, sex roles, etc. It is trial counsel's responsibility to elicit jurors' beliefs, opinions and attitudes and to inform jurors about the definition of sexual harassment, the extent of the problem in the work force, the responsibilities of employers to prevent such problems, reasonable actions taken by victims to remedy the problem, and nature of the emotional and physical injuries caused by sexual harassment and the appropriateness of damages as a means of compensating the plaintiff.

General goals for voir dire should include the following:

1. Communicate information about the case to jurors through requesting the trial judge to read a brief written statement to the jury which should be prepared for the judge's review prior to jury selection.

2. Make an opening statement to the jury in which you, among other things, introduce the plaintiff to the potential jurors, inform the jurors of the nature of the claims that they will hear and of the injuries and damages that will be sought by the plaintiff; and mention the defenses that will be raised by the employer and/or employee.

3. Use to the extent possible open-ended questions so to encourage a dialogue with potential jurors.

4. Questions to the panel as a whole should generally be avoided.

5. Attempt to communicate with jurors without the use of notes.

6. Engender trustworthiness with the jurors by the manner in which you communicate. Do not use a podium, admit weaknesses during the course of voir dire, do not ask questions that are so personal in nature so as to embarrass or inflame the jurors.

7. Be clear and to the point.

8. Discuss the burden of proof applicable in civil matters.

9. Avoid being wordy and communicate with the juror in lay person's terms.

Plaintiff's proposals for voir dire in sexual harassment cases which usually should be submitted in writing to the trial judge are as follows:

I. Sex Harassment in Work Place

A. Have you ever heard the term "sexual harassment"?

1. Where have you heard about it?

2. What do you think it would mean to be sexually harassed?

3. How serious a problem do you think sexual harassment is?

4. What do you think about a man in a work place who verbally harasses a woman or touches her body?

5. Do you think that might be considered harmless fun?

6. Do you think that harassment is more of a problem from a supervisor than from a co-worker? Why is that?

7. What do you think someone who is being sexually harassed should do about it?

8. What do you think the effect would be of ignoring the harassment?

9. Have you heard of any situations like this? How did it affect the situation for the woman to try to ignore it?

10. If you were being subjected to sexual harassment in the work place, do you think you might stay on the job? Why?

11. What if you thought you could stop the harassment by making the people who were bothering you change their attitudes?

12. Do you think you might try to go along with it to show you were tough enough to take it?

13. What if the employer had told you your charges were unfounded? Would it be okay to stay on the job?

14. Do you think sexual harassment (meaning unwanted sexual attention) could be a serious problem to a person?

15. Do you think someone could get very upset as a result of that unwanted attention?

16. Would you think differently about it if it happened on a repeated basis than if it happened only once or twice? How?

17. How do you think sexual harassment might affect a person's ability to perform their job?

18. What do you think about the fact that sexual harassment is against the law?

19. Do you know that there is such a law?

20. Do you understand that this law, which prevents sexual harassment of an employee by an employer or supervisor, means that people cannot be tormented, teased or harassed because of their sex?

21. Do you understand that this law does not apply only to a situation where an employer is trying to pressure an employee into a sexual relationship?

22. Do you think there is a need for this type of law?

23. Do you think that the lawmakers have gone too far in making laws to regulate how men and women should relate to each other on the job?

24. What do you think about someone suing their employer for sexual harassment?

25. Do you think it is possible that someone could feel forced to quit a job?

26. Do you think that people may sometimes feel harassed by their supervisors but may not complain because they are afraid they will lose their job?

27. Why do you think someone would stay on a job when they feel harassed or tormented?

28. How do you think that could happen?

29. What do you think about women who work outside the home?

30. Have you always felt that way?

31. Why do you think women decide to work outside the home?

32. Do you think that a woman who has children should work outside the home?

33. Have you read or heard about cases where people sued their employer claiming that they were sexually harassed on the job?

34. What do you think about these kinds of lawsuits?

35. Do you have any feeling that these matters should not be the subject of lawsuits?

36. Do you think that a woman might fabricate charges of sexual harassment just to get even because she lost her job?

37. Do you think that an employer should be responsible for unlawful acts, such as sexual harassment on the part of its employees or supervisors?

38. Do you think an employer has a duty to inform its employees that discrimination such as sexual harassment will not be tolerated?

39. Do you think that by not interfering in a situation where sexual harassment is occurring, an employer might be giving tacit approval to the harassment?

40. Do you think persons in the management position of a company would lie about events to protect themselves or their employees?

41. Some people say it's unfair for women to hold jobs usually held by men because it deprives family breadwinners of job opportunities. What do you think of that?

42. Have you ever worked with a woman in your job? Have you heard about, or been involved in, conflicts with women workers? If so, what happened? How do you feel about the situation now?

43. Would you be more likely to believe a male witness over a female witness?

44. Do you think someone could be injured by being sexually harassed?

45. What kind of injuries do you think might result?

46. What kind of emotional effect do you think unwanted sexual attention can have on a woman?

47. Do you think it is possible for a woman who has experienced this type of harassment to have physical problems as a result of the emotional stress?

48. Do you think that people should be awarded money compensation for sexual harassment?

49. Do you think that a person has more of a right to be compensated for physical injury, such as loss of a leg, than for emotional injuries, such as loss of reputation and suffering stress and anxiety?

50. Do you believe all people are entitled to be free from harassment on their jobs?

51. Do you think it is possible that a woman on the job can be driven to cry or yell because of harassment? (a) Do you think that a woman in a craft or trade job who cries or yells does not deserve to work in a trade or craft?

52. Is there anybody here who has not listened or read anything about the Clarence Thomas hearings?

53. Clarence Thomas' hearings have nothing to do with this case, correct? (a) Have any of you formed any opinions about women who complain about sex on the job based on the matters revealed in the Clarence Thomas hearings?

54. Do you understand that in addition to the legal requirement that you put aside any knowledge regarding any other sex harassment case, that the facts of this case are different than the facts of the Clarence Thomas case?

55. Do you understand that in addition to the factual difference that this case is being heard in court of law and that the kind of evidence that can come in court is different than the statements that can be made at a Senate hearing?

56. Does the fact alone of Clarence Thomas' confirmation make you skeptical of all women who claim sex harassment?

57. Without asking you your opinion of Clarence Thomas or the proceedings, would you agree that this case is unlike Anita Hill, if plaintiff did complain and file a lawsuit regarding her allegations?

58. Have you heard about cases where people claimed that they had been sexually harassed on the job? What have you heard? What do you think about those claims?

59. Have you seen or heard about incidents of sexual harassment in your work? If so, would you please describe the incidents? How do you feel about incidents like that?

60. Do you think that a woman might feel she has to stay in a job where she was being sexually harassed? Why do you think she might do that?

61. Were you ever in a position where the pressure to fit in made you tolerate things from others that you did not like or things that upset you? What was that situation?

62. Do you have sexual harassment standards or policies at the place where you work? What are they?

63. Do you think work places should have such standards?

64. If a work place has them, how do you think they should be enforced?

65. Is sexual teasing all right in a work setting like a law firm? Why do you say that?

66. Some people say that a woman does not get sexually harassed at work unless she encourages or consents to it. What do you think of that idea?

67. Some people say that a woman can always stop men from sexually harassing her if she wants to. What do you think about that? Why?

68. Do you believe that an employer has an affirmative obligation to ensure a woman who enters a previously all-male environment is not subjected to things that any reasonable woman could consider offensive?

69. I am going to read a list to you of several things that could take place in the work place. Do you agree that women should not be subjected to the following:

    a. sexually explicit talk;

    b. unwanted advances by men;

    c. explicit comments about their physical appearance whether complimentary or derogatory;

    d. being treated differently because of their sex;

    e. having to be at company functions where cakes are made in the shape of various parts of the female anatomy.

70. Do you believe a woman must physically resist all sexual advances in order for them to be unwelcome advances?

71. Do you believe a woman may claim sex harassment if she gives in to sexual advances?

72. Is there anything in your background or belief or morality that makes it impossible for you to award monetary damages?

73. Experts who will be testifying include a psychiatrist and psychologists. We want to ask you some general questions about your knowledge and experience in this area.

a. Have you or any of your close friends or relatives had any experience with or knowledge of psychiatry?

b. Have you ever studied psychology? If yes, please describe the nature of your studies.

c. Have you ever sought assistance of a psychiatrist or psychologist to help with a personal or family problem?

(1) Could you briefly tell us about the nature of your experience?

(2) Did you feel it was helpful or not?

(3) Why or why not?

(4) What are your thoughts generally about the psychiatric profession?

(5) What do you think a psychologist does?

(6) Some people think people can overcome most of their problems if they would just have a more positive attitude and set their minds to it.

(a) What do you think?

(7) Have you ever known anyone who became depressed and sought help from a psychiatrist or psychologist?

(a) Could you please tell me about it without mentioning their names?

74. Is there anything about the fact that there are no visible injuries that will preclude you from awarding appropriate monetary damages?

75. There has been some publicity about jury awards, and there has been some controversy about awards being too high.

a. Have you ever thought that juries award too much money to people for injuries whether psychological or physical?

76. Do you ever get the feeling that people are sometimes getting large amounts they do not deserve?

a. Why do you think this happens?

b. Who do you think is responsible?

c. Have you read or heard anything that caused you to believe this?

d. Do you think you might not want to compensate plaintiff because of your feelings about this?

77. Have you ever heard or read about million dollar awards?

a. Have you ever thought to yourself millions of dollars is too much, no matter what happened to the person?

b. If the evidence so provided, do you think you could award millions of dollars?

78. Do you think it's appropriate for jurors to be asked to decide cases involving large sums of money?

79. Does anyone have a monetary figure in mind as the limit they would award no matter what the evidence demonstrated?

80. Some of the allegations that plaintiff is making might be viewed by you as violations of the Penal Code. Do you understand that you must put aside any preconception you may have about criminal trial and/or law and decide this civil case according to the instruction of his Honor?

a. Is there anyone who because of the allegations thinks plaintiff must prove her case beyond a reasonable doubt?

b. If after hearing all the evidence and instructions on the law you find the plaintiff has proven her case against defendants by a preponderance of evidence, would you have any trouble returning a verdict for plaintiff?

TRIAL CONSULTING SERVICES IN EMPLOYMENT LITIGATION: MOCK TRIALS/FOCUS GROUPS AND JUROR QUESTIONNAIRES

David B. Graeven, Ph.D.
Trial Behavior Consulting, Incorporated
Transamerica Pyramid
600 Montgomery Street, 5th Floor
San Francisco, CA 94111-2702
(415) 781-5879

TABLE OF CONTENTS

More than any other type of case, the verdict in employment litigation, including cases with claims of sexual harassment, is dependent on juror biases. We base these observations on numerous mock trials and interviews with jurors throughout the country. For that reason, employment lawyers are much more likely to be interested in jury research and trial consulting services than lawyers handling other types of litigation.

Employment litigation is difficult because jurors bring strong feelings about their job experiences to the courtroom. In fact, the results of a nationwide poll of 803 respondents conducted for the National Law Journal and Lexis, shown below, indicates that one fourth of the U.S. work force feels it has been discriminated against in the workplace (San Francisco Chronicle, 1990). Of those who reported discrimination, about one-third said it had to do with their gender. One half of those who reported discrimination said they did something about it. In addition, almost all (80 percent) said they believe at least some employers discriminate in hiring and promotion, and half said all or most employers discriminate.

These attitudes about discrimination, which are often based on personal experiences, affect how jurors will react to the evidence and create problems for defense lawyers. Research has shown that although attitudes do not always predict behavior, attitudes formed as a result of personal experiences, such as those based on job experiences, are especially likely to affect an individual's behavior (Meyer, 1987).

Plaintiff's counsel also have to contend with jurors who react strongly against people who claim discrimination, particularly claims based on gender. Many employees have strong beliefs and stereotypes about members of various minority groups and these beliefs affect their evaluation of the evidence. Also many jurors are worried about their job security and often feel they are competing for scarce resources with members of minority groups in the job market. Thus these jurors will be less sympathetic to persons they see as receiving special treatment or those with whom they feel they are competing for a job.

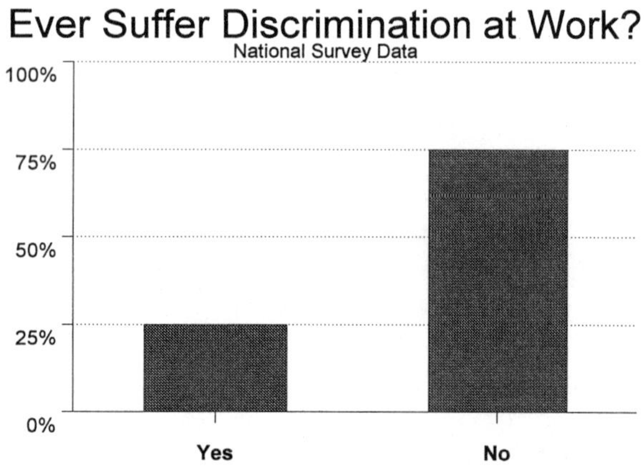

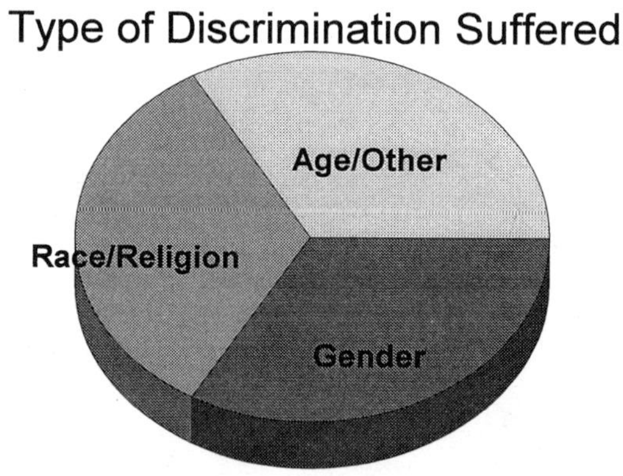

MOCK TRIALS/FOCUS GROUPS

Trial lawyers who handle sexual harassment and other types of employment cases are engaging increasingly in mock trial/focus group research. The main purpose of mock trials is to determine juror reactions to the themes, issues, and arguments that could be presented at trial. On occasion, an attorney may have two alternate case theories and would like feedback from jurors on the merits of the two approaches. When that occurs, two separate mock trials can be held and the results compared.

Focus group participants are selected so that they represent the demographic characteristics (gender, age, employment status, occupation, education, marital status, ethnicity) of prospective jurors in the jurisdiction where the case will be tried. Certain categories of persons may be excluded from participating. Examples of excluded categories include those who work with the defendant company, those who have experience with employment litigation, and those who have been summoned for jury duty. To eliminate the risk of disclosure, we usually exclude those working for the media and anyone who works in the legal field. The method used to recruit jurors and the population sampled should be carefully reviewed to ensure that no biases are built into the selection of mock jurors.

Structure of a Mock Trial

There are a number of formats for a mock trial. The most commonly used method in employment litigation is the four-hour session. This method usually includes live presentations by attorneys representing both sides, completion of questionnaires by jurors, and debriefing of jurors by a consultant. Usually attorneys are allowed a total of forty minutes to present their case. Variations in this method include video presentations by the attorneys rather than live and the use of more than one jury. Video presentations allow for more control in the arguments that will be presented. If a mistake is made in producing the video, it can be retaped. Also there is more flexibility in holding the session since the attorneys do not have to be present for the video presentation. Advantages of the live presentation are that the "reality" of the situation increases, there is greater juror involvement, and attorneys preparing for trial get more "plugged into" their case.

When the significance of a case can justify the expense, we usually have at least two juries listen to the case at the same time. The jurors are seated classroom-style during the presentation and are divided into two deliberating groups afterwards. This method provides more valuable feedback. If both juries focus on the same issues and produce the same verdict, there is greater confidence in the result.

One of the mistakes most often made in employment cases is to have a less experienced attorney take the role of opposing counsel. If the opposing counsel is less skillful, there may be a false sense of confidence about the strength of the case and the impact of opposing arguments.

Two other common formats are two-hour and all-day sessions. In the two-hour sessions, the process resembles what is more commonly called a focus group. The consultant presents a synopsis of the case and follows up by asking a series of questions of the jurors. Often a series of "what if" questions are asked to determine the impact of evidence that may or may not be excluded from the trial. When deposition videotapes of witnesses are available or a tape is made of an examination of the client, these sessions can be used to evaluate credibility and to develop suggestions for improvement in demeanor. If a lawyer has "client control" problems or problems getting the attention of his or her client, these sessions sometimes have the effect of conveying the risks involved in trying the case.

All-day sessions in employment cases usually include live or videotape presentations of witnesses and damages arguments. To obtain a representative panel of jurors who are full-time employees, these sessions are usually held on a weekend.

Regardless of their length, mock juries and focus groups are most helpful for showing lawyers how jurors think about the case. They are beneficial in providing metaphors, analogies, and images that can be used in argument. They also provide vivid indications of the types of arguments that are accepted or quickly rejected by jurors.

JUROR BIAS

Lawyers are concerned with removing jurors who may be predisposed to rule against their client. We find in our consultations that often a lawyer's main concern is to identify those jurors who are not telling their true feelings or not revealing their biases in a case. In fact, there are two types of distortions: jurors who overstate their biases, beliefs and predispositions in order to avoid jury service and those who understate or fail to fully explain their attitudes, beliefs, or opinions about a case so that they can serve as jurors. As frustrating as it can be, there is little a lawyer can do to keep a juror who does not want to serve. A lawyer or a judge can attempt to rehabilitate a biased juror by asking a series of questions ending with "You can be fair, can't you?", but often attempts to rehabilitate a juror who is motivated to avoid jury service are not successful.

We have found from assistance with jury selection and post-trial interviews of jurors in employment litigation, that intentional distortion by jurors in voir dire is *not* the main problem lawyers face in jury selection. It is comforting to note that a juror seldom consciously tries to get on a jury so he or she can deliver a verdict for or against one of the parties in employment-related litigation. It is more likely that jurors will overstate bias to avoid jury service than conceal biases to get on a jury.

The predispositions that are most critical for lawyers to discover in jury selection are those which relate to the primary issues and parties involved in the litigation. Social scientists often presume that their assumptions about juror behavior are shared by lawyers. However, our in-court observations of voir dire in gender-related employment litigation reveals that most lawyers' questions focus on employment history and different life experiences rather than the attitudes and predispositions that actually can affect juror evaluations of the evidence.

Research consistently shows that the attitudes and predispositions that jurors bring to a case affect the way they evaluate the evidence (Lord, Ross & Lepper, 1979; Ross, Lepper and Hubbard, 1975). In many civil cases that go to trial there is sufficient argument by both sides to produce a gray area where the outcome of the case is not clear. It is in the juror's evaluation of these disputed issues that juror attitudes are activated and can affect the outcome of the case.

Specific findings on the impact of juror attitudes on the evaluation of a case indicate that:

- When evidence supports juror beliefs it is more likely to be accepted at face value.
- If evidence goes against juror beliefs it is subjected to greater scrutiny than evidence that supports their beliefs.
- Jurors will be more likely to remember evidence that supports their beliefs.
- Jurors will find experts more credible if their testimony is consistent with juror beliefs.

Lawyers should be aware that jurors do not consciously decide in advance to go against one party or another in civil litigation or deliberately ignore evidence, but rather when the evidence is unclear, when experts disagree, or when credibility is at issue, there will be a tendency for jurors to believe evidence which supports their predisposition. The task for the litigator is to know in advance the critical juror predispositions or attitudes and to be able to identify them in the courtroom. The juror questionnaire, discussed later in this chapter, is an excellent device for revealing attitudinal information.

DESIGNING VOIR DIRE QUESTIONS FOR STRATEGIC ADVANTAGE

Voir dire represents a strategic dilemma. On the one hand, a lawyer needs to conduct extensive voir dire to identify those jurors predisposed against him or her. On the other hand, with extensive voir dire a lawyer also risks revealing to the opposing counsel those jurors predisposed in his or her favor. Unfortunately, many lawyers simply avoid this dilemma by conducting minimal voir dire. The more productive solution to this dilemma, however, is to design voir dire questions with this rule in mind:

"Bury your keeps and expose your strikes."

The use of this rule is best explained by example. This example comes from a wrongful termination case in which we were hired by defense counsel. Our goal in voir dire was to identify (expose) those prospective jurors most sympathetic to employees (our strikes). In so doing, however, we did not want to inadvertently identify those jurors most sympathetic to companies (our keeps).

Through prior research, we had identified a question which effectively distinguished between likely employee advocates and likely company advocates. The question read as follows:

"Do you think companies fire employees without good reason?"

As one might expect, those who said "yes" were more likely to be employee advocates, and those who said "no" were more likely to be company advocates. However, the question as stated was virtually *useless* for strategic purposes.

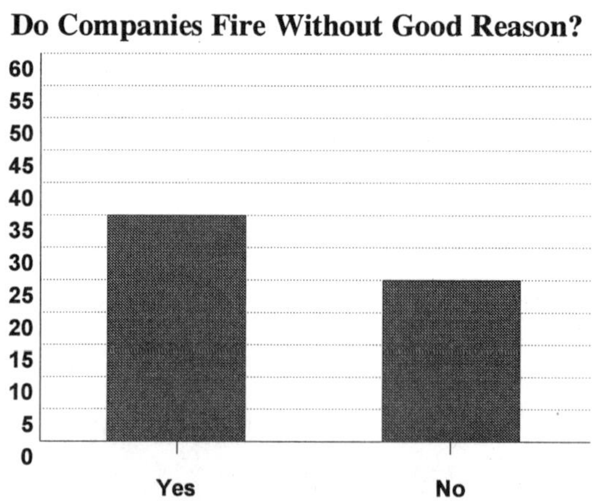

Figure 1

This question's lack of strategic value is illustrated in Figure 1. Based on a pre-trial community survey, we predicted that approximately 58 percent of the jury panel, or 35 prospective jurors (out of a panel of 60), would say "yes"-- companies do fire employees without good reason, and 42 percent, or 25 jurors, would say "no"-- companies do *not* fire employees without good reason. Thus, our question would have identified 35 likely employee advocates, all of whom would have been strike candidates. Based on the survey responses, more than one out of every two prospective jurors called into the box would have been considered a strike candidate. Not only would we have been unable to strike all 35 of these prospective jurors, but we also would not have known which of these 35 jurors would have been best to strike. Since it would not have provided us with a manageable list of top priority strike candidates, the question would have had little strategic value.

Fortunately, the question also would have been relatively harmless. This question would have identified 25 likely company advocates all of whom would have been considered strike candidates for the opposing counsel. Like ourselves, though, the opposing counsel would have been faced with too many strike candidates and would have had no way to identify who among the 25 would have been best to strike. So, the question would have neither helped us identify our top strike candidates, nor revealed our keeps (opposing counsel's strikes).

Strategic Defense Question

Instead of the original question, we used a slightly altered version of the question, which read:

"Do you think *most* companies fire employees without good reason?"

Those who said "yes" to this question were still employee advocates, but clearly the conviction they needed to say "yes" to this question is far greater than it would have been to say "yes" to our original question. Conversely, those who said "no" were still company advocates, but the conviction needed to say "no" was far less than it would have been to say "no" to our original question. The jury panel's responses to this question are presented in Figure 2.

As you can see from Figure 2, only 10 prospective jurors (17 percent) said "yes" -- *most* companies do fire employees without good reason. Rather than being overwhelmed with 35 strike candidates, we were able to focus our attention on the 10 jurors with the strongest convictions about the issue.

On the other hand, 50 prospective jurors said "no" -- *most* companies do *not* fire employees without good reason. With 8 out of every 10 prospective jurors qualifying as strike candidates, the opposing counsel clearly was unable to identify his top strike candidates from this question.

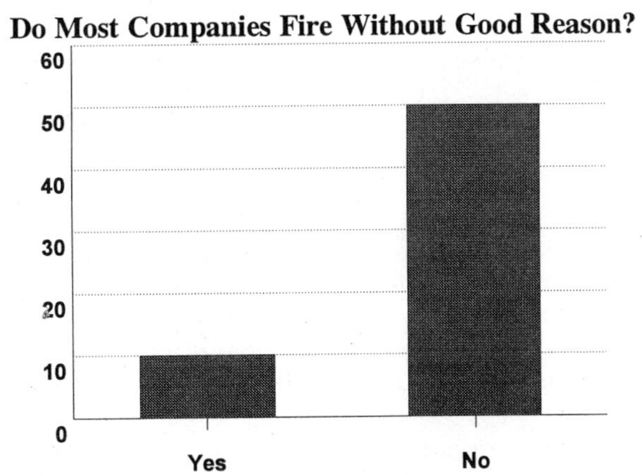

Figure 2

Thus, with a simple revision of our original question, we not only exposed our top strike candidates, but we also buried our keeps in a large, undifferentiated plurality of 50 jurors.

Strategic Plaintiff Question

This strategy can work for the other side as well. Had we been hired by the plaintiff's counsel, we would have rewritten the question in the following way:

"Do you think *some* companies fire employees without good reason?"

Those who said "yes" to this question still would have been employee advocates, but clearly the conviction needed to say "yes" to this question would have been far less than that needed to say "yes" to the original question. Conversely, those who said "no" would still have been company advocates, but the conviction needed to say "no" would have been far greater than that needed to say "no" to the original question.

In Figure 3, we present simulated responses to this question. As you can see, we would have expected 55 prospective jurors (92 percent) to say "yes" -- *some* companies fire employees without good reason and only five jurors to say "no" -- *some* companies do *not* fire employees without good reason. With this question, we would have exposed the plaintiff's top priority strikes (strong company advocates) and buried the plaintiff's keeps (strong employee advocates) in a large, undifferentiated plurality of 55 jurors.

Do Some Companies Fire Without Good Reason?

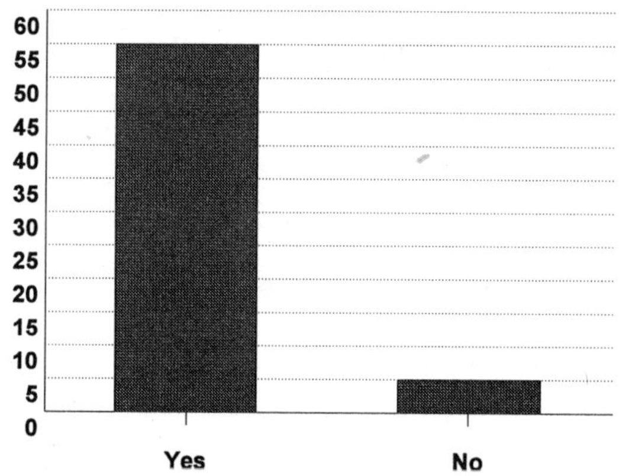

Figure 3

The Asymmetrical Question

The preceding example has demonstrated how we bury our keeps and expose our strikes through the use of what we call "the asymmetrical question." An asymmetrical question is one which is likely to elicit an unbalanced pattern of response. As our example demonstrated, an unbalanced pattern of response is quite effective at identifying individuals with pronounced biases and can be achieved with a simple rewrite of an ordinary question.

We have found that an asymmetrical question is most effective when asked to a group of jurors rather than to individuals. For example, to those in the box one might say, "How many of you think *most* companies fire employees without good reason? Please just raise your hand if you agree." These questions can also be used effectively in pre-trial juror questionnaires.

Conclusion

Although the rule demonstrated here was discovered through research, and the rule is best verified through research, its use does *not* depend on research. Rather, it depends on the ability of a lawyer to formulate effective questions and to anticipate jurors' responses. It is our belief that this rule cannot only help lawyers take advantage of the opportunities presented by voir dire but also help them to avoid the attendant risks.

THE USE OF JUROR QUESTIONNAIRES IN CIVIL LITIGATION

"I would have been flying blind without a juror questionnaire," a San Francisco litigator once remarked. He is not alone in this sentiment. More and more lawyers are relying on questionnaires for jury selection. A statewide survey of California Superior Court judges conducted by Trial Behavior Consulting, Inc. revealed that over 75 percent of judges had used a pre-voir dire juror questionnaire and most would consider using a questionnaire in an appropriate case. A sexual harassment case, due to its controversial nature, usually is the type of case where a questionnaire is seen as appropriate.

Why are juror questionnaires being used more? Simply put, jury selection has become more complex. Lawyers cannot rely on demographic formulas to select a jury. Our research shows that attitudes are far better predictors of juror behavior than demographic characteristics. It is very difficult, however, to assess personal attitudes during oral voir dire.

First, the courtroom is a very intimidating atmosphere for prospective jurors. Typically, they have little or no experience with the legal system, and most people are very uncomfortable speaking in public. Hence, prospective jurors are usually very reluctant to talk about experiences and attitudes which are very personal to them. Second, prospective jurors have a need to be perceived as "socially desirable" and do not want to express anything which may make them "look bad" to the court, to the lawyers, or to their peers (Suggs, 1981). Third, by listening to the answers previously given by others, individuals quickly learn which responses are acceptable and often merely agree with previous answers.

However, the questionnaire procedure should not take the place of the oral voir dire process. Oral voir dire is an opportunity to see how jurors react to questions as well as the lawyer. This "gut level" experience and rapport-building opportunity can never be adequately replaced by the questionnaire procedure.

A court-administered questionnaire can also significantly reduce the length of time necessary to select a jury. In such cases oral voir dire can be used simply to clarify certain written responses.

What Kinds of Questions are Best

A trial lawyer should have prospective jurors answer questions about their attitudes on salient factors in the case. For example, if a case deals with age discrimination, questions should be directed at attitudes toward employers, their commitment to the older workers, and the rights of employees. For sexual harassment cases, questions should focus on attitudes and experiences with gender-related issues. Of particular concern would be whether a juror feels claims about harassment are exaggerated or overstated, and whether employers are doing all they should to prevent harassment.

Measuring Attitudes

At first glance, measuring juror attitudes would seem to be a simple task. However, attitudes consist of a variety of dimensions-- some based on facts, some based on personal experiences, and some based on pure emotion. Attitudes also vary considerably in strength. The more dimensions of an attitude that are measured by a juror questionnaire, the more reliable will be the evaluation of the juror. This principle is used in developing reliable and valid questions for any psychological testing procedure.

Cause Challenges Based on Questionnaires

A properly designed juror questionnaire will also include a variety of questions directed to the issue of bias. If the questions are properly framed, the lawyers can move to challenge jurors for cause based on the jurors' sworn responses on the questionnaire. If dismissal for cause will not be granted on the basis of the questionnaire, then the lawyer may choose to request that oral voir dire of a biased juror be conducted in chambers.

Questions aimed at cause challenges should identify those jurors who have a personal financial interest in the outcome of the trial, who have biases against any of the parties, or who have such strong feelings about the case issues that they could not serve as fair and impartial jurors.

Are Questionnaires Always Useful?

Questionnaires are valuable if they elicit the *attitudinal* information needed to exercise intelligent cause and peremptory challenges. Questionnaires seeking only demographic information are not very helpful. Often times lawyers volunteer to limit oral voir dire in exchange for administration of a questionnaire. However, it is not worth sacrificing oral voir dire for a useless questionnaire.

<u>Recommended Steps for Questionnaire Administration</u>

1. One side makes a motion for court administration of a questionnaire.

2. If the court grants the motions, either the parties agree on questionnaire content, or they submit questions to the court for its approval.

3. Once the questions have been approved, the judge swears in the panel and administers the questionnaire.

4. The court, or one of the parties, makes copies of the completed questionnaires, distributes them to all parties, and returns the originals to the judge.

5. The judge announces the order in which all prospective jurors may be called into the jury box, thereby allowing for better determination of how and when peremptory challenges should be made.

6. The prospective jurors are sent home and called back the next day. This allows time for copying of the questionnaires and for lawyers and consultants to evaluate the responses.

7. The prospective jurors return the next day and oral voir dire begins. Lawyers use voir dire to clarify the responses to the questionnaire. Time to complete jury selection is thus significantly reduced.

PROSPECTIVE JUROR QUESTIONNAIRE OUTLINE FOR EMPLOYMENT-RELATED LITIGATION

This outline lists the range of topics typically covered in a questionnaire designed for employment-related litigation (Graeven, 1990). All questions can be open-ended, or they all can be close-ended. The open-ended format should be restricted to the more important attitudinal and experiential questions.

I. Title Page

The first page of the questionnaire typically lists the county, briefly explains the function of the questionnaire, and indicates that the juror is under oath. See Appendix for an example of a California state approved title page to juror questionnaires.

II. Demographic Characteristics

A. Background Questions

Address/Phone Numbers
Age
Occupation/Job Duties
Length of Employment/Employer
Current Job Status
Previous Employment (All Jobs)
Education/Special Training
Marital Status/Partner's Employment
Children's Ages/Occupations
Military Service
Labor Union Membership
Legal Experience

B. Lifestyle Questions

Organizational Memberships/Civil Rights Organizations
Leisure Activities
Television Shows/Radio News Programs
Main Sources of News

III. Jury/Litigation Experience

A. Previous Jury Service
B. Ever Been Sued
C. Ever Sued Anyone
D. Made Worker's Compensation Claim
E. Testified in Court or at Deposition

IV. Relevant Life Experiences (Employment-Related)

Involvement of Self, Family, or Friends with Similar or Same:

A. Case Facts

- Type of Company
- Type of Work
- Job Title
- Supervisory Experience
- Training in Affirmative Action/Discrimination in the Workplace
- Experience with Harassment/Discrimination
- Been accused of Harassment/Discrimination

B. Loss of Job

- Due to Merger
- Lack of Work
- Terminated for Any Reason
- Quit for Any Reason

C. Dispute With Employer

- Over Working Conditions
- Change in Job Description
- Complaints About Employer
- Complaints about Supervisor

D. Disputes With Other Employees

- Over Job Performance
- Over Work Attitudes
- Over Attitudes Toward Management

V. Attitudes (often the most critical area of inquiry for jury selection)

A. Attitudes Toward Litigation

- Feelings on Number of Lawsuits
- Feelings/Beliefs about Damages:
    - Lost Wages/Medical expenses
    - Pain and Suffering
    - Emotional Distress
    - Punitive Damages
- Beliefs about Impact of Damages/Awards
- Hesitation in Awarding Damages

B. Attitudes Toward Employees/Companies/Employers in General

- Trust in Companies/Employers

Beliefs about Integrity of Companies/Employers
Need to Regulate Companies/Employers
Feelings of Sympathy for Any Party
Desire to Help Any Party

C. Attitudes Specific to Disputes/Claims

Feelings about Employment Litigation
Awareness of Similar Cases
Necessity of Litigation
Belief in Benefits/Harm of Type of Litigation
Work Ethic of Employees
Feelings about Harassment/Discrimination Claims
Beliefs on Whether Incidents of Harassment are Increasing, Decreasing, or Staying about the Same

VI. Attitudes Toward Jury System/Ability to Serve

A. Willingness to Serve as a Juror

B. Anything Preventing Service for Estimated Length of Trial

C. Health Problems Interfering with Service

D. Religious/Philosophical Objections to Jury Service

E. Bias/Prejudice/Sympathy Toward Any of the Parties

VII. Signature of Juror Swearing That Questionnaire Answers Are True and Correct

BIBLIOGRAPHY

Graeven, D. (1990). Juror Questionnaire Adoption Packet. San Francisco: Trial Behavior Consulting, Inc.

Island, D. (1988). The Use of Juror Questionnaires in Civil Litigation. Research Notes, 1-2.

Lord, C.G., Ross, L., & Lepper, M.R. (1979). Biased Assimilation and Attitude Polarization: the Effects of Prior Theories on Subsequently Considered Evidence. Journal of Personality and Social Psychology, 37, 1098-2109.

Myers, D.G., (1987). Social Psychology (2nd Edition). New York: McGraw-Hill.

Ross, L., Lepper, M.R., & Hubbard, M. (1975). Perseverance in Self-perception and Social Perception: Biased Attributional Processes in the Debriefing Paradigm. Journal of Personality and Social Psychology, 32, 880-892.

San Francisco Chronicle, (July 12, 1990). "Twenty-Five Percent in Poll Have Felt Job Bias," San Francisco.

Suggs, D., & Sales, B.D. (1981). Juror Self-disclosure in the Voir Dire: A Social Science Analysis: Indiana Law Journal, 56, 245-271.

DAVID B. GRAEVEN, Ph.D.

David B. Graeven is President of Trial Behavior Consulting, Incorporated. He received his Ph.D. in Sociology from the University of Iowa. Dr. Graeven designs and evaluates mock trials, advises on case theory development, prepares witnesses, assists in jury selection, and conducts post-trial interviews of jurors. Dr. Graeven consults throughout the country in many litigation contexts including employment, general business, professional liability, product liability, toxic torts, intellectual property, and insurance bad faith. He delivers presentations to law firms and professional associations around the country, has published articles in a number of professional journals, and has been interviewed on many national media programs. Dr. Graeven has also served on the Board of Directors of the American Society of Trial Consultants. In addition to his trial work, Dr. Graeven served as Professor of Sociology in the California State University system for over twenty years.

APPENDIX

Juror Questionnaire for Civil Cases

Introduction and Instructions

Thank you for coming to court as a potential juror. Before the case can start, a jury must be selected. The judge and the people involved in the case need to know something about you in order to select jurors who can be fair to both sides.

Everyone has attitudes and opinions that are shaped by their life experiences. Sometimes these experiences can make it difficult to look at a certain issue in an unbiased and unemotional way. As a juror, you must return a verdict based on the law and on the facts proved in court, not on emotion or on other views not supported by the evidence. The judge will give you instructions on the law and how you should go about deciding the case. You must listen to and follow the judge's instructions.

The questions on this form are designed to help the court and the lawyers learn something about your background and your views on issues that may be related to this case. The questions are asked not to invade your privacy, but to make sure that you can be a fair and impartial juror. If there is any reason why you might not be able to give both sides a fair trial in this case, it is important that you say so.

The judge has decided to use this form to save time and to give you a chance to tell the court and the lawyers about yourself.

If there is anything you do not want to talk about in open court, please circle the question number. After you have finished the questionnaire, let the clerk know you have circled one or more question numbers.

Do not write on the back of any page. Use an additional sheet of paper.

If you are called to the jury box, your answers to this questionnaire become a matter of public record, just as if you had answered the questions aloud in the courtroom.

If you have trouble reading, understanding, or filling out this form, please let the court clerk know.

PLEASE REMEMBER THAT YOU ARE ANSWERING THESE QUESTIONS UNDER PENALTY OF PERJURY. YOUR ANSWERS MUST BE TRUE AND COMPLETE. THANK YOU FOR YOUR HELP IN SELECTING A FAIR JURY.

Form Approved by the Judicial Council of California
MC-001 (Effective July 1, 1993)

JUROR QUESTIONNAIRE FOR CIVIL CASES/Introduction and Instructions

PLAINTIFF'S OPENING STATEMENT IN A SEXUAL HARASSMENT CASE

Alison Wetherfield, Esq.
Visiting Professor
Tokyo University Faculty of Law

TABLE OF CONTENTS

1. GENERAL RULES

Studies of juror voting patterns and perceptions should send trial practitioners into deep depression. The general wisdom is that jurors are unimpressed by deft cross examination, clear direct examination, presentation of brilliant and abundantly qualified experts, exposure of lying witnesses and other highlights of the practice of our trade. Instead, 80 to 90 percent of jurors apparently come to a decision during or immediately after the opening statements of counsel. Clearly, nerves before delivery of the opening statement are justified and adequate preparation is essential.

The general rules to be found in any horn book and in common sense are as follows:

*** Be prepared.**

The opening statement is your chance to present your intimate knowledge of your client's *winning* case. If you don't have a simple, sincerely felt belief in the theory of your case by now, you should have settled. At this point, barring the surprises that come from witnesses in even the best-prepared case, you know all the ins and outs, strong points and flaws in your case and it should show. You should need no more than the most rudimentary notes on a yellow pad to remind you of the points you want to convey.

*** Be yourself.**

The jury doesn't have to like you or to consider you a better lawyer than your opponent, but it does have to believe you. Trying to come across as something you are not—whether a flashy orator or the jurors' oldest friend—will not help you. Being yourself is important (unless you are naturally pompous, arrogant and longwinded, in which case, get out of trial practice). Maintain eye-contact and smile (at appropriate junctures only of course). That said, do not be deceived that anything you do will make the jury mistake you for one of them. Realize that the jury perceives you as a lawyer with all the negatives and positives that brings.

*** Give the jury a clear guided tour of what the case is about.**

What is the crux of your case? Two or three sentences convey the gist of your client's claim, the defendant's wrongdoing and the injury suffered. It is far more important that the jury understand the heart of your case than that they grasp a complex chronology or technical point. Focus on the most important incidents and individuals in your case, not the cast of confusing background characters. Don't speak in legalese but don't talk down to the jury either. The facts, clearly presented, should speak for themselves.

*** Anticipate your opponent's statement.**

You know what the defense theory of the case is by now. Take advantage of going first to defuse it, briefly, charitably, but firmly. This will include touching candidly on your weak spots. It is far better to prepare jurors for these than to exaggerate the strength of your case. It is always worthwhile to alert jurors to expected important conflicting testimony.

*** Be flexible.**

Every case is different. Sometimes you will need to be brief, sometimes to tell a long story. Do not simply repeat a format that worked in one case if the next case or the next jury is totally different in focus.

Use the time to introduce yourself and your client to the jury.
The jury is even more tense than you. Use your time to get them settled in to their relationship as arbiters of your client's legal fate. Make sure they know your name and associate you fully with your client.

2. SPECIAL CONSIDERATIONS IN PRESENTING PLAINTIFF'S OPENING STATEMENT IN A SEX DISCRIMINATION/HARASSMENT/STEREOTYPING CASE

a. Sex composition of the jury

The jury's answers during voir dire should have alerted you to their basic viewpoints on sex discrimination. Voir dire questioning, however, is anything but a precise science. During your opening statement you will therefore be facing a group of people whose beliefs on the subject of sex roles and treatment of the sexes you will largely have to guess.

Academic studies suggest that, particularly in a sexual harassment case, you should be sensitive to the sex composition of the jury. Extreme differences in perception of events between the sexes are rare, but women and men respond very differently to situations involving sexuality. One study by social scientist Barbara Gutek involved the questioning of men and women about what their response would be to being approached sexually in the workplace. Only 15% of the men as contrasted with two-thirds (66%) of the women responded that they would be offended. In addition, surveys of men and women in the workplace suggest that the sexes' actual experience of sexual harassment at work are at great variance, which may affect their responses as jurors in a sexual harassment case. Two large scale studies of sexual harassment in the federal workforce by the U.S. Merit Systems Protection Board, published in 1981 and 1988, provide a fascinating portrait of the incidence of harassment and reactions to it. The 1981 study, "Sexual Harassment in the Federal Workplace: Is it a Problem?" found that 42% of all female federal government employees and 15% of all male federal government employees reported being sexually harassed during the 24-month period from May 1978 to May 1980. The 1988 study, "Sexual Harassment in the Federal Government: An Update," found that 42% of female federal government employees and 14% of male federal government employees said that between May 1985 and May 1987 they experienced some form of uninvited and unwanted sexual attention. Both surveys computed these percentages based upon their respondents' reporting of their experience of seven listed types of unwanted behavior:

(1) Actual or attempted rape or sexual assault
(2) Pressure for sexual favors
(3) Deliberate touching, leaning over, cornering or pinching
(4) Sexual looks or gestures
(5) Letters, phone calls, or materials of a sexual nature
(6) Pressure for dates
(7) Sexual teasing, jokes, remarks or questions

These figures suggest that far more women than men may be able to empathize with the plaintiff in a sexual harassment case based upon their own experience or philosophy. Obviously, one does not have to have been in a plaintiff's plight in most cases in order to render a verdict for a plaintiff, but the sex differences in perception and experience of harassment should be taken into account in planning presentation of a case to a jury.

For example, "sexual harassment," while an important phrase to use in any opening statement where the plaintiff's claims involve a sex discrimination cause of action, should not be the only phrase used to describe the totality of the plaintiff's experience, particularly in hostile environment cases before federal court juries. Such juries will have to determine as a factual matter whether a "hostile" or "abusive" environment exists in the workplace. Use your common sense in choosing your vocabulary so that both sexes can identify the hostility and abusiveness. Workers of both sexes, for example, appreciate the need for "respect" and "dignity" in employment, neither of which are enjoyed by a harassed worker, and understand the pain of workplace humiliation. Experiment with "buzz" words like these in outlining expected testimony. Emphasizing your client's professionalism and desire to succeed and explaining the harassing action as an obstacle to employment success may also help you to convey the injury better than reliance on the hope that all the jurors intuitively or through their own experience automatically understand "harassment" as a problem.

b. Sex of the advocates

All jurors form just as many opinions about the character of the advocates as about the parties and witnesses in any given case. Sonya Hamlin, in her book "What makes juries listen: a communications expert looks at the trial" (Harcourt Brace Jovanovich, 1985), describes a seminar exercise in which she asks a lawyer to demonstrate a two to three minute mini-opening statement. Afterwards she immediately asks the other seminar participants, who function as the "jury," several questions, including:

What kind of car do you think this lawyer drives?
What color is it?
Does she drink wine or beer?
How is her home furnished? - formal? - modern? - early American antiques?
What kind of movies does she like?

She reports that regardless of the content of the question, the audience answers vehemently, with absolute, definite and unshakable opinions. This amusing exercise well illustrates how judgmental we all can be and that you can expect the jury to be paying close attention to, and making snap judgments about, the lawyers who represent the parties. Your sex, in a sex discrimination case, will be part of this game.

Look at plaintiff's table and the defense table. Are there people of both sexes at both tables or does this look like a battle of the sexes? While the jury knows at some level that all the advocates are hired guns, jury members may be swayed by the fact that a woman is representing a male defendant or a man the female plaintiff. Jury reactions are hard to gauge on this. Some people are thrilled by an all female team in the traditionally male environment of the courtroom, others less than thrilled. Whatever the sex matrix of the opposing sides, it is worth being sensitive to how the jury perceives it. You may want to draw attention to a "girls versus boys" situation by making light of it, or to note subtly that your female advocate adversary "has been hired to put defendant's case for him."

c. Dealing with awkward expected testimony.

In any sex discrimination case, as a female plaintiff's counsel, you can expect that at some point the defendant will want to call other women from the same workplace to disavow the existence of any sex discrimination, stereotyping or harassment. Discovery and the pre-trial witness list should have alerted you as to what and whom to expect by the time you get up to deliver your opening statement.

As a general rule, the expectation of such awkward testimony should not dismay you. As a trial lawyer you know that there are many different true and false versions of the same incident, seen refracted through different eyes, and sex discriminatory incidents are no different. The defense witness may be lying out of fear of retaliation, loyalty to the employer or hope of advancement, or she may be truthfully testifying that she has experienced no sex discrimination while projecting her own experience, with no basis, onto your client. Either way, considcr how best to prepare the jury in your opening statement for testimony about the experience of other women because the jury members will want to be able to draw a clear and simple picture of this unknown workplace in their minds and the apparent inconsistent treatment and experience of some women will impede them. It may also confuse them, in a federal hostile environment case, in determining whether a reasonable employee would find the environment hostile or abusive. Consider, in such cases, bringing on an expert who can testify about the different ways, all "reasonable" women cope with a hostile work environment, ranging from denial through vociferous complaint, and to include discussion of this testimony in your opening statement.

d. Introducing expert testimony to the jury

The statistics revealing how early most jurors draw their conclusions about cases are perhaps most depressing for trial advocates who have persuaded their plaintiffs to hire trial experts at great expense. To ensure that you get your money's worth, it is clearly worthwhile to introduce the content of your expert's testimony to the jury in the opening statement and to pique their interest in what is to come.

As with any evidence the admission of which may be disputed, caution is advised. You do not want to promise the jury exciting evidence that they will never hear. If your opponent has already filed a motion to exclude your expert testimony, discussing it in opening is merely tempting an embarrassing objection from him or her that you are discussing potentially inadmissible testimony. If, however, you are fairly sure that the defense is not going to object to expert testimony, it is in your interests to touch on it. After all, the only expert testimony worth having is testimony that clearly explains the significance of other evidence and your opening statement should also be designed to have exactly that effect.

(i) Sex stereotyping. A brief excursus is warranted to urge counsel to consider using expert testimony on sex stereotyping and to explain some of its uses. Expert testimony about the study of sex-stereotyping by psychologists has been advanced by plaintiffs in a handful of sex discrimination cases thus far. It garnered a great deal of attention in *Price Waterhouse v. Hopkins,* 490 U.S. 228 (1989), in which it was offered by the plaintiff, Ann Hopkins, to clarify the role of sex discrimination in the decisional process for the denial of her promotion to partner at Price Waterhouse, the accounting firm. A U.S. Supreme Court plurality concluded that the expert witness' discussion of the sex discrimination evident from sex-stereotypical comments made about Hopkins by those evaluating her for promotion was obviously right, to the point of being "icing on the cake." A useful summary of empirical sex stereotyping research (which has been conducted by scientists for at least five decades and is generally accepted in the scientific community) is contained in the brief filed in the U.S. Supreme Court in *Hopkins* by *amicus curiae* the American Psychological Association through their counsel Ennis Friedman & Bersoff of Washington, D.C.

Perusal of the trial court opinion in *Hopkins* and of the APA brief reveals how useful sex stereotyping expert testimony can be to a plaintiff's side sex discrimination lawyer. It has particular use in hostile work environment sexual harassment cases in non-traditional work settings for women and has been so used by the author and her co-counsel Professor Sarah E. Burns of New York University Law School in *Robinson v. Jacksonville Shipyards, Inc.*, 760 F. Supp. 1486 (M.D. Fla. 1991). An explanation of cardinal points of sex stereotyping theory reveals these uses.

The study of stereotyping is the study of human categorization responses in thought and perception processes. In order to make sense of what we perceive, we tend to categorize people, events and objects by group. Perceiving people as divided into groups tends to maximize differences between groups and similarities within groups; for example, if we divide humans into groups by sex, we will tend to perceive women as being more similar to other women and more different from men and vice versa than they may actually be as individual people. When the person perceiving is a member of one of the groups into which he or she is dividing people, he or she tends to see members of the other group(s) less favorably. This categorizing process, applied in employment situations, can have discriminatory results if the categorizer does not recognize this tendency and check it. For example, when a male employer or co-worker categorizes a female employee based on her sex, he may evaluate and treat her in terms of things that are relevant to stereotypes of women as a group (her sex appeal, motherliness and so on), not in terms of her job skills and performance. This can lead to inappropriate decision-making (discrimination) and behavior (unwanted sexual attention/harassment) by the males. Such stereotyping, academic theory posits, is likely (to a statistically significant level) to occur in the presence of certain preconditions.

These preconditions include small numbers of a particular group, like women, in a setting where there are large numbers of another group, like men in a traditionally male workplace. The rarity of the former group suggests that stereotypes based on group membership will apply to them, that the group will be a focus of attention and that the behavior of the small group will be seen as different from and worse than the behavior of the large group by the large group's members, even when everyone is actually behaving in the same manner. In practical terms, this testimony, based on decades of empirical research, is very useful to help explain and defuse frequent defense testimony in hostile work environment sexual harassment cases that women actually create the problem by swearing and acting sexually more than the men do, which the women usually deny even if admitting to occasional foul language. It also helps to highlight the frequent stereotypes of women in defense witness testimony; it is very common to hear male witnesses describing any complaint by a woman as "hysterical" or "bitching" and so on while describing employment-related complaints by men in neutral or approving terms.

Other preconditions for stereotyping are also usually present in hostile work environments for women—a lack of women (the rare group) in positions of authority in the setting, and a non-professional ambience. Another useful feature of stereotyping research for trial testimony purposes is its positive finding that when people are made aware of their tendency to stereotype and given guidelines for how to avoid it, they are able to do so and to evaluate individuals according to relevant criteria. This testimony can be used to bolster the plaintiff's claim to the judge for relief in the form of a strict and enforced sexual harassment policy.

Hopefully this digression should have suggested to some plaintiff's counsel that sex stereotyping theory might be a useful topic for expert testimony in those difficult sexual harassment cases where women are perceived by the employer to be full participants in a hostile work environment and overreacting hysterics if they complain. Opening statements in such cases can be a real challenge for the advocate who is aware of the wide variety of conflicting testimony that is to follow. Reference to the common sense findings of generations of psychologists about our flawed perception processes may help jurors to sift through that testimony to form a picture of how the witnesses have formed their various pictures of their workplace.

(ii) Sexual harassment. Sexual harassment experts who have experience in counseling harassment victims and perpetrators and in training employers in sexual harassment elimination strategies can also be a boon for the plaintiff s advocate. For the purposes of the opening statement, perhaps the most useful expert testimony to describe to the jury (and judge) is that concerning how different people cope with sexual harassment and the need for, and effectiveness of, the different components of a workable sexual harassment policy.

Expert testimony on the former point helps to put your client's reaction into perspective and show, whatever it was, that it is a typical and reasonable reaction. If, for example, your client did not complain about harassment for a long time and simply chalked up absences from work, you can be sure that the defense will argue that her failure to complain shows that the problem was imaginary or nugatory and that she is simply seeking to excuse her malingering. Expert testimony drawn from counseling experience or from, for example, the Merit Systems Protection Board studies referred to above, will enable you to counter with evidence that a wide variety of actions are taken by victims. In the 1988 federal study only 15% of the self-identified female victims reported that they informed a supervisor of the problem, while others reported ignoring the behavior, avoiding the person, asking the person to stop, trying to make a joke of the behavior, threatening to tell others and/or going along with the behavior. This sort of testimony, and discussion of it in your opening statement, positions your client's behavior as mainstream, predictable and reasonable and helps to focus attention on the problem of harassment in the workplace, not on her response.

e. Explaining the need for adequate relief

One essential topic for inclusion in your opening statement is your client's need for adequate relief. Jurors who may be happy to see a sexual harassment policy put into place to protect other women may prove strangely reluctant to award large damages to the plaintiff. For the most part, where rape or other physical sexual assault is not in the fact pattern, the injury in sexual harassment cases is solely to the psyche, and while the trauma is undoubtedly great, it can be hard to convey this to a jury, particularly in parts of the country where seeing a psychiatrist or seeking other mental health care are stigmatized, and your client has not sought professional help. This problem requires sensitive handling in the opening statement.

As preparation, the plaintiff's advocate should become familiar with some of the literature on the emotional impact of sexual harassment, including the American Psychiatric Association Board of Trustees' "Statement on Discrimination Based on Gender and Sexual Orientation," 145 Am. J. Psychiatry 1494 (1988), which classifies sexual harassment as "potentially a severe stressor" similar to other stressors defined in the American Psychiatric Association's important diagnostic manual, "Diagnostic and Statistical Manual of Mental Disorders" ("DSM-III-R") (3rd Ed. 1987).

In the opening statement, as in direct examination of your client and of any health professionals you bring on to testify about her state, you will need to talk about the effects of the harassment in concrete terms readily understandable by the jury. Discussion of symptoms—sleepless nights, nausea, ulcers, hair loss, depression and so on—is far more compelling than bald statements about "emotional harm." Despite the Supreme Court's clear statement, in *Harris v. Forklift Systems, Inc.,* that a plaintiff may recover in a federal hostile environment case without having suffered a nervous breakdown, a jury may be reluctant to award damages for less. You should therefore clearly emphasize the impact of the harassment on the plaintiff's work performance and enjoyment of work and leisure time.

3. CONCLUDING THOUGHTS

All of the above may or may not be helpful in writing or thinking about your opening statement in any given case. As in every other area of trial practice, however, you only learn by doing it. At least when you and your opponent have sat down, having delivered your opening statements, an enormous pressure will be lifted. If the jury has basically decided the case you can now relax and enjoy the presentation of the rest of your case.

ALISON WETHERFIELD

Alison Wetherfield is a New York lawyer currently living in Japan where she is engaged in research and writing about the development of sexual harassment law in Japan, the U.S. and Europe, funded by a grant from the Abe Fellowship Program of the Social Science Research Council and the American Council of Learned Societies, with funds provided by the Japan Foundation Center for Global Partnership. Since 1992 she has also been a visiting professor at Tokyo University, teaching U.S. employment discrimination law and U.S. trial techniques, and a member of the Japan/U.S. Joint Project on Employment Discrimination sponsored by the Japan Institute of Labour.

Before moving to Japan, Ms. Wetherfield worked for six years at NOW Legal Defense & Education Fund, a public interest law firm in New York City founded in 1970. There, as staff attorney and Legal Director, Ms. Wetherfield litigated sexual harassment cases and wrote and lectured extensively on plaintiffs' sexual harassment litigation strategy. Ms. Wetherfield was trial counsel (with Professor Sarah E. Burns of New York University) for plaintiff in *Robinson v. Jacksonville Shipyards, Inc.*, 760 F. Supp. 1486 (M.D. Fla. 1991).

Ms. Wetherfield is a law graduate of Cambridge University, England, and Harvard Law School.

THE OPENING STATEMENT IN EMPLOYMENT CASES:
"Who do you believe? Me or your lying eyes?"

Robert B. Fitzpatrick, Esq.
Fitzpatrick & Verstegen
Universal Building North
1875 Connecticut Avenue, N.W.
Suite 1140
Washington, DC 20009-5728
202/588-5300

THE OPENING STATEMENT IN EMPLOYMENT CASES:

"Who do you believe? Me or your lying eyes?"

By: Robert B. Fitzpatrick, Esq.*
Fitzpatrick & Verstegen
Universal Building North
1875 Connecticut Avenue, N.W.
Suite 1140
Washington, DC 20009-5728
(202) 588-5300 (Telephone)
(202) 588-5023 (Facsimile)

The rules that plaintiff's counsel should adhere to in an opening statement in an employment case are no different than those to be followed generally in civil litigation. I have outlined below the most important rules that should be followed.

1. Never waive an opening statement.

2. Introduce the dramatis personae. Introduce the plaintiff's team of attorneys, the plaintiff, and the defense lawyers (make the SOB stand up and introduce him/her to the jury). Some attorneys even introduce the judge (be extremely careful). Consider, if the judge will permit, using photos of the witnesses as you tell the jury about the other actors in the play. Visuals are invaluable.

3. Make no promise that you cannot keep. Keep your contract with the jury. If you promise to prove something, the jury may think you have to prove it to win. The danger

of overstatement far outweighs the danger of understatement. Err on the side of understatement.

4. In describing the facts that you will prove, do not defy Newton's law, that is, do not ask the jury to believe what no one can believe.

5. In describing the facts that you will prove, do not extensively quote testimony to be given by your witnesses. If you do so, the testimony, when given at trial, will sound rehearsed and too pat.

6. Exude calm confidence. Let the jury know that it does not matter what the defendant says. Let them know that you have it together and are not afraid of anything.

7. If there is a weakness in your case (face it--there always is, or it would have settled), confront it. Do not avoid it. Annihilate it. Deal with it! If you have to overcome it to win the case, then deal with it at the outset. You would not be there if you did not have an answer.

8. Do not talk in legalese. Juries believe "proximate cause" is "approximate cause."

9. Do not talk about the plaintiff's case and the defendant's case. That is lawyer thinking, not jury perception. Their perception is the story.

10. Once and only once refer to your client as the plaintiff. Thereafter, use his/her name.

11. Maintain eye contact with the jury. Do not become a prisoner of your notes. Have your opening (talking points) on a single sheet of paper. If the court will permit you to be mobile, then get away from the podium--it is a communication barrier.

12. Talk in pictures. Become familiar with the day-time TV serials. Use analogies and metaphors. Tell them an interesting story. Have a story line--a theme.

13. Have a "hook." A hook is an advertising term describing a slogan, word, or phrase that grabs one's attention and sticks in their mind. Ideally, they evoke an image in a person's mind, and also are easy to remember. A hook can arouse the jury's interest and focus them on the major theme of your case immediately. That theme can then be carried throughout the trial and into closing.

14. Use theme reversal, i.e., take the defense's theme and start in your opening to undermine its theme.

15. If judge will allow you to be mobile, move about, but do not invade the jury's space too early in the trial. Remember you are forging new relationships with a bunch of strangers. This is akin to a first date--a courtship.

16. Do not refer to the jury as "the jury." Call them ladies and gentlemen. Be respectful. Treat them like individuals, not an entity.

17. When describing what you are doing in an opening, tell them it is like a preview of coming attractions at the movies.

18. Use blowups in opening. Get the court's ok in advance. Do not have a squabble at the outset in front of the jury. If there are one or two key documents, have them blown up and show them to the jury in your opening.

19. Do not say "we expect to prove that...." or "the evidence will show that...." Boring! Tell a story!

20. Do not start by telling the jury that what you say is not evidence. This has

been called "mimicking mediocrity." On a first date, you don't say "do not pay attention to anything I have to say." Well, don't say it to the jury you are courting.

21. Open a file at the start of the case called "opening" and put all those brilliant ideas (all the great metaphors) in there that you think of while out jogging. In fact, preparation of a working opening statement when you accept the case can be useful. Fine tune it as you proceed through pretrial preparation of the case, including tailoring discovery requests to your theme and opposing the inevitable motion for summary judgment.

22. If the case merits it and you can afford it, hire a focus group and "test market" the opening. The focus group's reactions should be used to modify the opening. Thus, if the theme does not sell to the focus group, go back to the drawing board to revise your theory of the case until it does resonate and sell to them.

23. If your case does not merit the expense of a focus group or you cannot afford one, then do a mock of your opening with your kids, your secretaries, etc. Make sure that non-lawyers understand the story and react positively to it.

24. If there is something unusual about damages, then explain it to them, but do not ask for money in the opening. That's like asking her to marry you on the first date.

25. Thank them for their service, but be careful not to patronize them.

26. Get in the particular shabby treatment. Thus, even if it is a breach of implied contract case with no emotional distress damages, let them know that the plaintiff was fired around Christmas.

27. Tell a good story. The human voice is a theatrical tool. Voice modulation, word pacing, silence, pitch--use them all.

28. Do not say "I think" or "I believe" the evidence will show blah, blah, blah. That is not courtship.

29. Remember that the plaintiff has primacy (you go first) and he who goes first has an advantage.

30. Repetition is the key to learning. Repeat key facts, buzz words, phrases that are critical to the story. Redundancy helps the jurors to remember.

31. You represent a person. You want the jury to get to know this person and to like this person. Stress not only what your client did for the company and the sacrifices he made, but also the number of years over which they were made.

32. In contrast, the defendant will almost always be a corporation or company. It is much more difficult for a juror to warm up to a fictional entity. Throughout your opening statement and the trial you should use references such as "defendant corporation," "the company," "the company's lawyer."

33. Similarly, your client was not terminated. Your client was fired. Your client's job was not eliminated, your client was eliminated.

34. Have a strong end to the opening. Summarize the story. Hit the theme. Hit the buzz words. Hit the talking points. End on a strong, positive note with a sentence or two that encapsulates the story.

ROBERT B. FITZPATRICK

Robert Brian Fitzpatrick is senior partner in the law firm of Fitzpatrick & Verstegen in Washington, D.C. where he represents clients in employment law and employee benefits matters. Mr. Fitzpatrick has specialized in employment law disputes for twenty-five years and has been described by the National Law Journal as being among the top employment lawyers in the country and by Washingtonian Magazine as "tops in employment law" in the Washington, D.C. area. He is included in the 1993-94 edition of *The Best Lawyers in America* published by Woodward/White, Inc.

Mr. Fitzpatrick is an active member of the American Bar Association (ABA) and the District of Columbia Bar, being a frequent speaker at Bar meetings and a participant in the activities of several sections of the ABA and the D.C. Bar. He has been Co-Chairman of the ABA's Committee on Individual Employee Rights and Responsibilities of the Labor and Employment Law Section; Co-Chairman of the Steering Committee of the Labor Relations Section of the D.C. Bar; Chairman and founder of the D.C. Bar's Committee on Individual Employee Rights and Responsibilities; Chairman of the Federal Bar Association's Labor Law and Labor Relations Section; and Chairman of the FBA'S Committee on Equal Employment Opportunity. He is an active member of the ABA's Employer-Employee Relations and Long Range Planning Committees of the Torts and Insurance Practice Section, and the Section of Dispute Resolution of the ABA.

Mr. Fitzpatrick is a prolific author in the field of employment law. Most recently his concentration has been on conflict resolution in the workplace. In that regard, he has written and lectured widely on mediation. Mr. Fitzpatrick is President of MENDS, a commercial mediation service.

Mr. Fitzpatrick received his J.D. Degree with honors from the George Washington University's National Law Center in 1967. He has been a member of the Bar of the District of Columbia since 1968.

THE DEFENSE SPEAKS—
THE OPENING STATEMENT

Harriet E. Cooperman
Weinberg and Green
100 South Charles Street
Baltimore, Maryland 21201
410/332-8600

The courtroom is completely silent, but for some sniffling sounds coming from a few of the jurors. The Plaintiff's counsel deliberately takes one step back, slightly smiles and nods to the jury, then slowly and steadily returns to her seat. She just has delivered an absolutely crushing opening statement, describing in graphic terms how that faceless, insensitive, profit-driven corporation [your client—the Defendant] has destroyed the Plaintiff's life. After twenty years of loyal and exemplary service to that Company, he was fired, on the spot, in front of his entire crew, merely because he was distraught over his dying son and arrived to work late one day. Then, turning and pointing at you and your client, the Plaintiff's counsel asks, "But was this Company content simply with firing Al and cutting him off completely after twenty years? No!" she answered, "They had to destroy him by spreading vicious lies and rumors that he was a drunk and drug addict, so he never again could get a steady job in the shipping community!"

You are beginning to sweat; your stomach is tied in knots. Then slowly the Judge peers down at you and says "Counselor, do you wish to deliver your opening statement?" You turn and look at the jury only to see twelve pairs of eyes staring at you with contempt and disdain. Do you run and hide? Do you ask the judge for a brief recess so you can convince your client to settle?

Of course not. But what can you do not merely to diffuse the tremendous impact that your opponent has had on the jury, but, further, to turn it around and convince the jury that your client truly is decent and caring, who acted properly and committed no wrong to the Plaintiff?

The opening statement is Defendant's perfect opportunity to get the jury on its side, making them see the case through the Defendant's eyes from the very outset. Yes, the Plaintiff tells his tale of woe first. But it is the Defendant who has the unique advantage of making the last speech, completely unrebutted, until closing argument. You can listen to the Plaintiff tell his story, and then respond to and weave those facts into your theme and explanation of the case, in a way that convinces the jury that it is only the Defendant's version that is believable and correct.

Your opening is critical. If properly presented it can direct the jury to follow the trial from your point of view; make them hear and absorb the evidence that you want them to remember and have them adopt your attitudes towards your client, the issues, what is fair and what probably happened. Significantly, you can emerge from opening as the thoughtful, credible and helpful teacher, who cares about the jury, works with them and gives them what they need to understand and decide the case. What you say and how you say it can hover over the entire trial, affecting the jurors' perceptions throughout the presentation of the evidence.

For most jurors this will be the first actual trial they ever have seen. Their understanding of what goes on in court, in all probability, is based on what they have seen on television and in the movies; and what they have read in the newspapers. They expect the lawyers to be as smooth and polished as the actors on *L.A. Law,* delivering their prepared script as if the words just flow naturally. They may further expect that the evidence will be presented to them in an organized and capsulized fashion so they will be able to follow the trial and understand the case with ease, as it unfolds before them.

The television/movie model is important for the trial lawyer to focus on. For although it is far from the reality of what goes on in the courtroom, it will remind you of where the jury is coming from, and what you must then do, in an environment foreign to the average juror, to present your case in a clear, understandable and convincing manner. Most significantly, it provides an excellent model to follow in preparing and delivering your opening statement in a way which the jury is used to and feels comfortable with.

YOUR OPENING AS THE COMING ATTRACTIONS

We all like coming attractions. We want to have an idea of what the movie or book is about before we commit our time to it. While jurors cannot simply walk out of a trial, they need and want to have a clear idea of what the case is about before the presentation of the evidence begins—who are the characters, what happened, what went wrong, and what evidence should I look out for. Since the evidence at trial is presented through witnesses and documents, in a piecemeal fashion, oftentimes out of order, and without any contemporaneous commentary tying it together, the coming attractions (opening) is particularly important to a juror's understanding of the case and what will unfold before them.

TELL A STORY

Before the development of written language, our ancestors recorded and repeated their history, from generation to generation, orally, through storytelling. The reason for this is quite obvious—There is nothing like a well-told story. A story is entertaining and able to capture and retain interest, much more so than a dry dissertation of factual and technical information; thus, it is much more often and easily remembered. In modern society, the dramatic story presentation remains overwhelmingly the most common means of disseminating information. A substantial percentage of the average person's leisure time is spent watching movies and television dramas and sitcoms. "Docudramas" have replaced documentaries. Even many segments on the nightly news are presented in a story fashion. It is the story that the public (your jury) can follow, understand, relate to, and, therefore, remember.

Every case, no matter how complex or technical, has a story to tell, complete with characters, plot, suspense and theme. From the very inception of your case you should begin to identify and develop your story. As discovery unfolds more facts, you should fill in the pieces by continually molding and developing your story. This story (the Defendant's version of the case and facts), should become the basis of your opening statement.

ESTABLISH THE THEME

Just as every case tells a story, every story (case) has one or two themes. It is essential to tell the jury your theme, at the very outset of your opening, and then repeat it at critical times throughout.

The theme, if explained and presented well, will serve as psychological anchors which the jurors can use to organize and understand the evidence and fall back on at difficult times during the trial.

LET US BEGIN

The jury is anxious and eager. They want to know right away what this case is all about. They do not want to wait and try to figure it out for themselves. Frankly, they also do not want to wait as you dilly dally before them for the first five to ten minutes of opening with prefatory remarks about civic duty, the American jurisprudence system and the like.

Get to the point. The first few minutes of your opening are critical. It is during this time that you, most likely, will make your impression on the jury—good or bad or blah. Use it. Get the jury's attention. Let them know who you are, who your client is and why you and they are there.

Your demeanor, at the outset as well as throughout, is critical. You *must* show the jury that you are confident. You believe in your client and in your case and therefore, so should the jury. If you fail to convey your strong belief in your case you will lose them—"why should I believe the Defendant's story if his own lawyer does not."

Introduce and humanize your client. This is key, especially when you are representing that big, faceless profit-driven corporation that fired the Plaintiff. Have the President or another appropriate representative of the Defendant present throughout the trial and introduce that person as "the corporation." Let the jury know that the Defendant is not some faceless steel, brick and glass building, but rather is made up of real people who think, feel, suffer and act just like them.

Set the tone of your case. Tell the jury your theme and imbed it in their minds. Let the jury know what your agenda is and how your opening will help them. In other words, perk the jury's interest from the start, involve the jury, and give them a reason why they should continue listening to you, rather than day dream about what they could be doing if they were not stuck there in the courtroom.

Now, tell your story. Remember, you want to capture and retain the interest of your audience. To do this you should follow the traditional techniques of good story telling. First, set the stage—"It was a deep, dark, stormy night. . ." Then, introduce the central characters around whom the story revolves. Next, you need to acquaint the jury to the problem (the issues of the case), followed by an explanation of the plot and the action that unfolds. Finally, you should suggest to the jury the conclusion, and how they have the power to decide that correct and happy ending to the story.

Present the story in a dramatic, humanistic and organized manner, giving the jury enough information so they can understand and follow the case, but not too much detail that they will be overwhelmed. Remember your television audience. Your jury is accustomed to getting their information in a capsulized fashion, within a few minutes (television shows average from 30 to 60 minutes, repeatedly broken up by commercials, approximately every ten minutes). Your jury's attention span is quite short. Don't forget your opening is the coming attractions, it is not the entire movie. Tell enough of the story to entice the jury so that they will want to stay for the feature presentation.

POINTS YOU NEED TO COVER

Emphasize critical evidence that you want the jury to focus on and remember. Explain why it is important. If done properly, when that witness testifies or that exhibit is introduced, the jury will be alert and prepared—it will stand out above the other evidence.

If your case involves complex yet critical expert testimony, prepare the jury for this. You need not and should not go into detail about what the expert will say. You should, however, tell the jury that there is certain critical evidence that can only be presented through an expert witness. Explain what an "expert" is and that the testimony may be technical and dry. Emphasize why it is so important to the case and that the jury should listen very carefully to the testimony. Define any key technical terms that the expert will use and promise to tie it up for them in closing.

Emphasize any weakness and inconsistencies in the Plaintiff's case. If the Plaintiff's story or theme is illogical or impractical or if it requires the jury to make certain assumptions which are incorrect or just not believable make sure to draw this to the jury's attention. Get the jury to view the case through your eyes and your perceptions. By revealing the Plaintiff's weaknesses, you can make the jury quite skeptical of the Plaintiff's credibility, his premise and therefore, his entire case. Remember, you speak last before the presentation of the evidence. Use this to your advantage.

Unfortunately, your case also has some weaknesses or difficult facts. If not it would have settled months (if not years) ago. You simply cannot ignore these problems hoping that they will remain hidden in a locked closet. Any decent Plaintiff's attorney will unlock these facts and parade them in front of the jury at the most opportune time, conveying the idea that this big, bad, mean corporation is trying to hide the truth from them. As defense counsel, you can diffuse this rather explosive weapon from the start. During your opening tell the jury about these weaknesses and problems. By doing so you will soften the impact of these bad facts by putting them in the proper light, explaining them away, and telling the jury that while these facts exist they should not affect the outcome you are asking the jury to reach. You may also score important points for being candid and up front with the jury—this lawyer is honest and believable, she really wants us to know the full case, not only the facts which are good for her client. These impressions will remain with the jury throughout the trial. When that "bad evidence" comes out, the jury already would have heard about it, thanks to you, and will be able to put it in its proper place (as you have so guided them).

Be careful not to overstate your case. Only tell the jury about those facts which you are certain you will be able to prove. If you make promises which you are unable to keep, the jury may remember them and, at the end, question your credibility, and ultimately your case. They may believe that those facts were critical to your case and, therefore, since you were unable to prove them, the jury may feel compelled to find against you. Better to understate your case, leaving the revelation of this uncertain evidence to the witnesses, and thus, pleasantly surprise the jury with such wonderful evidence which you can then argue from in your closing.

Explain that the story will come out during the course of the trial through witnesses and other evidence, such as documents. While in opening, you can tell them about the case in an organized chronological fashion, oftentimes the evidence is not presented so clearly. Explain to the jury that some witnesses are foundational, and at times witnesses need to be called out of order. This will help the jury understand the process, and they will be thankful to you for assisting them to do so.

Your Delivery As the Key

How you present your opening can be just as important as what you say during your opening. Again, remember the television/movie model. A convincing actor is the one who is believable and natural, not the actor who over-dramatizes or who tries to be someone he is not.

Opening statement is the lawyer's first real opportunity to make an impression on the jury. (For those of us in jurisdictions where there is no lawyer-conducted voir dire, it truly is the only such opportunity.) First impressions are lasting impressions. The moment you step up to deliver your opening you are under the jury's microscope. They will quickly determine what you are all about—are you there to help them or hinder and deceive them? Are you worthy of belief? Use the opening fully to your advantage. Here are some key points to remember:

- **Be the jury's guide and teacher.** The jury wants and needs to understand what will occur in the courtroom and what the case is all about. Let the jury know from the very start that you are there to help them do just that. Guide them through the trial process and explain the case in a clear, persuasive, but not argumentative manner. Speak to the jury as a friend and teacher, do not speak at them or down to them. Use your opening to develop this rapport with the jury—you are on their side and together you will reach the proper conclusion (which happens to be for your client).

- **Be yourself.** It is imperative that you come off natural, believable, likable and candid. The only way you can do this (unless you are Dustin Hoffman) is to be yourself. If you try to be someone you are not the jury will see right through it.

- **Be confident, positive and sincere.** Show the jury that you are self-assured and believe in your client and your case. If you do not, you should not be trying it. You also must be sincere. Avoid language which is too pat or too strongly worded, or lacks conviction. An opening which may come off beautifully, for an established folksy country lawyer will not work for a thirty year old big city attorney, and it will show. It will lack sincerity and will lose all credibility with the jury. Remember the cardinal rule—be yourself and confidence, credibility and sincerity will naturally follow. Your entire demeanor, the way you stand, your gestures, your facial expressions, your tone of voice, as well as how you phrase your words should be positive. This will go far in convincing the jury of the correctness of your position.

- **Be simple, clear and direct.** Large complex words serve absolutely no purpose other than to portray in the minds of the listeners the image of a speaker who is pompous, egotistical and arrogant, who thinks he is smarter than everyone else, and who is trying to impress them with his large vocabulary. Your opening, no matter how well thought out and eloquently given, will go absolutely nowhere if the jury does not understand what you are saying and cannot follow where you are going. The language you use must be simple, clear and direct, in terms that are readily understandable by the average person. Watch television and movies, listen to the language used and follow it in preparing your opening. Similarly, avoid legalese.

- **Be organized.** Explain to the jury what you intend to tell them in opening—give them a road map. Then as you tell your story and make your point, introduce each idea so they know where you are taking them and they can follow.

- **Be prepared, but be flexible.** Many lawyers wait until the eve of trial before they begin to think about and formulate their opening. This is much too late; the end result will be totally ineffective and waste of everyone's time. You should begin to start thinking about and develop your opening from the moment you take on the case. Identify your theme and theory, and develop your discovery and facts with this theme in mind, then put them together for your opening.

  Organize your basic points and ideas, and jot down key words, and, if, necessary, a very brief outline. Do not write out your opening. If you do so you will be wedded to a speech. Then, when you forget a word or line, which you inevitably will do, you probably will become totally lost. If you write out your opening you may feel compelled to read it (so you can be assured that you will not forget a single word). This can be disastrous. It is almost impossible to come across natural, sincere and credible when you obviously are reading from a script. In all likelihood your opening will be stilted and boring, and will turn off the jury completely. Practice your opening in front of your staff, children, and, if no one will listen to you, a mirror or video camera. Study what works, and change that which does not. Preparation is important, but do not overly prepare. You do not want your opening to come off as memorized or too pat or even too smooth. The jury will not burst out in hysterical laughter or think you are totally inept merely because you misstate a word, or need to pause for a moment to rephrase or regain your thoughts. More likely, you will appear natural, believable and human. Remain flexible at all times. You should be able to incorporate necessary responses to points made by Plaintiff's counsel in her opening.

- **Watch your body language.** Your thoughts and attitudes are conveyed not only by the words you use, but also by your facial expressions, gestures and other body language. You should be aware of and in control of your expressions and habits. Use thoughtful expressions and gestures to your advantage; do not let bad habits sabotage an otherwise effective opening. As with language, do not use overly exaggerated expressions or gestures, they will seem unnatural or simply too distracting. Videotape your opening and you will identify your peculiar annoying habits—pulling hair, scratching your head, jiggling change in your pocket, waving arms, etc. Now, stop it!

- **Speak directly to the jury.** Maintain eye contact with the entire jury, but do not stare at or concentrate on a single juror. If permitted by the court, give your opening in front of the jury. You want to speak directly to the jury, and this is quite difficult to do if you are at a distant podium or counsel table. Stand up near the jury, but do not get too close. You have not yet developed a rapport with the jury, and if too close, you may be invading their space and making them feel uncomfortable.

  If you can do so comfortably, try to move during your opening to keep it interesting or to make to point. Do not pace, or the jury will feel like they are watching a tennis match. Again you must make sure that such movement is acceptable with the local rules and your judge.

- **Create interest and suspense with your voice.** Change your tone and inflection to make different points. At critical moments pause for emphasis. Use your voice in such a way that it sounds believable, but not overly dramatic, put on, or incredible.

- **Imbed your theme.** Establish your theme at the very beginning. Like a good ballard, repeat it throughout, and remind the jury of your theme at the conclusion of your opening.

- **Tell a good story.** Tell your story naturally, and let it flow. A good story should tell itself. In other words, do not over-dramatize. You want the jury to focus on your story, not you, the story teller. It is the substance of what you are saying that you want them to remember and follow throughout the trial.

- **Words and pictures.** Your story should be told through a careful selection of words, and if permissible and susceptible, pictures and other visual aids. In contrast to those self-destructive big words, descriptive, creative and active words can be winners. Think about your case, and how and what words can best describe not only what occurred but the images you are trying to instill in the minds of the jury. Repeat these words throughout your opening to create that appropriate mental image.

  Remember the old saying—a picture is worth a thousand words? In today's multi-media society this becomes even more evident. Most people have become conditioned to learning and remembering information through the use of pictures and other visual images. Television largely has replaced radio. Even songs have been transformed into music videos. A visual image can be an excellent reinforcing teaching aid—just like a blackboard for a teacher. If you have a piece of powerful demonstrative evidence, which you know will be admitted into evidence, consider showing it to the jury and using it during your opening. Charts outlining the chronology or other details of the case also may be useful tools. To avoid unnecessary interruptions (objections) during your opening, you should obtain the court's permission before using such visual aids. You also should consider using the courtroom as your stage to demonstrate certain points or to describe the scene.

- **Repetition**. Your theme and key points need to be stated, repeated, stated again and recapitulated. An excellent teaching method is to explain the same things a number of times but differently each time. In other words, be repetitive but do not be redundant. Only by repetition and re-emphasis can you be assured that hopefully all, or at least most, of the jurors will follow, understand and remember.

- **Avoid the common opening cliches**. Do not give the jurors a sermon about the importance of jury service. It usually comes off as stilted and insincere, and merely wastes critical time at the beginning of opening, when you should be catching the jury's attention and establishing rapport.

  Do not tell the jury that what you are about to say in opening is not evidence and should not be considered as such. By doing so you have just undermined your entire opening. The jury will wonder why you are standing up there wasting their time, and will turn you off.

  Do not say "I believe the evidence will prove. . ." Just tell them your story. Let the jury know that you are certain about your case and this is what it is about.

- Finally. **Be Brief.**

CONCLUSION

You have now completed your opening statement. You have ended on a high note, once again reminding the jury of the theme of your case, and how your suggested outcome is the only conclusion they logically could reach. They now are ready, willing and eagerly waiting to hear the evidence in the light most favorable for the Defendant.

HARRIET E. COOPERMAN

Harriet E. Cooperman is head of the Labor and Employment Law Practice Group for Weinberg and Green in Baltimore, Maryland. She brings to the Firm more than sixteen years of experience in the area. She earned her Juris Doctor degree from the University of Maryland School of Law and her undergraduate degree from the Cornell University School of Industrial and Labor Relations. Ms. Cooperman is a former Chairperson of the Section on Labor and Employment Law of the Maryland State Bar Association and is a frequent national speaker and author on labor issues relevant to management involved in manufacturing, wholesale, retail and service industries.

THE USE OF STEREOTYPE EXPERT WITNESS TESTIMONY IN EMPLOYMENT DISCRIMINATION ACTIONS FOLLOWING THE HOPKINS v. PRICE WATERHOUSE DECISION

Karen Kaplowitz, Esq.

Alschuler, Grossman & Pines
Los Angeles, California 90067

and

Rebel Ely, Esq.

Los Angeles, California

The Use of Sex Stereotype Expert Witness Testimony in Employment Discrimination Actions Following the Hopkins v. Price Waterhouse Decision

By Karen Kaplowitz, Esq. and Rebel Ely, Esq.[1]

The Supreme Court's 1989 decision in Hopkins v. Price Waterhouse launched a new era in the use of experts on sex stereotypes. Hopkins v. Price Waterhouse, 490 U.S. 228, 109 S.Ct. 1775 (1989), remanded 737 F.Supp. 1202 (D.D.C. 1990), aff'd 920 F.2d 967 (D.C. Cir. 1990). Although expert witness testimony was admitted prior to Hopkins in employment discrimination actions, it was rarely utilized to expose damaging sexually stereotypical behavior. The Supreme Court ruled in Hopkins that evidence of the existence of sex stereotypes is admissible evidence of discrimination. Sex stereotype experts are, therefore, likely to become more common in future state and federal employment discrimination actions.

I. The Use of Expert Witnesses Before Hopkins v. Price Waterhouse

Even though experts have not been used often in the past on sex stereotyping, historically courts often admitted evidence of stereotypes in discrimination actions. For example, in the landmark 1971 California Supreme Court sex discrimination case Sail'er Inn, Inc. v. Kirby, the Court rejected various stereotypes about women's ability to tend bar which the state advanced as a defense. Sail'er Inn, Inc. v. Kirby, 5 Cal.3d 1 (1971).

The Court found that there was no empirical evidence to support the State's claim that a male bartender or owner must be present in a liquor establishment to preserve order and to protect patrons because a woman could not perform such a task. Sail'er Inn, Inc., at 9. The Court also found that it was difficult to believe that women working behind bars would be more subject to the dangers of inebriated customers than cocktail waitresses already permitted to work among drinking customers. Id.

The Court also found that there was no evidence to support the "peculiar and wholly unacceptable generalization that women in bars, unrestrained by husbands or the risk of losing a liquor license, will commit improper acts" nor any data to support the contention that women bartenders would have an unwholesome influence on the public or "any less incentive than male bartenders to obey the laws governing the sale of alcoholic beverages and the rules set down by their employers in order to retain their jobs and promote their own well-being." Sail'er Inn, Inc. at 20.

In a recent employment discrimination case in which the defense used an expert witness on sex stereotypes, EEOC v. Sears, Roebuck & Co., the District Court found that the segregation of women in lower-paying jobs was the expression of the women's own choices. EEOC v. Sears, Roebuck & Co., 628 F.Supp. 1264 (N.D.Ill. 1986) aff'd 839 F.2d 302 (7th Cir. 1988). The Court rejected the EEOC's claim that Sears had engaged in sex discrimination in hiring and promoting men into commission sales jobs while relegating women to much lowerpaying jobs.

In the controversial EEOC case, the Court invoked women's stereotyped experience in the family as the underlying reason for a variety of "feminine" traits and values that supposedly lead women to "prefer lower-paying, noncommission sales jobs." The Court stated that:

> Women tend to be more interested than men in the social and cooperative aspects of the workplace. Women tend to see themselves as less competitive. They often view noncommission sales as more attractive than commission sales, because they can enter and leave the job more easily, and because there is more social contact and friendship, and less stress in noncommission selling. EEOC v. Sears, Roebuck & Co., 628 F.Supp. at 1308.

To support these broad assertions, the Court cited the testimony of an expert witness Sears hired. Dr. Rosalind Rosenberg, an historian, testified for Sears and attributed the motherly characteristics of women's personalities directly to their traditional domestic roles. EEOC at 1308 & n. 42. She testified about sexual stereotypes which she opined justified Sears' hiring and promotion procedures. She stated that:

> Throughout American history women have been trained from earliest childhood to develop the humane and nurturing values expected of the American mother. Women's participation in the labor force is affected by the values they have internalized. For example: women tend to be more relationship-centered and men tend to be more work-centered. Women tend to be more interested than men in the cooperative, social aspects of the work situation. These differences in female and male self-perception present difficulties for women in traditionally masculine occupations.

Offer of Proof Concerning the Testimony of Dr. Rosalind Rosenberg, EEOC v. Sears, Roebuck & Co., 628 F.Supp. 1264 (N.D. Ill. 1986).

Although in cases like Sears and Sail'er Inn, Inc., evidence of sex stereotypes has been considered, neither case involved an expert specifically designated as a sexual stereotype expert witness.

II. The Use of Sexual Stereotype Expert Witnesses in the Hopkins v. Price Waterhouse Case

The Supreme Court's acceptance of the sexual stereotype expert witness in Hopkins will undoubtedly change the method of, if not the focus on, addressing sexual stereotypes in proving employment discrimination.

The Hopkins case is the first major overt statement of the propriety of using a sexual stereotype expert. The Supreme Court held that the denial of partnership status to a female employee based on her "abrasive" personality constituted sexual stereotyping violative of Title VII. Ann Hopkins, the plaintiff, was nominated for partnership after four years of employment at Price Waterhouse, a "big eight" accounting firm. Although the Price Waterhouse partners believed her highly qualified for partnership based on the quality of her work and her ability to bring new clients into the firm, Hopkins' candidacy was delayed for one year and then not further considered because of her deficient "interpersonal skills." Hopkins then resigned.

Many of the comments in the partners' evaluations of Hopkins were described in terms of her sex. For example, the partners wrote that she needed to take a "course at charm school," "she may have overcompensated for being a woman," "many male partners are worse than Ann", and "she is a lady using foul language." The Court concluded that such comments, <u>whether from opponents or supporters</u>, showed that Hopkins was being judged by stereotypical criteria.

The Supreme Court approved of the District Court's reliance on testimony by an expert witness named Dr. Susan Fiske, a social psychologist, Associate Professor of Psychology at Carnegie Mellon University, and expert in sexual stereotyping. Dr. Fiske testified that Hopkins' partnership denial was heavily influenced by the male partners' sexist expectations and attitudes which the Court found had impermissibly infected Price Waterhouse's partnership promotion process.

The Court of Appeals found that a discriminatory motive existed in spite of the fact that the partners' sexist evaluation comments could have been unconsciously motivated. The appellate court also found that the absence of ill-will did not vitiate the finding of a discriminatory motive given the fact that Ms. Hopkins was treated less favorably than male candidates due to her gender.

The United States Supreme Court reversed the judgment of the Court of Appeals with respect to Price Waterhouse's liability and remanded the case for further proceedings. Although the Court was unable to agree on an opinion, six members of the Court agreed that (1) on some showing by the plaintiff in a Title VII action that an illegitimate factor such as gender entered into an employment decision - which showing had been sufficiently made by the plaintiff Hopkins - the employer may be required to prove, by a preponderance of the evidence, that it would have made the same decision regardless of the presence of the illegitimate factor; but (2) the courts below had erred in requiring Price Waterhouse to prove this point by clear and convincing evidence instead of by a preponderance of the evidence.

On remand, the United States District Court for the District of Columbia held that (1) Price Waterhouse failed to show that it would still have placed Hopkins' partnership candidacy on hold even in the absence of sexually-biased evaluations, (2) Hopkins was entitled to be made a partner, and (3) Hopkins was entitled to back wages, to be reduced by her failure to mitigate damages. Hopkins v. Price Waterhouse, 737 F.Supp. 1202 (D.D.C. 1990). The District Court decision was recently affirmed by the United States Court of Appeals for the District of Columbia. Hopkins v. Price Waterhouse, 920 F.2d. 967 (D.C. Cir. 1990).

III. The Consequences of the Hopkins v. Price Waterhouse Decision: Using a Sexual Stereotype Expert Witness in Your Practice

The method the Hopkins attorneys used to present the testimony of Dr. Susan Fiske raised several problems during trial.[2] For example, the judge constantly interrupted the lawyers and the witness during the direct examination and cross-examination to ask his own questions of the witness. His inquiries were largely prompted by his confusion over the qualifications of the witness, the empirical basis for the witness' conclusions, the analytical substance of the witness' opinions, and the witness' methodology. Each of these areas is instructive.

A. The Expert Witness' Qualifications

Dr. Fiske was a social psychologist who had specifically studied gender stereotyping, authored numerous publications, and acted as Associate Professor of Psychology at Carnegie Mellon university. Her qualifications were sufficient for the Court to accept her testimony. In general, however, there are no clear guidelines articulated by any court as to what criteria legitimate a witness as an expert in sexual stereotyping. Certainly formal education, job experience in a field where gender issues frequently arise, and previous experience appear to be crucial.

Plaintiffs might offer experts on sexual stereotypes from other disciplines, such as clinical or research psychologists, therapists, sociologists, personnel managers, authors and/or professors in a related area with an advanced degree. There is no authority as whether alleged experts without the type of specific background *Hopkins* offered would qualify as experts.

The lack of clear formulation of the requisite qualifications for a sexual stereotype expert leaves the door wide open for opposing counsel to attack the legitimacy of such expertise. If the expert's experience is clinical in nature, the opposing attorney can attack the number of clients treated and the resulting scientific basis for any opinions the expert offers in trial.

On the other hand, if the alleged sexual stereotype expert's experience is research-oriented, then the opposing attorney may find the expert vulnerable to attack for lack of real life experience. The lawyer can inquire about the number of questionnaires the expert's research has produced, the potential absence of honesty and sincerity in questionnaire responses, and the concrete application of theories the expert's studies have produced.

The less specific the qualifications of an expert, the more vulnerable the expert may be to a challenge that the testimony is not a proper subject of expert testimony and invades the province of the trier of fact. One could argue that triers of fact have historically considered sex stereotyping and that a sex stereotype expert is simply a device to argue and give emphasis to facts easily considered by the trier of fact based on his or her own life experience. As one author noted, "the courts border on taking judicial notice of the cultural phenomenon."[3]

In Hopkins, the defense did not challenge the plaintiff's expert's qualifications on cross-examination. TR 567. The defense's later efforts to discredit the expert's opinion on the grounds that it was "gossamer evidence" was, therefore, rejected by the appellate courts. Hopkins v. Price Waterhouse, 109 S.Ct. 1775, 1793 (1989). Defense counsel must assert and preserve all such objections at trial.

B. The Expert Witness' Basis for Opinions

In the Hopkins case, the defense counsel questioned the empirical basis upon which Dr. Fiske formulated her opinions about Ms. Hopkins and Price Waterhouse's promotion criteria. The Court focused on the number of hours Dr. Fiske spent becoming familiar with the documents describing sexually stereotyped comments. On cross-examination there was also an issue as to whether Dr. Fiske had done a complete statistical analysis of the Price Waterhouse partnership procedures. The defense counsel also inquired in depth on cross-examination into the number of written Price Waterhouse documents Dr. Fiske examined in preparation for her testimony.

Experts using numerical data or synthesizing their data will be more persuasive than those who testify in generalities. Courts appreciate specificity and percentages. Intangible theories unsubstantiated by facts do not persuade judges that the sexual stereotype expert's testimony is credible.

C. The Expert Witness' Opinions

One problem during the Hopkins direct examination and cross-examination was the expert's difficulty in framing her opinions in concrete language that the Court and the attorneys could understand. The testimony could have been more persuasive had it described her conclusions in lay language rather than in social psychologist jargon. For example, the judge who asked Dr. Fiske to render her expert opinion remarked, "You are not telling me anything. You have got to talk to a layman, madam. You are not talking to one of your colleagues and so I have got to understand what you are saying, you understand." Transcript of Record ("TR") 542. In response to the judge, Dr. Fiske stated

> What I'd like to do is talk about some of the factors in a particular organization and particular setting that would tend to encourage stereotyping, and one of the factors is that if there are very, very few people, say very, very few blacks or very, very few women or very, very few men within a particular level of an organization those people are very much likely to be thought about in terms of their category, in terms of their race or in terms of their sex. TR 543

Dr. Fiske answered the judge's question in such an abstract way that her opinion was effectively non-responsive. The judge stated "I mean we have got to talk about people dealing with people in a business context. Does that lady have an opinion that she is going to offer in this case?" TR 544. When finally pressed by the judge, Dr. Fiske concluded in a single sentence, "I am confident that stereotyping played a role in the decision about Ann Hopkins." TR 545.

A sexual stereotype expert witness might also be more effective by describing sexual stereotyping in terms of the particular context of the plaintiff rather than the general context of the plaintiff's organization. To effectively overcome suspicions about the validity and helpfulness of the sexual stereotype expert's testimony, lawyers should counsel their witnesses to be as specific as possible about the plaintiff. Conversely, defense counsel will exploit any ambiguity.

With respect to the issue of the degree of certainty required of the expert's opinion, there was a minor question in the Hopkins judge's mind as to how much of a role gender stereotyping played in the decision not to promote Ann Hopkins into partnership. Typically, reasonable certainty is required. The expert must thus state his opinion in terms of probability rather than possibility.

The test of whether an expert's testimony expresses a reasonable probability as opposed to mere conjecture that an event occurred is not based upon the semantics of the expert or the attorney or the use of any particular language. Instead, reasonable certainty is determined by looking at the entire substance of the expert's testimony.

D. The Expert Witness Methodology

Dr. Fiske offered her analysis and opinions at an organizational level rather than at an individual level. Dr. Fiske stated that "The level of analysis at which I draw conclusions about stereotyping is occurring within an organization. I do not try to identify particular individuals as stereotypers or not stereotypers." TR 569. Dr. Fiske's methodology was based on her area of expertise in organizational behavior. The trial court, however, appeared to be more persuaded by Dr. Fiske's detailed description of Ann Hopkins' specific situation at Price Waterhouse rather than more abstract conclusions about sex stereotyping within the Price Waterhouse organization. Thus the more individualized the expert's testimony, the more persuasive it is.

E. Preparing the Expert Witness for Cross-Examination

In advance of the trial, it is critical to have deposed the plaintiff's sex stereotype expert witness. In Hopkins, the expert was a rebuttal expert who had not been deposed prior to trial. To avoid this uncertainty, depose the expert first. If the case merits the expense, a defense consulting sex stereotype expert should be present at the plaintiff expert's deposition.

At the expert's deposition, it is critical to discover all information to which the expert has been exposed, whether or not the expert has relied on it. If the expert has relied on other experts, identify those experts. Discover everyone whom the expert has spoken with, all written materials provided to the expert, and all meetings the expert attended. If the expert has contacted other experts or witnesses, ask what the expert knows about the others' positions. It is sometimes also an opportunity to obtain damaging admissions made by parties and their lawyers to the experts at meetings.

It is imperative to learn whether the expert has retained all documents provided to or created by the expert in the course of the assignment. The expert's failure to retain all documents or drafts of reports may provide the basis for exclusion of the expert's testimony.[4] To avoid being sandbagged at trial, one must determine at the deposition whether the expert's work has been completed, or what additional work the expert plans to do.

With respect to each opinion of the sexual stereotype expert, the deposition is the opportunity to examine closely all evidence upon which the expert relied. Opposing counsel should establish whether the expert asked for additional information from the plaintiff which was not provided. If the sexual stereotype expert relied on deposition testimony, establish which depositions the expert reviewed.

If possible, it is helpful to obtain prior testimony from the plaintiff's expert to see whether the expert's assumptions vary from case to case or depend upon the party for which he or she is testifying.

IV. Conclusion

The _Hopkins_ decision will encourage the use of sexual stereotype expert witnesses in future employment discrimination litigation. The _Hopkins_ holding ensures that sexual stereotyping can, under certain conditions and on a case by case basis, constitute sex discrimination under Title VII. A complainant who argues that sex stereotyping is discriminatory must demonstrate that comments were made or behavior took place, that the comments or behavior included sex stereotypes, and that those stereotypes were relied upon in making an employment decision which adversely affected the plaintiff.[5]

Plaintiffs may applaud the availability of such experts to attack implicit, unspoken assumptions based on sex stereotypes in the employment context that have been hard to address in the past.[6] Plaintiffs may also, as in Hopkins perceive a sex stereotype expert as a way to overcome difficult facts. Price Waterhouse had a powerful argument that even the plaintiff's supporters found her to be abrasive and offensive to coworkers. The sex stereotype expert effectively diffused the impact of this testimony. Defense counsel may, of course, in some situations be able to make use of a sexual stereotype witness for the same purpose, to neutralize otherwise harmful evidence. For example, in a sexual harassment case hinging on the plaintiff's consent, a sex stereotype witness might testify that because of prevalent stereotypes, any reasonable person would have interpreted the plaintiff's behavior as evidencing consent.

But it is important to remember that sexual stereotype expert witness testimony may not necessarily be admissible because not all sex stereotyped behavioral expectations are permissible bases of employment actions under Title VII.[7] For instance, some personality, appearance, and grooming requirements will survive Title VII scrutiny.[8]

However, sex stereotype expert witness testimony will become increasingly useful to defendants and plaintiffs alike as the courts tend to accept its validity and reliability. For the past five years or so, plaintiffs have successfully employed sexual stereotype expert witnesses to explain problem areas where there is an inconsistency between the plaintiff's behavior and the plaintiff's claims. The most effective defense weapon in such a situation is the strategic use of common sense. The jury and judge can readily focus on and understand logical, facial contradictions between the expert's testimony and the plaintiff's behavior.

Thus far, defendants have not employed sexual stereotype expert witnesses with as much frequency as plaintiffs have. There is no reason why defense attorneys should not consider using sexual stereotype expert witness testimony to substantiate claims that the plaintiff overreacted to a given situation, that the plaintiff's behavior was inconsistent with his or her claims, that the defendant was non-discriminatory in its employment practices, and that the work environment was tolerant by nature. Creative defense attorneys have yet to reap the rewards such testimony can offer them in litigation.

BIBLIOGRAPHY

ARTICLES

Bellace, "Comparable Worth: Proving Sex-Based Wage Discrimination," 69 Iowa L. Rev. 655 (1984).

Cava, "Taking Judicial Notice of Sexual Stereotyping," 43 Ark.L.Rev. 27, 40 (1990).

Cohen, "Price Waterhouse v. Hopkins: Mixed Motive Discrimination Cases, The Shifting Burden of Proof, and Sexual Stereotyping," Lab.L.J. 727 (1989).

Eichner, "Getting Women Work That Isn't Women's Work: Challenging Gender Biases In The Workplace Under Title VII," 97 Yale L.J. 1397, 1404 (1988).

Konrad and Gutek, "Impact of Work Experiences on Attitudes Toward Sexual Harrassment," Administrative Science Qtrly., Vol. 31, No. 3, pp. 422-438.

Nieva and Gutek, "Sex Effects on Evaluation," Academy of Mgmt. Review, Vol.5, No. 2, pp. 267-276.

Note, "Permissible Sexual Stereotyping Versus Impermissible Sexual Stereotyping: A Theory of Causation," 34 N.Y.L. Sch. L. Rev. 679 (1989).

Note, "Sex Discrimination in Newscasting," 84 Mich.L.Rev. 443 (Dec. 1985).

Schlei and Grossman, Employment Discrimination Law (2d ed. 1983).

Schlenker and Gutek, "Effects of Role Loss on Work-Related Attitudes," Jrnl. of Applied Psychology, Vol. 72, No. 2, pp. 287-293.

CASES

Federal

Barker v. Taft Broadcasting Co., 549 F.2d 400, 401 (6th Cir. 1977).

EEOC v. Sears, Roebuck & Co., 628 F.Supp. 1264 (N.D.Ill. 1986), aff'd 839 F.2d 302 (7th Cir. 1988).

Hewlett-Packard Company v. Bausch and Lomb, Inc., 116 F.R.D. 533, 540 (N.D. Cal. 1987).

Hopkins v. Price Waterhouse, 490 U.S. 228, 109 S.Ct. 1775 (1989), remanded 737 F.Supp. 1202 (D.D.C. 1990), aff'd. 920 F.2d 967 (D.C. Cir. 1990).

William T. Thompson Co. v. General Nutrition Corp., 593 F.Supp. 1443, 1456-1457 (C.D. Cal. 1984).

State

Sail'er Inn, Inc. v. Kirby, 5 Cal.3d 1 (1971).

Thor v. Boska, 38 Cal.App.3d 558, 567 (1974).

ENDNOTES

1. The authors would like to acknowledge the gracious assistance of Los Angeles, California lawyers Nancy Bornn; Stuart P. Herman, Esq. of Herman & Wallach; Andrew C. Peterson of Paul, Hastings, Janofsky & Walker; Barbara Lindemann Schlei of Seyfarth, Shaw, Fairweather & Geraldson; Washington, D. C. lawyers Stephen E. Tallent, Wayne A. Schrader and Theodore J. Boutrous, Jr. of Gibson, Dunn & Crutcher; Boston, Massachusetts lawyer Nancy Gertner of Dwyer, Collora & Gertner; and Catharine Kissee-Sandoval, Esq., Law Clerk to Judge Dorothy Nelson of the Ninth Circuit Court of Appeals in the preparation of this article. Note that in June, 1991, Barbara Lindemann Schlei and Paul Grossman, authors of Employment Discrimination Law (2d ed. 1983), published a new text on sexual harassment, which contains chapters on evidence and discovery. Karen Kaplowitz, Esq. of Alschuler, Grossman & Pines, and Peter M. Sloan, Esq., formerly with Alschuler, Grossman & Pines, contributed a chapter to the text.

2. Gibson, Dunn & Crutcher made available the trial transcript of Dr. Fiske's testimony, which is obtainable upon request from the authors.

3. See Cava, "Taking Judicial Notice of Sexual Stereotyping," 43 Ark.L.Rev. 27, 40 (1990).

4. Hewlett-Packard Company v. Bausch and Lomb, Inc., 116 F.R.D. 533, 540 (N.D. Cal. 1987) (the trier of fact has the right to know everything experts consider and to see drafts); Thor v, Boska, 38 Cal.App.3d 558, 567 (1974) (a party's suppression of evidence indicates consciousness that case is weak or unfounded); William T. Thompson Co. v. General Nutrition Corp., 593 F.Supp. 1443, 1456-1457 (C.D. Cal. 1984) (destruction of evidence results in default judgment and $450,000 in sanctions).

5. See Cohen, "Price Waterhouse v. Hopkins: Mixed Motive Discrimination Cases, The Shifting Burden of Proof, and Sexual Stereotyping," Lab.L.J. 727 (1989).

6. See Eichner, "Getting Women Work That Isn't Women's Work: Challenging Gender Biases In The Workplace Under Title VII," 97 Yale L.J. 1397, 1404 (1988).

7. See Note, "Sex Discrimination in Newscasting," 84 Mich.L.Rev. 443 (Dec. 1985).

8. See Barker v. Taft Broadcasting Co., 549 F.2d 400, 401 (6th Cir. 1977), holding that employer grooming codes requiring different hair lengths for men and women bear such a negligible relationship to the purposes of Title VII that such a requirement is not a target of the Act.

KAREN KAPLOWITZ

Karen Kaplowitz, a 1971 graduate of the University of Chicago Law School, is a partner at Alschuler, Grossman & Pines, Los Angeles, California, where she concentrates on employment litigation on behalf of employers, business dissolutions, and litigation involving the entertainment industry. She is a member of the board of the Association of Business Trial Lawyers and its Treasurer for 1993-94. She is a Vice-Chair of the Employer-Employee Relations Committee of the Tort and Insurance Practice Section of the American Bar Association and has participated in its programs at the ABA Annual Meetings in 1989, 1990 and 1993, and in the TIPS National Institutes on Sexual Harassment in 1991 and 1992. She has published and written extensively on employment litigation.

Rebel Laura Ely practices civil litigation in Los Angeles, California. She was graduated from Yale University, and the University of Michigan Law School.

CROSS EXAMINING THE PLAINTIFF IN A SEX HARASSMENT CASE

By Homer L. Deakins, Jr.

Ogletree, Deakins, Nash, Smoak & Stewart

Atlanta, Georgia

CROSS EXAMINING THE PLAINTIFF IN A SEX HARASSMENT CASE

By Homer L. Deakins, Jr.
Ogletree, Deakins, Nash, Smoak & Stewart
Atlanta, Georgia

The cross examination of the plaintiff in a sex harassment case tried before a jury is critically important to the defense, primarily because it sets the stage for the believability of the defendant's case. If the plaintiff is shaken during cross examination, the jury will be anxious and open minded when the defense witnesses take the stand. On the other hand, if the plaintiff steps down from the witness stand with the jury's sympathy for her plight, there is a grave question whether the defense witnesses will even be heard by the jurors.

The goals of cross examination are: (1) to make the jury believe the plaintiff is incredible; and (2) to soften the brunt of her direct testimony through admissions. In most sex harassment cases you pursue both goals, but with varying degrees of vigor, depending on what you have to work with. If you can accomplish the first goal, you are on the way to winning the case; jurors rarely reward people they consider to be liars. If you accomplish the latter goal, at least the jury should be awake when you begin the presentation of your defense. Learning how to accomplish these two important purposes may be primarily a matter of experience, but there are a few general guidelines you should keep in mind.

1. The single most important aspect of cross examining the plaintiff is advance preparation. Before the trial begins, you should prepare a detailed written outline of the entire examination. The outline should cover all aspects of the plaintiff's testimony; it is easier to delete, than to add to, once you are in the heat of battle. Your outline should not only take into account the statements of the plaintiff in her deposition, to the EEOC, to the State Unemployment Commission, to the employer, to prospective employers and to anyone else, but also the relevant statements of all other witnesses and all other discovery and pleadings. The outline should include a reference system, which will lead you to all records you will need in conducting the examination.

Discovery in sex harassment cases is normally exhaustive (and should be), and there should not be any evidentiary surprises while the plaintiff is on the stand, if you meticulously examine all discovery evidence in the preparation of your outline. Typically, the most critical document you will scrutinize is the plaintiff's deposition. Contradictions and admissions drawn from this earlier sworn testimony can be of immeasurable value. In order to be sure you do not miss any opportunities, you should have in your hands at the trial very specific notes, keyed by subject matter, of everything the plaintiff has said on relevant points.

Once you examine all of the other evidence produced during discovery, you may also find that other very fruitful sources of information come from the plaintiff's other witnesses, such as her medical experts and treating physicians. Fellow employees of the plaintiff are also excellent sources of persuasive facts to jurors. If they are to be used as witnesses for the defense, their testimony should be taken into account in your cross examination outline.

After the trial opens and before the plaintiff is called to the stand, you should revisit the cross examination outline regularly and make necessary revisions. As only one example, an overly zealous plaintiff's attorney, in his opening statement to the jury, may turn out to be a worthwhile source of contradiction to the plaintiff's earlier statements.

Your outline should be organized in the way you think will persuade the jury of your case. How the plaintiff's lawyer organizes direct examination is almost totally irrelevant. Don't do like so many lawyers, by cross examining the plaintiff from your notes taken during direct examination. Examine the witness from your outline, which should contain penciled-in notes of any gems coming out of the plaintiff's direct examination. If possible, make your cross examination tell an interesting straight-forward story that reinforces your theory of the case.

2. Regardless of the thoroughness of your examination of the plaintiff during her deposition, you can never be certain how the plaintiff will appear as a live witness at trial. The only thing you can predict with reasonable certainty is that she will be more impressive and better prepared than she was during the deposition. Sometimes the contrast can be dramatic. There is little you can do in advance to prepare for such changes, except to know that they will occur and realize that while the plaintiff testifies on direct

examination you must decide what your attitude toward her will be on cross examination. Try to see who the jury sees. Is she actually hostile? Is she really angry with your client? Has she become an advocate? If the answer to these questions is affirmative, be certain to keep the witness in check from the start. Begin by telling the witness you will be asking questions that will generally require only a "yes" or "no" answer and that you will never seek hearsay evidence. "We only want to know what you know, not what somebody told you happened." This should give you some aid in securing the loose cannon to the deck. If, on the other hand, the plaintiff's direct examination exhibits a hurt, innocent child who loves the whole world, including your client, your job must be carried out with the appearance of less aggressiveness.

Ease into the examination. Jurors sympathize with witnesses until there is significant impeachment. Unless you have some bullet proof impeachment, avoid leaping into hard questions immediately. Introduce yourself and explain to the jury your relationship, or lack thereof, to the plaintiff. Ask the plaintiff a few introductory questions, which will put her at ease.

3. Once you begin your examination, it is critical that you control the witness. Cross

examination should never sound like direct examination. If you allow the witness to repeat large portions of her earlier testimony, the only thing you accomplish is to reinforce that testimony in the jurors' minds. Too many lawyers have the bad habit of beginning cross examination with questions which begin with the words "Do I correctly understand your testimony to be ..." or "Did you testify on direct examination that ..." Such questions should only be used sparingly in order to set up for the cross examining questions, and even then the questions should be phrased in such a way that the answer is always "yes."

Typically, you control the witness by asking only leading questions. You should put words into the witness' mouth to make the witness say what you want her to say, not what she wants to say. The hallmark of an effective cross examination is when the witness never says anything beyond "yes" or "no." Whatever else you may do, never ask the plaintiff a question that starts with "Why?" Never permit the plaintiff to explain anything.

It is especially important that you ask questions which will be easily understood by the plaintiff and the jury. You do not want to leave the impression of being the Harvard lawyer asking questions of a deprived head-of-household female. Do not use legal phrases. Use plain English and the simplest words possible. Otherwise you run the risk of the jury not understanding the question. The jury may be smart, but it may not be sophisticated.

The other person you need to control during cross examination is yourself. Don't quarrel with the witness; it could adversely affect your demeanor with the jury. Don't ask questions in an accusatory manner. The jury has a lot of sympathy with a person in the witness box. The advantage of the lawyer in being able to ask questions and insist on answers to them is obvious to the jury. Unnecessary hostility is likely to backfire. If the plaintiff refuses to answer your questions, ask the judge to instruct her to answer the questions. This shows that you are in control of the examination without showing hostility.

This is not to say that there may not be a time for a raised eyebrow, a series of rapid-fire questions or even righteous indignation. To some extent, the jury gets its cue from counsel on how to respond to testimony, and you should not neglect this role. The problem is to strike the proper balance without putting on a transparent act. One good way to approach this balance is to keep from being hostile with the plaintiff, even if you know she is lying, unless the jury can see that you have a good reason for it.

The best chance you generally have of showing the jury that the plaintiff is lying is through direct contradiction in her earlier statements. When you are presented with such an opportunity, don't rush it. First, pin her down to her current story, but only to the extent necessary to establish the contradiction. Then confront her with the contradictory document. Usually it is her deposition. Emphasize the importance of her deposition, or other sworn statement, with questions such as:

> Ms. Smith, you have previously given testimony in this case by deposition, have you not?
>
> Prior to giving that deposition, you swore to tell the truth, did you not?
>
> Was the oath the same as the oath given before you began your testimony in this court room? (If there is any hesitation given by the plaintiff, quote her the oath.)
>
> Do you recognize this transcript as a copy of your deposition?
>
> Were you given any opportunity to review the deposition after it was typed up and

> before it was filed, to be sure what you said was true?
>
> Did you make any changes after reading the deposition?

Then, you are prepared to confront the plaintiff with the contradiction. Once you have done so, you are prepared for your final question on the point:

> Which statement is true and which is false: the statement you swore to on deposition or the statement you swore to earlier today?

4. Another important point in cross examination is to always stick to the old adage, "Never ask a question the answer to which you do not know." The trial is a poor place to start learning the plaintiff's views on anything.

5. Always remember that the first step to persuasion is having the jury remember. If you are brief, it is more likely the jury will remember. Address only those areas where you can make points with the jury. Try to close your cross examination with a crescendo. Prepare your line of questioning so that you have saved your best questions for last. Never sit down after asking a question on which there was an objection sustained.

6. Avoid asking one question too many. Know when you have obtained everything possible helpful from the plaintiff, and then stop.

HOMER L. DEAKINS, JR.

Homer L. Deakins, Jr. was born in Longview, Texas, where he attended public school. He attended Southern Methodist University and received a degree in Business Administration in 1957. Thereafter, he attended the University of Texas School of Law, receiving an LL.B., cum laude, in June 1960.

Mr. Deakins is the managing partner of the law firm of Ogletree, Deakins, Nash, Smoak & Stewart, which maintains offices in Atlanta, Georgia, Washington, D.C., Albany, New York, Raleigh, North Carolina, Nashville, Tennessee, and Greenville, Charleston and Columbia, South Carolina. This law firm specializes in representing corporate and public sector employers in employment law and labor relations.

In addition to being a member of the American Bar Association, Mr. Deakins is a member of the Georgia, District of Columbia, South Carolina, Texas, Tennessee, and New York State Bars. He is also a member of the Lawyers Club of Atlanta.

Mr. Deakins has been a frequent management spokesman before congressional committees on proposed labor and civil rights legislation.

ATTACKING A STONE WALL—EXAMINATION OF THE ALLEGED SEXUAL HARASSER

Joseph Posner
16311 Ventura Boulevard, Suite 555
Encino, California 91436-4303
818/990-1340

Those of us who grew up in the 40's and 50's remember the exploits of the legendary radio (yes, radio) and television lawyer Perry Mason. Quick of brain, quicker of mouth, he slashed, parried and thrust until the real killer couldn't stand it any longer and shouted out his confession in an emotional orgasm of guilt.

In a real life sexual harassment case, on the other hand, that scenario is about as likely to happen as Saddam Hussein is to turn to democracy. If you think that miscreant police officers, leveraged buyout specialists and producers of defective products hide behind the wall of silence, when it comes to sexual harassers you ain't seen nothing yet. These people give a whole new meaning to the phrase stonewall.

Nonetheless, at some point in the trial the plaintiff's attorney is going to have to examine the harasser. I recommend that plaintiff call the harasser as a witness during the case in chief. This means that the attorney's first job is to make sure that the harasser shows up. Generally, in suits under the California Fair Employment & Housing Act (FEHA), we name the harasser as a co-defendant with the company. Under California Code of Civil Procedure Section 1987, we can compel the harasser's attendance in trial by a simple notice. If you are in a jurisdiction which doesn't have this simple procedure, make sure that you have subpoenaed personally the harasser for trial. Do not rely upon assurances by defense counsel that the harasser will indeed be present.

You must then decide when in the line up of witnesses to call the harasser. Many plaintiffs' practitioners will start with the plaintiff, because she will be able to tell the entire story, or at least most of it, to the jury. If you are lucky enough to have other persons whom the harasser victimized, you might consider calling the plaintiff first, the harasser (who will deny that he ever did anything wrong) second, and the witness-other victim third, to offer a direct rebuttal to what the jury just heard. On the other hand, if you have several other witness-other victims, you might want to call one of those witness-other victims before the harasser, and then another one afterwards, in order to sandwich the harasser between the two.

If you happen to have a witness who overheard the harasser make abusive or hostile remarks toward the plaintiff, then you might put on the plaintiff, the harasser and then the witness. When you question the harasser, ask him specifically whether he said certain things on certain dates: "Mr. Jones, on October 3, 1990, did you say to Sam Smith, 'I am going to get that bitch, no matter what it takes?'" If Mr. Jones gives an evasive or rambling answer, let him talk as long as he wants; then look at him and say, "Sir, all of that's interesting but I don't think you answered my question. My question was: "Mr. Jones, on October 3, 1990, did you say to Sam Smith, 'I am going to get that bitch, no matter what it takes?'" Keep doing this until he answers. Continue with other short, pointed questions on whether he did certain things on certain dates at certain locations. Then put on the witness who overheard him make the nasty remarks and have the witness testify to what Mr. Jones really said or did.

Another approach is to call the harasser as your first witness, especially if he happens to be a particularly obnoxious individual. Ask a series of short, pointed questions either to which you know the answer, or to which the answer really doesn't matter. In this way, you will limit the scope of what the defense is able to ask the harasser during this phase of the testimony. Do not, however, excuse the harasser at the end of this segment of testimony; make sure that the court orders that he remain present for additional testimony, as needed.

But no matter when you call the harasser, be sure that your plaintiff is at counsel table looking him straight in the eye. If possible, also have some of the other victims-other witnesses (with their husbands or significant others if available) in the audience as well. These people should be cautioned not to vent too much emotion at the harasser, but simply, again, to look him straight in the eye. You will find that in many instances, the harasser will not be able to look at your client or the other victims, and will instead look down or stare off during his answers.

Although the defenses and the harassers vary, of course, they can be categorized generally into three types:

1. It never happened (H1);
2. She welcomed it (H2);
3. I was only joking and that's how she took it (H3).

Who are sex harassers? Obviously, just about anybody could fit the bill. But one study indicated that in the majority of cases (1) the harasser is usually a man; (2) the harasser usually acts alone; (3) the harasser is usually older than the victim; (4) the harasser usually is married; (5) the harasser is usually someone of the same race or ethnic background, and (6) the harasser is often a repeat offender. U.S. Merit Systems Protection Board, Office of Merit Systems Review and Studies, Sexual Harassment in the Federal Workplace: Is It a Problem?, Washington D.C., March, 1981, cited in Sexual Harassment in Employment, Labor Defense Network, October 13, 1985, page 4.

In my opinion, although I agree with these findings, the study left off one key item: In most instances, the harasser is somebody within the corporate hierarchy who has real or apparent power over the plaintiff, i.e., the ability to make decisions about her job and/or to take actions which can make her miserable. I believe that in the majority of cases, the issue in sexual harassment is not sex; it is an abuse of power. Because the harassers pick on and bully those over whom they have power in a work situation, I believe that the majority of them get more thrills from the exercise of this power than from the sex (if any) itself. In many instances you will find that the harasser was the owner or the president or the division head or unit manager or some other relatively high ranking person in the corporate hierarchy. This often means that the harasser is used to being the one in charge, has a sense that he can do no wrong, and is outraged at the charges against him. Hedin, Assessment of Damages in Sexual Harassment Litigation: A Plaintiff's Perspective, Minnesota Institute of Legal

Education Seminar on Sexual Harassment in the Work Place, March 1, 1991 describes the harasser thus:

> "A self made businessman or high policy maker would not have achieved his success without considerable ability, creativity, ambition and self-confidence. Many of these men have such strong personalities that they are not challenged by subordinates. At least in their own business environment they believe they can do no wrong. Thus, when they are accused of even the cruelest acts of sexual harassment, they cannot bring themselves to admit error. Depositions of these men frequently erupt into monologues about their acts of charity and the civic awards they have received. Their acts of harassment are justified as 'jokes' or acts of 'friendship' toward a female employee who 'didn't complain at all'. The result of this mentality is that the case becomes nearly impossible to settle."
>
> Ibid., pp. 5-6.

The reader will see that such a profile fits in the categories H1 and/or H3 above. This defendant will not like being on the witness stand. He will definitely not like answering questions; after all, in his company he is the one that asks the questions, not answers them. Given that he will not admit his guilt, what should you do?

Keeping in mind that you must retain control of the witness (see above), ask the harasser questions designed to bring out his arrogance and megalomania. For example, if the harasser is a chief executive officer, ask questions such as "You make nearly all the important decisions in the company, right, sir?" Or "You are the ultimate authority in the company, right?" Or "When you tell your employees to do something, you expect them to do it, right?"

If possible, while asking these questions, get across to the jury that this person enjoys the trappings of power and its exercise. For example, if a key encounter happened at a company conclave at the local country club, ask him "Now, let's see, you got to the country club around 10:00 in the morning in the company limousine, sir, right?"

At some point ask the harasser point blank if he ever made any sexual advances to your plaintiff. With H1 you will get an outright denial and with H3 you will get a denial, too, because he will attempt to justify same as "I was only joking". But keep asking the questions at various times during your examination. If you are lucky enough to have other victims as witnesses, ask him point blank if he ever asked any other employees for sex.

For example, you might ask the harasser such things as whether he made the remarks which he did on the evening when he and the plaintiff were working late, whether he believes that a woman's place is to be a full time mother, whether he ever said something about the bad time of the month, whether he ever told any dirty jokes or made any sexual comments (and here I would ask him exactly and explicitly if he used the words to which the plaintiff already would have testified), whether he ever remarked about the physical attributes of women in general and the plaintiff in particular, whether he ever asked the plaintiff anything about her own sex life or personal relations with a husband or male friend, and whether he ever made any threats either directly to the plaintiff or to other persons about the plaintiff.

But I would not ask these questions as a litany, one after the other, lock-step fashion. I would intersperse those questions into other parts of my examination. I might dwell upon the harasser's desire to climb up the corporate ladder and how important achieving more power in the company was to him, especially if he boasted that his wife worked full time and his family was thus dependent on him for support.

The idea here is to keep asking pointed questions, even when you know you will only get denials. Remember that these people do not like their authority questioned. Also, many of them feel they have a right to the sexual favors of their subordinates because of their powerful position, and you need to demonstrate such an attitude to the jury.

What about H2? These people also usually exhibit the typical harasser characteristics, with this difference: They think they are the office Lothario. In addition to their power in the organization, they are often proud of their supposed sexual attractiveness and/or prowess. They may well admit that they called the plaintiff at home, in the evening, but according to them the plaintiff welcomed the call because she welcomed their attentions generally. To these kinds of people, you can ask questions such as "If you didn't want phone calls at home at night and you got them, you'd be upset, right?" They will attempt to weasel out of an answer, but basically they will have to answer yes or they will seem like complete fools. Again, be persistent; get them to answer a simple yes to a simple question.

Other such questions you can ask might include "Well, if somebody approached you and wanted sex and you didn't want sex, you would be offended or annoyed, right?" or "If someone interrupted your work at a time when you didn't want to be interrupted, you'd be pretty upset, right?" and other such inquiries.

Again, do not expect admissions. Your goal here is to show the jury that the harasser thinks he is God's gift to womankind, so anything he does is okay, and he can't conceive of being rejected.

How do you handle the matter when the company "investigated" the sexual harassment charges? If the harasser is a top executive or other powerful person, the chances are that any investigation was just a cover-up. If you know, for example, that the supposed investigator and the harasser went back together a long time, you could ask the harasser such questions as "You knew (the investigator) for a long time, right?"; or "You and (the investigator) used to work together at the XYZ Company, right?" or "You recommended (the investigator) for a job at this company, right?" or "You are friends with (the investigator's) boss, right?".

The company, of course, will never admit that its investigation was a sham. Your task is to show that the investigative system was inherently biased.

Remember that harassers do not walk around with a big red "H" on their chests. Do not expect confessions, and do not expect the truth. Portray the harasser's personality for the jury to see, and hope that the contrast between his demeanor, attitude and the like and that of your plaintiff will lead the jury to decide that your plaintiff is the one telling the truth.

JOSEPH POSNER

- Trial and appellate lawyer in Los Angeles area. Principal in Joseph Posner, Inc., a professional law corporation, Encino.

- Practice concentrates on representing plaintiffs in wrongful firing, discrimination, employee harassment and related tort litigation.

- Won one of first sexual harassment cases and one of first physical handicap discrimination cases tried to a jury in Los Angeles County.

- Argued landmark wrongful firing cases of Tameny v. Atlantic Richfield and Gantt v. Sentry Insurance before California Supreme Court. Argued and/or briefed other landmark tort cases in the appellate courts, including Rojo v. Kliger, Shoemaker v. Myers, Foley v. Interactive Data, and others.

- Speaks and lectures on firing and harassment cases before many legal, professional, business and educational groups.

- Regular columnist on tort topics for Los Angeles Daily Journal. Authored many other articles for legal and lay publications.

- J.D., Loyola University Law School; M.S., University of Southern California; B.S., UCLA.

EMPLOYER V. INDIVIDUAL HOSTILE ENVIRONMENT LIABILITY

When the Employer and the Harasser Are *Not* "In Bed" with One Another

Allison C. Blakley
Fox and Grove, Chartered
311 S. Wacker Drive
Suite 6200
Chicago, Illinois 60606

INTRODUCTION

The Supreme Court's recognition of a cause of action for sexual harassment based on the hostile environment theory has caused great consternation for employers, who are uncertain just how far society expects them to take the fight against "intimidating, hostile, or offensive" work environments.[1] As the courts grapple with the message of the Supreme Court's *Meritor Savings Bank, FSB v. Vinson* decision, and scholars criticize the Court for the decision's ambiguities,[2] employers must bear the risk in interpreting and applying the decision. Business owners and leaders are understandably concerned that their workplace environments might be branded as "hostile" without their notice of or participation in any particular acts of harassment.[3]

The substantive and procedural difficulties inherent in the dual-liability scheme of agency law create a hostile environment paradigm which poses many tactical choices for employers and their counsel when confronted with sexual harassment litigation. When an employer is charged with a sexual harassment violation due to the acts of supervisors, managers, co-workers, or even third parties, the interests of the corporation may well be divergent from those of the actual "harasser." In addition to the important and obvious goals of prevention, this paper outlines some of the strategic concerns of employers in avoiding liability for attenuated acts of employees and third parties who had been adequately informed of the inappropriateness of their conduct.

I. AN INTRODUCTION TO EMPLOYER LIABILITY FOR SEXUAL HARASSMENT

A. *Meritor* and the Equal Employment Opportunity Commission Guidelines

Although the hostile environment cause of action is based on the Civil Rights Act of 1964,[4] neither the original nor the recently amended language of that Act specifically mentions sexual harassment.[5] The Supreme Court definitively recognized that sexual harassment caused by a hostile environment was actionable under Title VII in *Meritor Savings Bank, FSB v. Vinson*.[6] The Court, however, largely left the standard of employer liability for the lower courts to define,[7] noting only that "we do agree with the Equal Employment Opportunity Commission that Congress wanted courts to look to agency principles for guidance in this area."[8]

The Equal Employment Opportunity Commission ("EEOC") has issued guidelines that outline the basic parameters of employer liability for hostile environment harassment.[9] The EEOC also has issued a more particular *Policy Guidance on Current Issues of Sexual Harassment* which attempts to specifically tackle the employer liability issues left open in *Meritor*.[10] Most post-*Meritor* decisions have relied heavily on a careful analysis of analogous common law agency principles and the EEOC's recommendations.[11]

B. Supervisor Liability

Meritor did little more than rule out the extremes in establishing the standard for employer liability. The Court concluded that employers cannot be held automatically liable for supervisors' sexual harassment; it also held that employers were not automatically insulated from liability because they lacked notice of the harassment's occurrence.[12] Between these extremes lies a broad continuum of potential liability, left to the determination of the lower courts and the EEOC.

The EEOC interprets *Meritor* to allow two avenues of employer liability: direct and imputed.[13] Direct liability attaches for any sexual harassment by supervisors[14] of which the employer had actual or constructive knowledge.[15] Thus, an employer is directly liable if it has first-hand knowledge of the harassment, if it learns of harassment via an internal grievance procedure, or if the affected employee actually files a charge of harassment.[16] Employers are also subject to direct liability under a constructive knowledge theory if the conduct is pervasive enough to create an inference of knowledge or of purposeful ignorance of improper conduct.[17]

Liability for harassment may be imputed to the employer if a supervisor's actions are found, under analogous common law agency principles, to fit any of the following scenarios:

1. The supervisor's actions are viewed as being within the scope of employment;[18]

2. The employer becomes aware of sexual harassment, yet refuses or fails to bring it to an end or prevent it from reoccurring;[19]

3. The supervisor is somehow vested with apparent authority that third parties reasonably believe (because of the employer's conduct) he possesses;[20] or,

4. The employer fails to take remedial action in regard to past, unrelated incidents of harassment that may lead employees to believe such conduct is regularly tolerated.[21]

The introduction of agency principles into the equation endows the federal courts with great latitude in attributing liability to employers via broad or narrow readings of common law agency principles applied to the facts of each case.[22] This latitude can be criticized for varying what was meant to be a uniform federal scheme, or complemented for allowing the various federal districts to create a "laboratory" of case law upon which Congress or the Supreme Court can eventually act with greater insight. Regardless, employers anxiously await precedent under these standards to enable them to respond with more certainty when faced with sexual harassment litigation.

C. <u>Co-worker and Third Party Liability</u>

Under the EEOC guidelines, employers may also bear liability by implication for sexual harassment caused by non-supervisory co-workers[23] and even non-employees under certain fact situations.[24] Any time that the employer (or its agents or supervisors) "knew or should have known" of sexually harassing conduct somehow connected to the harassed employee's work environment, the employer risks liability.[25] Employers may defend against such liability by a showing of "immediate and appropriate corrective action."[26] Importantly, the employer's *subsequent* remedial conduct can preclude liability in these instances.[27] Moreover, to the extent the courts and the EEOC recognize that all employees have the right to be free from an intimidating or hostile work environment, any employee affected by the hostile environment, even if the hostile conduct is not directed at that particular employee, has standing to challenge the hostile environment.[28]

II. EMPLOYERS' TACTICAL CONCERNS

A. General Issues

An employer faced with sexual harassment litigation attributable to the actions of one of its employees will face important strategic decisions. The first inquiries will likely involve a certain amount of soul searching. Were our policies sufficient to warn the alleged harasser that we forbade sexual harassment? Were our policies consistently enforced and effectively communicated? Were we on notice that improper conduct was occurring or likely to occur? Should we seek settlement to avoid harmful publicity? How should we reprimand the perpetrator?

To best avoid sexual harassment litigation, employers should undoubtedly attempt to prevent as much improper conduct as possible (see part III, below). When an employer has carefully created and implemented anti-sexual harassment policies, however, it should not be condemned for exploring avenues to avoid expense and liability for employee actions it considers to be independent, attenuated, and in direct violation of the employer's policies. To suggest otherwise would amount to little more than a pure deep-pocket theory of insurance against sexual harassment in the workplace not contemplated by Title VII or the Supreme Court.[29]

B. Proof Issues in the Case in Chief

In many instances individuals and employers are both named as defendants for the same or overlapping conduct, the employer under Title VII and its state parallels, and the individuals under various tort or other theories and, in some cases, Title VII.[30] In these instances, the employer is faced with a major threshold decision: whether to dispute the occurrence of the sexual harassment conduct, or whether to focus on proving that liability should not be imputed regardless of the truth of the complainant's assertions. The choices are obviously not mutually exclusive, and will turn on the particular facts of the case.

Under the EEOC guidelines, however, "direct" liability will usually be preventable by focusing on proof that the charges lack merit since the employer will be principally liable for the conduct. Cases involving potential indirect liability will more likely encourage the employer to challenge first the occurrence of the conduct and, second, the agency relationship. Note, however, that this will not always be the case. Consider the situation where a highly valued employee suffers from harassing conduct by a lesser-valued co-worker. Despite the fact that the employee might be named as a defendant under various tort theories for tactical purposes, the employer and the harasser's interests in the proof of the case might be entirely distinct. In these situations, employers must be aware of the difficulties that may await them in distinguishing their interests from those of the harassing employee.

C. Settlement Dilemmas

A recent case exemplifies the important advantages employers can effect by creatively handling a sexual harassment claim. In *Biggs v. Surrey Broadcasting Co.*,[31] an employer preempted a great deal of cost and troubling publicity by settling one of its advertising salesperson's sexual harassment and discrimination claims. The Company then filed an indemnification suit in Oklahoma state court against the male sales manager who admitted the acts of improper conduct alleged by the complainant. The Oklahoma Court of Appeals reversed the trial court's holding, ruling that it was proper for the company to seek indemnification from the tortfeasor (its employee) responsible for the harassment.[32]

On the available record, the court noted that it appeared that the complainant's claim would have survived a directed verdict; that the Company would likely be liable for the management employee's harassment under the agency principles of *Meritor*; and that the company had taken prompt remedial actions in response to the harassment complaints.[33] Thus, the Company's settlement of the case was appropriate in order to limit its exposure to a larger damage award, and its attempt to seek indemnification was proper under established, state-law indemnification principles.

The Court of Appeals then remanded for additional factual findings. The primary issues of fact would be whether the Company reasonably assessed its risk of federal Title VII litigation and of the complainant's odds in winning a large damage award in that litigation at the time it settled the case. Next, the court noted that the alleged harasser should have an opportunity to prove that the Company was jointly liable because it knew or should have known about the harassment, or because it failed to take appropriate remedial actions and thus that indemnification might be improper under the facts of the case.[34]

The *Biggs* case presents an interesting look at a situation where the employer effectively satisfied multiple goals by settling a situation already beyond the prevention stages. First, the employer likely avoided a great deal of adverse publicity[35] and protected its assets by recognizing its probable liability. Second, the employer's decision to take prompt remedial actions and to seek facts (instead of blindly siding with the alleged harasser) created a favorable factual record and may allow it to fully recover its settlement expenditure in state court. Finally, and perhaps most importantly, the employer sent a clear message to the community and to its other employees that it considers sexual harassment inappropriate, and that the responsible harasser may end up paying the price for his own conduct.

Consider momentarily the criteria the *Biggs* court required in endorsing the employer's decision to settle the case brought against it. The court required a "reasonable" analysis of the merits of the case and of the possibilities of a "large" damage award. The court suggests that the employer would be unable to settle its case and later seek indemnification from the harasser without resort to its prescribed analysis of risk.[36] Employers might wonder how seriously the court intends to enforce its required assessment of the **reasonableness** of the risks involved and of how **large** the potential damage award might be. Can an employer factor into this analysis the negative publicity that a finding of sexual harassment liability would bring?[37] If so, should an employer with a higher public profile be able to settle sexual harassment cases that plaintiffs are less likely to win at trial or that are less likely to exact a high damage award? If an employer is found to have "unreasonably" settled a case, will it be estopped from seeking indemnification or contribution from the harassing employee(s)? Any attempt to "weigh" the employer's right to settle in such a manner would inevitably raise such issues.[38]

Although victims of sexual harassment have, in some instances, successfully brought suit against individual employee harassers under Title VII, sexual harassment plaintiffs have typically been unable to join individual employee harassers under Title VII.[39] Accordingly, most victims of harassment who wish to hold their harassing supervisors, co-workers, or third parties individually liable to proceed either under pendent tort claims or in the state courts themselves. In cases where the harasser's improper conduct is evident or admitted, an employer must be aware of the possibility that the harasser will attempt to share or shift as much liability as possible toward the "deeper pocket" employer. Plaintiffs may forego difficult-to-prove intentional infliction of emotional distress or other state law actions if they are able to recover large compensatory and punitive damage awards from the employer.[40] Thus, despite the seeming inconsistencies, individual harassers may, in certain cases, forego the often incredulous "nothing really happened" defense in lieu of the possibility of shifting the cost of the harassment to the employer. Supervisory harassers might downplay their own misconduct and argue that "everyone was doing it" or at least that "everyone was aware of it" in order to shift the blame. The possibility of harm to a well-intentioned employer whose employee has violated stated, enforced policies against sexual harassment argues in favor of courts' bestowing more discretion on employers to "settle first" and seek indemnification or contribution later.[41]

None of this is to suggest that employers should be able to escape, with impunity, liability for a bona fide hostile environment. Employers with obvious complicity in or knowledge of the sexual harassment and employers who fail to remedy, investigate or warn their employees will remain fully accountable. Plaintiffs' attorneys would be unlikely to settle such meritorious suits for anything less than they are worth--a figure that will inevitably rise given the Civil Rights Act of 1991.[42] Similarly, courts are unlikely to allow guilty employers to collect much, if anything, from the offending harasser employee in an action for contribution. Thus, employers who settle suits in which they negligently, recklessly or intentionally allowed the sexual harassment to occur will pay the price.

Employers do have the available deterrent force of severely sanctioning harasser employees commensurate with their misconduct. Discharging the harassing supervisor, however, carries its own risks. Such actions may lead to additional, ancillary litigation without dispelling the employer's reputation for maintaining a "hostile environment." Thus, it seems appropriate that courts encourage the individual(s) directly responsible for the wrongful conduct to share the employer's burden for resultant sexual harassment liability.[43]

D. Potential Cross Complaints

Another important consideration for employers is the possibility of various counter or cross claims by employees who are accused of sexual harassment. The employer faces a bit of a "Catch-22" in this regard, between the demand for prompt and effective remedial action and the risk of lawsuits brought by accused harassers under federal and state civil rights statutes;[44] tort theories such as defamation,[45] tortious interference with economic advantage,[46] and intentional infliction of emotional distress;[47] various contract theories of breach[48] and wrongful discharge;[49] and even the Constitution.[50]

Fortunately, most of these cases have been unsuccessful for the alleged harassers because of the strong federal policy favoring employer prevention of harassment, with many courts imposing only good faith investigation requirements.[51] However, one author warns that "[c]onduct that creates a hostile work environment has been treated unevenly in arbitration."[52] Regardless, employers must carefully investigate employee allegations of sexual harassment before making conclusory accusations given that viable countersuits are both probable,[53] and expensive despite the merits of the harasser's ultimate claims.

III. PREVENTING VICARIOUS LIABILITY BY ESTABLISHING EFFECTIVE ANTI-HARASSMENT POLICIES

Since federal courts began recognizing claims for sexual harassment, an enormous amount of ink has been spilled in advising employers about the need for effective sexual-harassment prevention policies and procedures.[54] As the Ninth Circuit recently noted, "To avoid liability under Title VII, employers may have to educate and sensitize their workforce to eliminate conduct which a reasonable victim would consider sexual harassment.[55] The *EEOC Guidelines* stress prevention, recommending that employers:

> take all steps necessary to prevent sexual harassment from occurring, such as affirmatively raising the subject, expressing strong disapproval, developing appropriate sanctions, informing employees of their rights . . . and how to raise the issue of harassment under Title VII, and developing methods to sensitize all concerned.[56]

The *Meritor* Court suggested the importance of effective sexual harassment policies when it noted that the employer's contention that the harassed employee's failure to utilize the grievance procedure "should insulate it from liability might be substantially stronger if its procedures were better calculated to encourage victims of harassment to come forward."[57]

In *Meritor*, the grievance procedure in place was deemed ineffective due to its requirement that the employee initially complain to her supervisor--who was the very subject of her harassment complaint.[58] Thus, the first lesson for employers is to create a flexible complaint system that ensures employees' an "open door" policy for making complaints of harassment. The United States Merit Systems Protection Board, in response to a survey showing widespread problems with harassment in the federal sector, has outlined the following list of additional recommendations for the prevention of sexual harassment claims:[59]

1. Training: Employers should tailor their training/educational programs to the individual need of each agency and include the entire workforce, not just supervisors. Training should cover the range of situations and conduct that could be considered sexual harassment, and agencies should conduct periodic "equality control" reviews of training efforts.

2. Policy statements: Such statements should define the types of behavior that may constitute sexual harassment, state the range of penalties that may be levied against an offender, and clearly state that sexual harassment is against the law and will not be tolerated.

3. Enforcement action: Strong and effective sanctions against sexual harassment should be publicized and implemented. It should be clear that such sanctions apply to harassers who make submission to sexual advances a condition of employment, as well as those who create or contribute to creating an offensive or hostile work environment.

4. Complaint and investigation procedures: Employers should quickly review both formal and informal complaints of sexual harassment and provide prompt relief for harassed employees. Sensitive, knowledgeable people of both sexes should be chosen to hear complaints. Efforts should be made to reduce the number of days it takes to resolve such complaints. A goal of 120 days is reasonable. Grievance procedures should be well advertised.

5. Additional preventive efforts: Periodic random, anonymous surveys to assess the work environment in a particular department or office may be a useful preventive mechanism. Followup interviews of all parties involved in formal or informal settlements

> of complaints also may check recurrence of the problem.[60]

CONCLUSION

After *Meritor*, the importance of effective remedial conduct has become a vital aspect of handling sexual harassment claims.[61] However, as one commentator has noted:

> An employer may find it awkward or uncomfortable handling sexual harassment complaints that draw it into the social as well as business relationships of its employees. However, the approach should be no different for the sexual harassment than for any other complaint of employment discrimination.
>
> * * *
>
> In-depth investigation of sexual harassment complaints is not always easy. An employer will normally be reluctant to question employees about the sexual conduct of others. The oft-expressed concern is for possible slander. Employee morale may also be a factor. An employer, however, must weigh these concerns against the statutory mandate that it maintain a nondiscriminatory environment.[62]

Employers should heed the prudent advice of the EEOC, the Supreme Court, and the other commentators in attempting to create an atmosphere where employees are fully cognizant of sexual harassment issues. Employers must also be aware of the hazards in instinctively assuming that sexual harassment litigation will pit them and the

the alleged harasser against the complaining employee. Employers should guardedly protect their own interests in avoiding liability for their employee's sexual harassment once they have taken all reasonable steps to protect their work environments from such conduct. To do so will reinforce the message that sexual harassment is outside the scope of the employer's intended relationship with its employees, and will ultimately help sensitize the workforce to the evils of its continuation.

NOTES

* The author wishes to thank Michael L. Sullivan from Fox and Grove, Chartered for his assistance with this paper.

1. The Supreme Court recognized both the "quid pro quo" and the "hostile environment" causes of action to prohibit sexual harassment in Meritor Savings Bank, FSB v. Vinson, 477 U.S. 57 (1986). This paper assumes a working knowledge of these causes of action in an attempt to avoid unnecessary duplication of the vast commentary on *Meritor* and its progeny. Quid pro quo causes of action are beyond the scope of this article. For scholarly writings on virtually every notion of sexual harassment, see compilations of writings cited in R. Turner, *Employer Liability Under Title VII for Hostile Environment Sexual Harassment by Supervisory Personnel: The Impact and Aftermath of* Meritor Savings Bank, 33 HOWARD L.J., 1, 3, n.3 (1990); also see the bibliography compiled by B. Stanton entitled *Sexual Harassment*, 10 CAP. U.L. REV. 697 (1981).

2. *See, e.g.* Note, *The Aftermath of* Meritor: *A Search for Standards in the Law of Sexual Harassment*, 98 YALE L.J. 1717, 1730 (1989) (by M. Vinciguerra) (noting that the Supreme Court's "refusal to delineate the scope of employer liability for sexual harassment . . . assures the perpetuation of confusion in this area.").

The issues employers face with respect to the fight against "intimidating, hostile, or offensive" work environments become even more problematic with respect to harassment based on all types of protected classes. In November of 1993, the EEOC issued a Notice of Rulemaking on Harassment. The purpose of the Proposed Guidelines on harassment is to "emphasize that harassment based upon race, color, religion, gender, age, or disability is egregious and prohibited by Title VII, the ADEA, the ADA, and the Rehabilitation Act." EEOC Notice of Rulemaking on Harassment, Guidelines on Harassment Based on Race, Color, Religion, Gender, National Origin, Age, or Disability, 8 FEP Manual (BNA 1993) 403:521, 522, to be published at 29 C.F.R. Part 1609, [hereinafter, *Proposed Guidelines*]. The *Proposed Guidelines* clearly state that harassment on the basis of gender or gender-based animus, in addition to harassment of a sexual nature, is actionable under Title VII. Harassment based on race, color, religion, age, or disability is beyond the scope of this article. Employers should be aware, however, that harassment extends beyond that which is attributable to sex and gender.

3. Lack of notice to the employer has been held indeterminative in cases involving supervisor harassment. *See, e.g., Meritor*, 477 U.S. at 72 ("absence of notice to an employer does not necessarily insulate that employer from liability); Yates v. Avco Corp., 819 F.2d 630, 636 (6th Cir. 1987) (noting that the *Meritor* Court "made it clear" that notice to the employer of sexual harassment is not an absolute requirement to hold the employer liable); Sparks v. Pilot Freight Carriers, Inc., 830 F.2d 1554, 1558 (11th Cir. 1987)

(unnecessary for plaintiff to establish that she gave anyone notice of sexual harassment to hold employer liable for supervisor's conduct, when bringing mixed hostile environment and *quid pro quo* action); *Watts v. New York City Police Dep.*, 724 F. Supp. 99, 106 and n. 6 (S.D.N.Y. 1989) (employers failure to "put in place strong policies and procedures to belie" apparent authority may make employer liable without notice for certain supervisory conduct).

4. 42 U.S.C. § 2000e-2(a) (1982) states the following:

> It shall be an unlawful employment practice for an employer (1) to fail or refuse to hire or to discharge any individual, or otherwise to discriminate against any individual with respect to his compensation, terms, conditions, or privileges of employment , because of such individual's . . . sex . . . or, (2) limit, segregate, or classify his employees or applicants for employment in any way which would deprive or tend to deprive any individual of employment opportunities or otherwise adversely affect [her or] his status as an employee, because of such individual's . . . sex . . . .

5. Originally, federal courts refused to hold sexual harassment actionable under Title VII. *See, e.g.* Corne v. Bausch & Lomb, Inc., 390 F. Supp. 161 (D. Ariz. 1975), *vacated on other grounds*, 562 F.2d 55 (9th Cir. 1977); *see generally*, A. CONTE, SEXUAL HARASSMENT IN THE WORKPLACE: LAW AND PRACTICE at 12-19 (1990) [hereinafter, SEXUAL HARASSMENT IN THE WORKPLACE]. The recent amendments to Title VII are collectively entitled *Civil Rights Act of 1991*, and are codified as S. 1745 (amending 42 U.S.C. § 2000e) (1982)), do not add language specifically covering sexual harassment claims.

6. 477 U.S. 57, 106 S.Ct. 2399, 91 L. Ed. 2d 49 (1986).

7. The Court's majority found the factual record in *Meritor* insufficiently detailed to rule on the various specifics of employer liability in that case. *Meritor*, 477 U.S. at 472.

8. Meritor, 477 U.S. at 72. The Court went on to note, "Congress' decision to define `employer' to include any `agent' of an employer, 42 USC § 2000e(b) . . . , surely evinces an intent to place some limits on the acts of employees for which employers under Title VII are to be held responsible." Employers should also be cognizant that state civil rights laws may hold employers to a higher degree of vicarious liability than does Title VII, either on their own terms or by a particular state's more expansive views of agency liability.

9. EEOC Guidelines on Discrimination Because of Sex, 29 C.F.R. § 1604.11 (1988) [hereinafter, *EEOC Guidelines*]. *See also* 45 Fed. Reg. 25024 (1980). The Supreme Court made several references to the *EEOC Guidelines* in the *Meritor* decision, including the comment that "[s]ince the Guidelines were issued, courts have uniformly

held, and we agree, that a plaintiff may establish a violation of Title VII by proving that discrimination based on sex has created a hostile or abusive work environment. Meritor, 477 U.S. at 66. The EEOC guidelines define hostile environment harassment as "conduct [that] has the purpose or effect of unreasonably interfering with an individual's work performance or creating an intimidating, hostile, or offensive working environment. 29 C.F.R. § 1604.11 a(3).

The courts as well as the EEOC recognize that discrimination based on gender-animus also creates a hostile or abusive environment which is actionable as harassment under Title VII. *See Hall v. Gus Construction Co.*, 842 F.2d 1010, 1014 (8th Cir. 1988) (harassment which occurred because of the sex of the victim, although not of a sexual nature, is actionable harassment under Title VII); *Robinson v. Jacksonville Shipyards*, 760 F. Supp. 1486, 1522 (M.D. Fla. 1991) (harassment motivated by animus against women, even though not of a sexual nature, constitutes sex discrimination under Title VII); *Proposed Guidelines*, 403:522.

10. *EEOC Policy Guidance on Current Issues of Sexual Harassment*, 8 FEP Manual (BNA 1991) 405:6681 [hereinafter, *EEOC Policy Guidance*]. The *Proposed Guidelines* on harassment follow the principles enunciated in the *EEOC Policy Guidance*. 403:524-525, 527-528.

11. *See, e.g., Sparks,* 830 F.2d at 1557 (citing the Restatement (Second) of Agency, and noting that acts of an employer's agents [supervisors] are acts of the employer for which the employer is directly liable); Ellison v. Brady, 924 F.2d 872 (9th Cir. 1991) (relying heavily on EEOC recommendations); Hicks v. Gates Rubber Co., 833 F.2d 1406 (10th Cir. 1987) (analysis of the Restatement (Second) of Agency in examining the appropriate employer liability standard); Hall v. Gus Const. Co., Inc. 842 F.2d 1010 (8th Cir. 1988) (analyzing and comparing agency principles and the EEOC guidelines).

12. *Meritor,* 477 U.S. at 72, 73. Single instances of harassment will rarely be sufficient to create employer liability for hostile environment sexual harassment. *EEOC Policy Guidance* at 6690. The *Proposed Guidelines* recognize, however, that "an isolated instance of such conduct particularly when perpetrated by a supervisor -- can corrode the entire employment relationship and create a hostile environment." 403:524.

13. *EEOC Policy Guidance* at 405:6695-6696.

14. *Id.* Under the EEOC's proposal, high-level managers, officers, directors, and the like would also be directly responsible for harassment of which they had actual knowledge. *See, e.g.,* Ross v. Twenty-Four Collection, Inc., 681 F. Supp. 1547, 1551 (S.D. Fla. 1988) (cited in SEXUAL HARASSMENT IN THE WORKPLACE at 69, n.22.); *Hall*, 842 F.2d at 1015 ("a company will be liable if management-level employees knew, or in the exercise of reasonable care should have

known, about a barrage of offensive conduct); Hamilton v. Rodgers, 791 F.2d 439 (5th Cir. 1986). The distinction between supervisory and non-supervisory employees is most important in the analysis of quid pro quo actions where the employer is liable for supervisory sexual harassment without regard to employer knowledge. Note that the distinction, while less important in hostile environment actions, remains noteworthy because of the proof distinctions between "direct" and "imputed" liability in the EEOC's schematic.

15. *EEOC Policy Guidance* at 6695; *Sparks*, 830 F.2d at 1558 and n. 4 (employer directly liable for supervisor's sexual harassment under agency principles); Huddleston v. Roger Dean Chevrolet, Inc., 845 F.2d 900 (11th Cir. 1988) (same); Jones v. Wesco Investments, 846 F.2d 1154 (8th Cir. 1988) (direct liability imposed under actual or constructive knowledge standard). *Proposed Guidelines*, 403:524-525, 527-528 (applying the same standard as the *EEOC Policy Guidance*).

16. *EEOC Policy Guidance at 6695.*

17. *Id. Hall*, 842 F.2d at 1016 (foreman who observed some instances of improper conduct should have discovered all of the harassment because of the incidents were pervasive); *see also Lipsett, infra* note 25.

18. *EEOC Policy Guidance* at 6697. The EEOC suggests that this scenario will rarely occur, since an employer would not likely authorize its supervisors to engage in sexual harassment, and thus the harassing supervisor's actions would fall outside the scope of employment, much like most intentional torts fall outside the scope of employment in traditional agency law. Exceptions to this principle include situations where an employer becomes aware of, yet fails to stop the harassment, thus bringing the conduct within the scope of the employment relationship.

19. The *EEOC Guidelines* note that the employer's remedial actions must be "immediate and appropriate," should "express[] strong disapproval," and should include "appropriate sanctions." 29 C.F.R. § 1604.11(d) and (f); *see also* Paroline v. Unisys Corp., 879 F.2d 100, 106 (4th Cir. 1989) (plaintiff states a hostile environment claim when employer who anticipated or reasonably should have anticipated that she would become the victim of sexual harassment has failed to prevent it); *Hall*, 842 F.2d at 1015.

20. The *Meritor* Court hinted, and the EEOC has adopted the position, that an "effective, widely disseminated, and consistently enforced employer policy against sexual harassment, and an effective complaint procedure" can help prevent such apparent authority. *See Meritor*, 477 U.S. at 72, 73 (while the existence of a policy and grievance procedure are not dispositive, the victim's failure to utilize an effective complaint procedure might insulate the employer from liability); *EEOC Policy Guidance* at 6697-6698; *Sparks*, 830 F.2d at 1560.

The *Proposed Guidelines* recognize that an employer may be liable for harassment engaged in by supervisors, "regardless of whether the employer knew or should have known of the conduct, where the harassing supervisory employee is acting in an 'agency capacity.'" 403:527. An agency capacity is determined by the "circumstances of the particular employment relationship and the job functions performed by the harassing individual shall be examined." *Id.* Additionally, apparent authority exists where "the employer fails to institute an explicit policy against harassment which is clearly and regularly communicated to employees, or fails to establish a reasonably accessible procedure by which victims of harassment can make their complaints known to appropriate officials who are in a position to act on complaints." *Id.*

21. *EEOC Policy Guidance* at 6697-98; Zabkowicz v. West Bend Co., 589 F. Supp. 780 (E.D. Wis. 1984); *Watts*, 724 F. Supp. at 108 (atmosphere of hostility in past instances is relevant to a case involving a different harassing employee).

22. *Compare Sparks*, 830 F.2d at 1558 (broad analysis of agency liability) with Carrero v. New York City Hous. Auth., 668 F. Supp. 196 (S.D.N.Y. 1987); *aff'd in part, rev'd in part*, 890 F.2d 569 (2d Cir. 1989) (narrower agency analysis); Steele v. Offshore Shipbuilding, Inc., 867 F.2d 1311, 1316-17 (distinguishing *Sparks* as a mixed hostile environment/*quid pro quo* action).

23. It is not always clear whether an employee is a supervisor under traditional federal definitions. Courts will likely analyze the issue under factors similar to those set forth in the National Labor Relations Act, 29 U.S.C. § 152(1) (defining supervisor within the meaning of the act). *See also Hall*, 842 F.2d at 1016 (construction foreman is both a co-worker and a supervisor of employee); Maturo v. Nat'l Graphics, Inc., 722 F. Supp. 916, 924 (D. Conn. 1989) (binery co-worker held to be supervisor mainly due to his ability to assign tasks to plaintiff and apparent authority); Hunter v. Countryside Ass'n for the Handicapped, Inc., 723 F. Supp. 1277 (N.D. Ill. 1989) ("client supervisor" of employer held to have insufficient internal supervisory duties to impute sexual harassment liability to employer); Kouri v. Liberian Services, 55 FEP Cases 124 (E.D. Va. 1991) (personnel director held without "sufficient authority" to impute liability).

24. EEOC Guidelines, 29 C.F.R. § 1604.11(a) (1988); *EEOC Policy Guidance* at 6695 and n. 29. Non-employee harassment might be imputed to the employer if its clients or customers act improperly with the encouragement or consent of the employer, or perhaps, without any remedial action. Additionally, the EEOC will consider the "extent of the employer's control over non-employees and any other legal responsibility that the employer may have had with respect to the conduct of such non-employees on a case-by-case basis." *Proposed Guidelines*, 403:527.

25. *EEOC Policy Guidance* at 6695; *see also* Lipsett v. University of Puerto Rico, 864 F.2d 881 (1st Cir. 1988) (openly practiced

sexual harassment, well-known among employees will likely result in inference of employer knowledge); *Yates*, 819 F.2d at 636 (6th Cir. 1987) (employer is liable if it "knew, or upon reasonably diligent inquiry should have known," of the harassment).

26. *EEOC Policy Guidance* at 6695, n.29; *Ellison*, 924 F.2d at 882 (reasonableness of employer's remedy will depend on its ability to stop the harassment--temporary transfer of the victim of the harassment was insufficient); Swentek v. USAIR, Inc., 830 F.2d 552 (4th Cir. 1987) (employer's full investigation followed by issuance of written warnings for harasser to refrain lest he be terminated was sufficient to preclude liability); Barrett v. Omaha National Bank, 726 F.2d 424 (8th Cir. 1984) (employer held not liable when, within 4 days of victim's report of harassment, it investigated the report, reprimanded the harasser, placed him on probation, and warned of discharge in the event of a recurrence); *see also* note 19 *supra*.

27. *See EEOC Policy Guidance* at 405:6699-6701 (noting that the EEOC will administratively close claims of sexual harassment that they investigate and find to have been promptly and properly remedied by the employer).

28 *Proposed Guidelines*, 403:523, 526.

29. The fact that such a comprehensive scheme was not contemplated by *Meritor* is evidenced, for example, by the Supreme Court's express refusal to hold employers strictly liable for their employees' acts of sexual harassment. *See supra* note 8.

30. *See infra* note 38 and accompanying text.

31. 56 FEP Cases 289 (Okla Ct. App. 1991).

32. *Id.*

33. *Id.* at 290.

34. *Id.*

35. One commentator notes that "[e]mployers are so squeamish about the publicity engendered in [sexual harassment] cases . . . that an unscrupulous plaintiff can achieve a quick settlement and destroy another employee's career." D. Machlowitz & M. Machlowitz, *Preventing Sexual Harassment*, Oct. 1987 A.B.A.J. at 78.

36. Another indemnification issue regarding settlement scenarios involves whether an employer's insurance coverage will cover damages resulting from sexual harassment by one of its employees. Employers should investigate whether they have tortious liability insurance coverage, and if so, whether it will cover statutory sexual harassment liability. Some policies contain exclusions for "intentional acts," and may exclude coverage for principal or attenuated liability. *See generally* SEXUAL HARASSMENT IN THE WORKPLACE

at Chap. 11, § 11.5 (discussing cases that have upheld and reflected insurance companies' attempts to avoid liability for sexual harassment damages).

37. *See supra* n.34 and accompanying text. Given the recent amendments to Title VII allowing jury trials in cases alleging intentional discrimination--encompassing virtually every allegation of sexual harassment--the publicity concerns of employers are likely to rise. Note also that the amendments will now permit punitive and compensatory damages in these cases, again raising the ante for employer liability. *Civil Rights Act of 1991*, S. 1745 § 1977A(b) and (c) (amending 42 U.S.C. § 2000e).

38. In addition, employers might argue that setting standards (other than the parties' agreement) for settlement is antithetical to the oft-stated purposes of the employment-based civil rights laws i.e., to eradicate the discrimination and to put employees who have suffered wrongful discrimination back to work. Thus, employers who settle in the favor of an employee who has been harassed in a hostile environment can be acting in the spirit of Title VII, and should be allowed to do so freely. Airline Stewards & Stewardesses Ass'n Local 550 v. American Airline, 573 F.2d 960, 963 (7th Cir. 1978), *cert. denied*, 439 U.S. 876 (1978) ("[i]t is a well-settled principle that the law generally favors the encouragement of settlements." *Cf.* Ford Motor Co. v. EEOC, 458 U.S. 219, 228 (1982) (citing Albermarle Paper Co. v. Moody, 422 U.S. 405, 417 (1975) for the proposition that "the `primary objective' of Title VII is to bring employment discrimination to an end" and McDonnell Douglas Corp. v. Green, 411 U.S. 792, 800 (1973) for the proposition that "the preferred means for achieving [this goal is through] "cooperation and voluntary compliance.").

39. Title VII only covers wrongful employment actions by employers, labor unions, and employment agencies. 42 U.S.C. § 2000e(b)-(d) and §2000e-2(a)-(d). Courts have recognized, in some circumstances, that a supervisor employee harasser may be individually liable for purposes of Title VII. *See Vakharia v. Swedish Covenant Hosp.*, 824 F. Supp. 769, 786 (N.D. Ill. 1993) *on reconsideration in part*, (under Title VII, "individuals may be held personally liable for civil rights violations they commit while working as agents of larger institutions, provided that their individual liability is based on individual acts distinct from institutional policies set by their superiors"). For the most part, jurisdictions considering this issue are split on the issue of whether individual liability may be imposed. Courts which impose liability usually do so based on the participation of the supervisor or manager as a decision-maker with respect to the discriminatory act under Title VII. *Gaddy v. Abex Corp.*, 884 F.2d 312, 318-19 (7th Cir. 1989); *EEOC v. Vucitech*, 842 F.2d 936, 942 (7th Cir. 1988); *Robinson v. Jacksonville Shipyards, Inc.*, 760 F. Supp. 1486, 1527 (M.D. Fla. 1991); *but see Henry v. E.G.&G. Missouri Metals Shaping Co., Inc.*, 837 F. Supp. 312, 314 (E.D. Mo. 1993) (refusing to follow other courts finding a distinction between individual and official capacity). Courts refusing to

recognize individual liability rely on the damages allowable under Title VII. Since only equitable relief is allowed and since such relief can be provided only by the employer, such courts find that individual liability is not appropriate. *Harvey v. Blake*, 913 F.2d 226, 227-28 (5th Cir. 1990); *Weiss v. Coca-Cola Bottling Co.*, 772 F. Supp. 407, 410-11 (N.D. Ill. 1991); *Bertoncini v. Schrimpf*, 712 F. Supp. 1336, 1340 (N.D. Ill. 1989); *Seib v. Elko Motor Inn, Inc.*, 648 F. Supp. 272 (D. Nev. 1986). The Civil Rights Act of 1991 amended the damages provisions of Title VII to allow compensatory and punitive damages under Title VII. The inclusion of compensatory and punitive damages has prompted at least one court to reject the rationale that Title VII damages are of the type only an employer would be required to provide; since compensatory and punitive damages are of the type individuals pay, a rationale exists for imposing individual liability on employee harassers. *Bridges v. Eastman Kodak Co.*, 800 F. Supp. 1172, 1180 (S.D. N.Y. 1992). For a discussion of this issue, *see Bertoncini*, 712 F. Supp. at 1339-40, collecting cases on the issue of individual liability under Title VII. The Supreme Court recently refused to review the issue of individual liability under Title VII. *Miller v. LaRosa*. U.S. Sup. Ct. No. 93-659, 2/221 94.

40. *Cf. Steele*, 867 F.2d at 1315 (finding insufficient publication of supervisor's harassing comments to hold him liability under invasion of privacy theory).

41. The employer's ability to hold its agents liable for the failure to exercise reasonable and ordinary care in their relationship is a longstanding principle of the common law which comports with the Supreme Court's recognition that such principles are applicable to the sexual harassment cause of action. *See generally*, Restatement (Second) of Agency, § 380, *et seq*.

42. *See supra* note 36.

43. *See Juarez v. Ameritech Mobile Communications, Inc.*, 746 F. Supp. 798, 806 (N.D. Ill. 1990) (court dismissing Title VII sexual harassment claims against employer and advising that an action against the responsible employee would have been more appropriate).

44. *Elrod v. Sears, Roebuck & Co.*, 56 FEP Cases 1246 (11th Cir. 1991) (alleged harasser brings ADEA suit arguing that employer's harassment allegations against him were pretextual); *Rush v. Metro Transit Auth.*, 51 FEP Cases 1217 (D. Kan. 1989) (employee discharge for sexual harassment brings Title VII action arguing that termination was racially motivated); *Yates*, 819 F.2d at 637-39.

45. *Johnson v. Int'l Minerals & Chemical Corp.*, 40 FEP Cases 1651 (D.S.D. 1986) (supervisors argue that they suffered from public scorn and ridicule); *McAlear v. Kasak*, 225 Mont. 113, 731 P.2d 908 (1987); *cf. Erickson v. Marsh & McLennan Co.*, 55 FEP Cases 1179 (N.J. Sup. Ct. 1990) (alleged harasser argues that his ultimate termination was in retaliation for beginning legal action to clear his name of sexual harassment charges--defamation suit brought

regarding subsequent poor job recommendation).

46. *Jordan v. Hudson*, 690 F. Supp. 502 (E.D. Va. 1988) (postal employees argue that their accusers interfered with their contractual rights to their jobs).

47. *Johnson v. Int'l Minerals & Chemical Corp.*, 40 FEP Cases at 1651-52 (supervisors argue that they suffered from public scorn and ridicule).

48. *Scherer v. Rockwell Int'l*, 56 FEP Cases 215 (N.D. Ill. 1991) (alleged harasser argues that his written employment contract was broken since his actions did not fit its definitions of "misconduct" and he was given improper notice); *Anderson v. Hewlett-Packard Corp.*, 694 F. Supp. 1294 (N.D. Ohio 1988) (supervisor argues breach of contract despite his "constant" sexual remarks, insinuations and threats).

49. *Williams v. Maremont Corp.*, 875 F.2d 1476 (10th Cir. 1989) (wrongful discharge suit brought on alleged handbook contract).

50. *Lyons v. Barrett*, 851 F.2d 406 (D.C.C. 1988) (government worker terminated for alleged sexual harassment deserves fifth amendment hearing to provide opportunity to clear his name).

51. *See, e.g.*, *Williams v. Maremont*, *supra* note 48 (public policy gives the employer broad discretion in its efforts to eliminate sexual harassment and thus employer can discipline for conduct "which could be interpreted" as sexual harassment).

52. SEXUAL HARASSMENT IN THE WORKPLACE at 419 (citing cases where clear sexual harassment has been ruled in arbitration to not merit termination of the harasser).

53. *Cf.* *Lyons*, 851 F.2d at 410, 411 (the court noting that discharge for sexual harassment would clearly "imperil [the alleged harasser's] standings and associations in his community" and that the alleged harasser would have to live with the possibly "false and defamatory impression created by the circumstances of his termination).

54. *See, e.g.*, W. Kandel, *Current Developments in Employment Litigation, Sexual Harassment: Persistent, Prevalent, but Preventable*, EMPL. REL. L.J., (1988); G. Siniscalco, *Sexual Harassment and Employer Liability: The Flirtation That Could Cost a Fortune*, 6 EMPL. REL. L.J. 277 (1981); D. Machlowitz & M. Machlowitz, *Preventing Sexual Harassment*, Oct. 1987 A.B.A.J. at 78.

55. *Ellison*, 924 F.2d at 882 (citing 29 C.F.R. § 1604.11(f) which notes that "[p]revention is the best tool for the elimination of sexual harassment."). Note that there is some disagreement whether sexual harassment cases should consider the sensitivities of the reasonable person, or more specifically, the reasonable woman. *Compare*, *Ellison*, 924 F.2d at 879-891 (endorsing a reasonable woman

standard); Andrews v. City of Philadelphia, 895 F.2d 1469, 1482 (3d Cir. 1990) (same); *Yates*, 819 F.2d at 637 (same); Vermett v. Hough, 627 F. Supp. 587 (W.D. Mich 1986) (same); *with Ellison*, 942 F.2d 872, 884-885 (J. Stephens, dissenting on the reasonable woman standard); Rabidue v. Osceola Refining Co., 805 F.2d 611, 620 (adopting a reasonable person standard); Ross v. Double Diamond, Inc., 672 F. Supp. 261 (N.D. Tex. 1987) (same). *See also*, Note, *The Aftermath of* Meritor: *A Search for Standards in the Law of Sexual Harassment*, 98 YALE L.J. 1717, 1737-38 (1989) ("the standards for accessing women's psychological harm due to harassment must begin to reflect women's sensitivity to behavior once condoned as acceptable").

56. *EEOC Policy Guidance* at 6699 (citing 23 C.F.R. § 1604 11 (f)).

57. *Meritor*, 477 U.S. at 73.

58. *Id.*

59. *See* United States Merit Systems Protection Board, *Sexual Harassment in the Federal Government: An Update* at 11, 45 (1988). The recommendations of the Board apply equally to the private sector.

60. *Id.* at 46-48.

61. *See supra* notes 19 & 26 and accompanying text.

62. *Sexual Harassment and Employer Liability: The Flirtation That Could Cost a Fortune*, *supra* note 53 at 290.

CROSS-EXAMINATION OF A DEFENDANT IN A SEXUAL HARASSMENT LAWSUIT

Mark S. Rudy
Rudy & Zieff
San Francisco, California

I. Primary objectives of cross-examination of defendant.

As in any other litigation, cross-examination of a defendant in employment discrimination litigation should always be conducted with a specific objective in view. Counsel should pursue one or more of the following goals in cross-examination:

1. To develop favorable matters that have been left unsaid on direct examination;
2. To introduce all of a conversation or document, if the witness testified to only a part out of context;
3. To demonstrate that the witness is lying;
4. To establish that the witness could not have seen or hear heard what he claimed;
5. To test the witness's ability to hear, see, remember, and relate with accuracy what he testified to;
6. To establish the witness's bias or prejudice;
7. To establish any interest, peculiarity or otherwise, the witness may have in the outcome of the trial;
8. To impair the credibility of the witness, e.g. by inducing him to admit that he made statements on a prior occasion contrary to

his testimony and direct examination, or by laying the foundation for proof of contradictory statements;

9. To bring to the attention of the jury that the witness testifies evasively, hesitantly, belligerently, or so slowly that he seems to be struggling to support his testimony in chief;

10. To establish that the witness has been coached and has memorized his testimony; and

11. To impeach the witness in any other way permitted by law.

II. At the outset of cross-examination of the defendant, it may be appropriate to present the following general questions:

Q. When did you last talk to the attorney calling you as a witness about the facts of this case?

Q. How many times have you discussed this case with the attorney?

Q. Have you discussed the testimony or the case with any of the persons involved, including Murray Planet or any of your partners?

Q. Have you been allowed to read the deposition that you gave in this case?

Q. Have you any financial interests in the outcome of this case?

Q. Since this trial started, have you talked with the other witnesses about what their testimony was or is going to be?

Q. Within the course of this trial, have you taken any notes on what you have heard or seen?

Q. How many times before this trial started did you discuss this case with anyone who is to be called as a witness?

Q. Did you discuss the facts with anyone who was to be a witness in order for each of you to refresh your memory about what has been seen or heard?

Q. Was such a discussion entered into so that your testimonies would agree with one another?

Q. Have you read any textbooks, or other writing on the issue of sexual harassment in preparation for your testimony here today?

III. Specific subject matter to be covered on cross-examination.

In a sexual harassment lawsuit, it is imperative that counsel for plaintiff examine the defendant on several different legal areas as follows:

1. The witness's knowledge, or lack thereof, of laws and regulations relating to employment discrimination including

specific reference to the Equal Employment Opportunity Commission Guidelines on Discrimination because of Sex. 29 C.F.R. Section 1604.11.

2. The extent of any of defendant's internal policies and practices on discrimination or sexual harassment. This includes examining the witness on both prevention and remedy practices and polices. During the course of examination on this subject matter, have the defendant admit that its policy has been to treat employees fairly and even-handedly. Then, during the course of further questioning, demonstrate that the handling of Mary Smart's claim of employment discrimination was, in fact, violative of defendant's past practices and policies.

3. Determine those persons responsible for implementing and enforcing the employment practices and policies of defendant.

4. Establish that past practices of defendant with regard to the handling of other employment problems. Again, the purpose of this inquiry is to show disparate treatment in the manner in which Mary Smart's problems were handled.

5. Determine the policies and practices of the law firm for investigating all employment problems and complaints.

During the course of cross-examination of Percy Grand, have him admit that the law firm had no formal policies regarding handling and remedying internal employment discrimination issues notwithstanding the fact that the firm employed labor and employment law specialists as both partners and associates.

6. Inquire of the defendant regarding his attitudes, beliefs, and opinions about professional women in the work place.

7. Have the defendant admit that environmental sexual harassment is a type of employment discrimination as well as quid pro quo discrimination; and that intimidating hostile or an offensive working environment that reasonably interferes with an individual's job performance is actionable.

8. Have the defendant admit that a partner is authorized to make representations regarding employment guarantees such as representations regarding the partnership track, salary increases, promotions, etc.

9. Cross-examine generally regarding issues of ratification, acquiescence, and notice relating to acts of associates of the law firm such as Murray Planet.

IV. Cross-Examination relating to the Mary Smart matter.

The objective of this line of questioning is to fully ascertain the role that the defendant played in all aspects of Mary Smart's employment relationship with the defendant law firm. The objective is to demonstrate that Percy Grand and his subordinates, including Murray Planet, differentially treated Mary Smart throughout the course of her employment tenure with the firm. Inquiry in this area should include the following topics:

1. The defendant's role, if any, in the hiring of Mary Smart. Have the defendant admit that partners such as Sam Eggy had the authority to make employment promises as alleged by Mary.
2. Determine the role, if any, the defendant played in supervising Mary and evaluating her performance.
3. Cross-examine in detail through the use of leading questions Percy's knowledge of an acquiescence in alleged to be discriminatory by Mary Smart.
4. Determine on cross-examination that the defendant did little or nothing to prevent and remedy the various acts of discriminatory treatment raised by Mary.

5. Cross-examine Percy regarding the circumstances under which Mary Smart left the law firm including who was involved in the decision to ask her to leave, the reasons for it, and the precipitating event(s) leading up to the separation. It is important to establish through Percy that similarly situated male associates, with comparable or worse performance records, were not asked to leave the firm. Although the law firm of Eager, Angst & Maloney did not have formal employment policies, it is worthwhile to establish through Percy that it has always been the practice of the firm to provide progressive discipline and counseling to those associates who are deemed to have performance problems. Then, it should be demonstrated that Mary was asked to leave despite not having been progressively disciplined, or offered counseling.

6. That since Mary Smart has raised a claim for emotional distress, inquiries should be made in order to show Percy Grand and Murray Planet were, in fact, out to get Mary Smart for non-legitimate business reasons.

V. Conclusion.

In essence, the goal of cross-examining Percy Grand is to show that the defendant law firm Eager, Angst & Maloney was totally insensitive to employment issues and problems facing its professional women employees; and that it acquiesced and ratified unlawful activity. As with any other cross-examination, the inquiry should be well-prepared, clearly focused, concise, and undertaken through the use of leading questions for which the examiner can anticipate the response.

CROSS-EXAMINING

THE

PLAINTIFF'S PSYCHIATRIST

Karen Kaplowitz, Esq.
Alschuler, Grossman & Pines
1880 Century Park East
Twelfth Floor
Los Angeles, California 90067-1694
(310) 277-1226

CROSS-EXAMINING THE PLAINTIFF'S PSYCHIATRIST

The plaintiff's psychiatrist has just finished describing clearly and persuasively the post-traumatic stress disorder or other disorders the plaintiff claims she suffers as a result of your client's harassment.

It is your turn. How do you cross-exam the plaintiff's psychiatrist?

Some lawyers opt to forego the cross-examination, figuring they are better served by calling their own expert and in effect cross-examining the plaintiff's expert through their own. In some situations, this is a sound strategy, particularly when the time span between the testimony of the plaintiff and defense experts is not long. For example, instead of asking the plaintiff's expert about the significance of facts which she did not appear to have taken into account, you can ask your own expert about the reliability of a diagnosis which did not take into account such facts. Cross-examining the plaintiff's expert through your expert eliminates the risk of an excellent expert's repeating strong testimony or a weak expert's fixing the problems or omissions in her testimony. If you ask a weak expert about facts which do not appear in her report, the expert might try to fill the gap by suggesting that that fact was taken into account although not highlighted in the report.

However, there are risks inherent in the decision to waive cross-examination. In most trials, the absence of a cross-examination is unusual, and most jurors have a psychological need to explain and understand the unusual. This need could lead jurors to manufacture theories over which the lawyer has no control. For example, jurors might conclude the lawyer was intimidated by the psychiatric jargon or that the testimony took the lawyer by surprise and he was unable to develop a meaningful line of cross-examination.

Even with a weak expert, the testimony may have been perceived as significant to the naive juror. That juror must be educated by the cross-examination in order to understand the flaws in the expert's testimony. Furthermore, if settlement negotiations are underway or still possible, a blistering cross-examination of any plaintiff witness can translate into dollars saved for the defendant.

In most cases, the lawyer is well-advised to proceed with cross-examination. There are so many fruitful areas to pursue in cross-examining a plaintiff psychiatric expert, the well-prepared defense lawyer can almost always weaken -- sometimes fatally -- such testimony. The following are suggested areas for cross-examination.

1. <u>The "Bought" Expert</u>. It is common to paint experts in cross-examination as the paid tools of the lawyer and party who hired them by, for example, questioning about their hourly rates or the size of their fees. In the case of psychiatrists, there is usually an extra opportunity for raising an inference of pecuniary motivation. In Los Angeles, some psychiatrists who are both clinicians and forensic witnesses charge double their clinical rates for their forensic work.

In such a case, the inference of the psychiatrist's testimony having been bought is clear. If the psychiatrist is strictly a forensic witness, one can also question whether the expert is aware if the plaintiff or her counsel approached other psychiatrists first, conveying the notion that the plaintiff "shopped" until finding a cooperative expert.

2. <u>Lack of Relevant Experience.</u> From the expert's deposition, you know what the expert's normal experience is. It is your job on cross-examination to distinguish the expert's background from the plaintiff's case. If you can establish the expert's normal work consists of evaluating competency to stand trial, the jury may doubt the expert's own competency to evaluate non-criminal plaintiffs such as highly educated professionals or middle managers. If you can establish that the expert has never evaluated someone like the plaintiff, the "expert" has become more of a novice. One must be careful not to trivialize this line of

questioning. If the plaintiff is a Lithuanian, born after World War II who emigrated to the United States in 1955 and lived in Chicago, the fact that the psychiatrist has never evaluated any Lithuanians from Chicago hardly discredits the psychiatrist.

3. Examiner Bias. If you have discovered that the expert often works with plaintiffs' lawyers, by all means bring it up. There are many referral networks among experts and lawyers that may suggest bias. The referral network can work in both directions. In a recent case, a psychiatrist referred his patient to a lawyer in order to generate a source of money in order for the patient to pay the psychiatrist's bills. If the expert works mainly for plaintiffs, bring that up.

If the expert is the plaintiff's treating psychiatrist, a whole new sphere of cross-examination is opened up. Ask the expert to discuss the phenomenon of "therapeutic alliance." Ask whether it is harder to be objective about a patient in therapy versus a plaintiff evaluated solely for a lawsuit. Further, a treating psychiatrist may have an indirect financial stake in the outcome in the case. If the expert has suggested long-term therapy to the plaintiff, ask what the projected cost will be to the patient. Not surprisingly, a lot of experts will be uncomfortable with such issues.

4. The Misled or Underinformed Expert. The most effective technique for undermining the jury's confidence in the psychiatrist is to establish that the psychiatrist was underinformed either because the plaintiff failed to disclose key facts to the psychiatrist or because the psychiatrist otherwise failed to discover key facts. For example, if you have uncovered that the plaintiff has asserted similar claims on other occasions, although never filed another lawsuit, a psychiatrist who did not know this fact has either been misled or failed to ask the right questions. You need to uncover as many facts as possible about the plaintiff's life, from medical records, employment records, hospital records, co-workers or other witnesses to impeach the facts on which the psychiatrist's diagnosis was based. If the psychiatrist attributes the plaintiff's mental distress to alleged trauma on the job, you need to question the psychiatrist closely about the effects of other factors you have uncovered that may have caused the alleged mental distress. If you can establish that there are facts which the plaintiff did not disclose to the psychiatrist, you will also have an easier time suggesting that the plaintiff may be malingering, that is, faking or exaggerating the extent of her psychiatric distress. Medical records are often a source of helpful evidence. If the plaintiff sought a non-psychiatric physician in the same time period as the alleged trauma took place and the medical records omit any reference to sleep problems or emotional disturbance, such medical records provide a powerful indication of internal inconsistencies in the plaintiff's medical story.

5. Attacking the Integrity of Psychiatry. One popular approach to cross-examining psychiatric experts is to attack the field of psychiatry itself and its lack of reliability. Before embarking on this course, you should read Ziskin & Faust's "Coping With Psychiatric and Psychological Testimony."[1]

In some communities, this type of attack may be successful. Some people are highly distrustful of the reliability of psychiatrists. If you intend to pursue this course of attack, you should question prospective jurors during voir dire about their attitudes toward psychotherapy. Since their attitudes may depend on whether they have had psychotherapy themselves, a potentially embarrassing topic, such inquiry might be better suited for a confidential jury questionnaire, rather than public voir dire.

6. Your Attitude Toward the Expert. Dr. Stephen Raffle of Oakland, California, who testifies frequently in employment cases and whose practice is three-quarters medical-legal, emphasizes that the most effective cross-examination he has endured has been by examiners who behaved civilly. If the examiner is abrasive or combative, and jurors perceive that there is a battle raging between the lawyer and the witness, lawyers should expect a good expert to win.

Stanley L. Brodsky makes a similar point in his excellent treatise "Testifying In Court: Guidelines and Maxims for the Expert Witness."[2] He notes that eliciting "collaborative criticism" from a psychiatrist can be highly effective. This is where the lawyer, using a friendly or at least scientifically inquisitive tone, asks the expert to discuss the limitations of psychiatry in diagnosing or treating the relevant dysfunction. Since psychologists and psychiatrists are trained to question methodology, including their own, some professionals are not at all reluctant to engage in a scholarly discussion of the limits of their field. The witness is in essence "collaborating" with the cross-examiner in undermining her own testimony.

7. Use of Your Own Expert. Your own expert is highly valuable in reviewing your opponent's report, assisting and preparing for your opponent's deposition and generally in determining what the opponent's expert has omitted or failed to consider. Also, your own expert can determine whether psychological tests should have been used by the plaintiff's expert, or if plaintiff's expert did use psychological tests, whether he used the right ones. If plaintiff's expert did conduct the appropriate tests, and you obtain the raw data, your own expert can re-analyze the data to check the validity of plaintiff expert's conclusions. In order to help you cross-examine the plaintiff's expert, your own expert does not necessarily have to examine the plaintiff personally. However, to be most effective

as a witness, your own expert usually does have to personally examine the plaintiff. Otherwise he is vulnerable to attack as the less informed of the two battling experts.

8. Obtaining Prior Testimony. Another effective technique for challenging the credibility and integrity of an expert is to obtain her testimony from previous trials and point out inconsistencies between that testimony and her current testimony. Experts are nonplussed by having to reconcile their own disparate opinions. For example, perhaps Dr. Expert previously testified for the defense and stated that the inability to perform Task X was a necessary condition for a diagnosis of post-traumatic stress. But in this case, where plaintiff claims she is suffering from post-traumatic stress, plaintiff is competently performing Task X. This sets up a situation where the re-direct will be defensive in tone. (It also rattles plaintiff counsel who wonders what other skeletons you have uncovered, not only from this witness but from others as well.)

It is also valuable to talk to other lawyers who have cross-examined this expert. Not only can they provide valuable information about the expert's strengths and vulnerabilities from their own perspective, but perhaps also from the jurors' perspective, if they spoke to jurors after the verdict.

Conclusions. For extensive questions for cross-examination, see Ziskin & Faust, supra. Whether or not you accept their premise that psychiatric and psychological testimony is unreliable and should be attacked as such, their lines of questioning should prove very helpful. In sum, do not be phobic about cross-examining the plaintiff's expert. The jury will not normally replace its own innate sense of reason about human nature with a psychiatric diagnosis which you have demonstrated is unreasonable or unreliable.

The author gratefully acknowledges the insights of Dr. Stephen Raffle of Oakland, California and Dr. Vicki Stone of Los Angeles, California in connection with preparation of this article.

BIBLIOGRAPHY

Brodsky, S.L. (1991). "Testifying In Court: Guidelines and Maxims for the Expert Witness." Washington, D.C.: American Psychological Association.

Ziskin, J. & Faust, D. (1988). "Coping With Psychiatric and Psychological Testimony" (Vol. 1-3, 4th Edition). Marina del Rey, CA: Law and Psychology Press.

ENDNOTES

1. Ziskin, J. & Faust, D. (1988). "Coping With Psychiatric and Psychological Testimony" (Vol. 1-3, 4th Edition). Marina del Rey, CA: Law and Psychology Press.

2. Brodsky, S.L. (1991). "Testifying In Court: Guidelines and Maxims for the Expert Witness." Washington, D.C.: American Psychological Association.

THOUGHTS ON ARGUMENT

Craig Needham
Caputo, Liccardo, Rossi, Sturges & McNeil
San Jose, California

It is my view that arguments get down to a simple formula:

LAW + FACTS = VERDICT!

In short, you integrate the law, which comes from the judge, into the facts, which comes from the evidence. In blending those two elements together, you try to persuade the jury to reach a certain verdict.

You need to spend some time emphasizing that the jury is only to use the law and the facts that developed during the trial. Lawyers have tremendous powers to marshall the facts at a trial (subpoenaing witnesses, depositions, interrogatories, requests for admissions, production of documents, etc.); you should use each of these tools at least once in trial, just so you can make this point in argument. Since lawyers on both sides of the case have the same powers, fairness dictates that the jury consider only those facts which the lawyers have produced during the evidence phase of the trial. It is not fair to do it any other way.

It follows, therefore, that any argument utilizing facts (or inferences) which are not based on the evidence, are not only unfair, but should demonstrate a fundamental weakness in the position proffered. I believe that juries do not understand the tremendous powers and responsibilities that attorneys have in civil litigation. Every argument should incorporate this concept.

You should use straight logic and simple language. On the one hand, you don't want to be so academic on the law that you lose the jury; on the other hand, you don't want to be so fact oriented that the jury loses the implication of those facts toward a verdict.

Most verdicts are now special verdicts. The special verdict form is a useful tool in your argument. By going through the questions that the jury must analyze, you have a ready outline to blend the law and the facts. Many lawyers use the special verdict form at the end of their argument by way of summary.

I think there are several important issues that the plaintiff must point out, in one way or another, during argument of a sexual harassment case:

1. Plaintiff is here for compensation, not a gift. He/she does not seek charity or sympathy. Charity is a demeaning thing in a court of law.

2. Each item of compensatory damages should be evaluated. The lawyer must argue the totality of the effects on the plaintiff's life that occurred as a result of the conduct of the defendant. While

this kind of argument is "fact specific", you must be ready to discuss the damages in terms of the effect on the plaintiff's self-esteem and his/her relationships with other people. It is one thing to say that the plaintiff is angry, depressed, sad, etc. It is far more effective to talk about how it has affected his/her relationships with other people as well as his/her own feelings of self-worth.

3. You must make clear that sexual harassment (as defined by the parameters of the instructions) is wrong. You must have no apologies for that. This is not a "good ol' boy" theory which implies compensation can only be justified in the most egregious case. Sexual harassment in any form is wrong and should be compensated. It is important to differentiate between sexual harassment and forms of sexual overtures or encounters which are either not improper or not the subject of the lawsuit.

4. In my view, you must discuss the dollars you are asking. Leaving damages "up in the air" does not fulfill your responsibility to give the jury guidelines in working through the formula mentioned above. You must point out that what you are doing is "lawyer talk" and that the final decision must be theirs alone. You should not shrink from the opportunity to suggest damages in specific amounts to the jury. This should be done in opening argument, which will force the defense to respond to the amount. This will provide great soil for your rebuttal argument.

5. You must, of course, talk about the defendant's conduct. It is from the conduct of the defendant that you can derive specific intent. It is from the conduct of the defendant that you can focus the arguments that lead to punitive damages, assuming you have that issue in your case. The defendant's conduct must be discussed in terms of the defendant's knowledge at the time of the conduct. For example, if the defendant knows a particular plaintiff is susceptible to certain forms of harassment, it will undoubtedly get the jury more sympathetic to your side. Repetition of conduct, which in and of itself may seem "no big deal", is also important to emphasize. It is of obvious benefit to the plaintiff to show a pattern of conduct as opposed to isolated incidents. All of the specific instances should be put together to form a picture, or "mosaic", of the defendant's sexual harassment profile.

6. Finally, and most importantly, you must individualize your plaintiff. You must talk about the effects of sexual harassment on your client as opposed to generalities of how sexual harassment hurts people. You must bring home to the jury that this case is about your client. You can concede that the effects of the defendant's conduct may be entirely different, all the while pointing out that is irrelevant. You force the defendant to talk about your client on damages and not make generalities. Use of the damage instructions in your argument is very helpful on this point.

CLOSING ARGUMENT IN THE SEXUAL HARASSMENT CASE: A DEFENDANT'S VIEWPOINT

Douglas L. Williams
Schwartz, Kelm, Warren & Rubenstein
Columbus, Ohio

CLOSING ARGUMENT IN THE SEXUAL HARASSMENT CASE: A DEFENDANT'S VIEWPOINT

I. Closing Argument is Alive and Well

Much has been written about the importance of the opening statement. Supposedly, a large majority of jurors make up their minds during the opening statements. My experiences and conversations with jurors after a trial lead me to doubt this conclusion.

The opening statement is truly an important aspect of any trial. However, when the jurors hear the opening statement they do not yet understand the case. Many times, lawyers deliver an opening statement assuming that the jurors understand the case as well as they do. They don't. This means that in the opening statement lawyers have to speak in general terms to jurors who know very little about the case. Another problem with opening statements is that you cannot be sure at the time that all of your evidence will be admissible, how your evidence will be received by the jurors, and whether plaintiff will be able to rebut your evidence. You also won't reveal any surprise evidence you may have waiting for the plaintiff. Lastly, in most jurisdictions the opening statement cannot be argumentative.

Moreover, the purposes of the opening and closing statements are different. The purpose of the opening statement is to tell the jury a bit about the facts of the case, to establish rapport with the jury and to persuade the jury that your side of the case has merit. As a trial develops--as witnesses testify on direct and cross-examination and exhibits are introduced--you are able to put the bits and pieces of evidence before the jury. The closing argument gives you the opportunity to correlate all of these bits and pieces, weave them together and persuade the jury to accept the version of the facts most favorable to your client. In other words, the closing statement is your last opportunity to persuade and to communicate with the jury. And unlike the opening statement, the lawyer can be argumentative and is now communicating with jurors who, hopefully, have an understanding of the case.

With so much significance placed on the opening statements, lawyers often prepare the closing statement the night before the argument. This is a mistake. From the very beginning of trial preparation, the lawyer should be working with the theme of the case and outlining how that theme will be presented to the jury in both opening and closing statements. The simpler and more straightforward the theme, the easier this will be. The earlier the lawyer begins the more convincing the closing argument will be.

II. Defendant's Closing Argument in Sexual Harassment Cases

From the defendant's perspective, closing arguments in sexual harassment cases present several problems. First, the plaintiff's theme in closing will normally be based on a sympathetic chord. Further, plaintiff will normally end its closing on a strong emotional appeal. Thus, after plaintiff's argument the defendant's lawyer must change the jury's mood promptly and redirect the jury's attention positively to the defendant's case. For example, you can say, "Now you have just heard a very emotional, impassioned presentation by Ms. Smith. Of course, that is her side of the story and what she would like to believe. But let's now look at what the facts really are." Defendant must convince the jury that no matter how sympathetic the plaintiff's case may seem, sympathy does not change the facts or the law. The defendant's closing argument must try to get the jury to consider the case on a factual basis, as distinguished from an emotional basis. This is exceedingly difficult because most jurors believe that sexual harassment does take place in the workplace.

It is my opinion that in sexual harassment cases it is a mistake for the defendant to attack the plaintiff head on. Most jurors do not like to conclude that a plaintiff is lying. Similarly, most jurors will recognize that it takes a certain amount of courage for a woman to come forward and complain of sexual harassment. Jurors are more comfortable concluding that the plaintiff was mistaken, misinterpreted what happened or has faulty memory as opposed to concluding that the plaintiff is lying. Thus, the better approach to take when possible is to develop a theme that allows the jury to rule on the defendant's behalf and, at the same time, believe that everyone is telling the truth. Remember that except for the obvious liars, jurors like to believe most people are trying to tell the truth. For example, defendant might argue, "It would appear at first blush that the plaintiff lied to you, but it may be hard to believe that she would take the stand and swear to tell the truth and then deliberately lie to you. Instead of that, please let's try to understand. Maybe she thinks she's telling the truth and let us see how this came about." This allows the jury to decide the case without painting the plaintiff a liar.

This approach is most appropriate when the factual clash in the case is over whether the alleged sexually harassing conduct occurred, or whether the conduct constituted sexual harassment. With respect to whether or not harassment took place, a defendant might agree that a plaintiff has convinced herself that she was sexually harassed in an unconscious attempt to divert attention from her own deficient job performance. A jury might also believe that a plaintiff believes she's been harassed after her affections were not returned by the male employee she has accused, or because her personal life is troubled in some other respect. A defendant may also argue that even if a male employee's conduct or overtures were sincerely considered harassing by the plaintiff that she did not actually demonstrate that such conduct was unwelcome, even if she has convinced herself otherwise. Also, if the defense to a sexual harassment claim is that no harassing conduct occurred, there may be an emotional, sympathetic angle to play as well. A mistaken accusation of sexual harassment against a male employee(s) may jeapordize his employment and his family life if the jury accepts the plaintiff's characterization of harassment as true. With this offsetting sympathetic element, the jury may guard itself against allowing sympathy to influence its analysis of plaintiff's accusations.

In hostile environment cases, the focus can more easily be directed away from the plaintiff's credibility to issues of whether the alleged harassment was "severe" or "pervasive," and whether the company should be held responsible for any such harassment. In many jurisdictions the jury must decide not whether the plaintiff felt the harassment to be severe or pervasive but how the reasonable person in the plaintiff's position would have viewed the conduct. It may be effective to ask the jury in closing argument if the conduct alleged by the plaintiff would be harassing if the roles were switched: if it had been the plaintiff who had acted in that way towards a male employee in her position. To use the fact pattern in this case, what if a male associate walked in on a group of female associates laughing and joking over the sexual paraphernalia sold by the firm's client? Or, if it had been a male associate asked to work with a female client representative who had indicated her romantic interest in him? While there might be legitimate examples of conduct that could be more offensive to women than to men, a defendant can argue that an overly paternalistic application of the laws against sexual harassment could reduce women once again to a stereotype of vulnerable, helpless individuals who must be protected in a way that may reduce their opportunity to participate equally in the workplace.

Also critical in hostile environment cases is the issue of the employer's liability for any alleged harassment. Defendants can argue in closing statement that while plaintiff may be sincere in her belief that harassment occurred, she did not make the appropriate attempt to eliminate the harassment or bring such harassment to the attention of the appropriate company official. Jurors may be inclined to hold well educated, professional women to a higher standard, and require them to clearly address the harassing conduct and establish its unwelcome nature. For example, the plaintiff in our fact pattern wanted her firm to relieve her from working with an amorous client before she had determined if a simple discussion with the client explaining her inability to return his interest could have removed the perceived sexual tension. A jury may accept that a woman who achieved the plaintiff's level of success in law school and with ambitions to become a successful lawyer has not exerted a sufficient effort to determine if she could personally correct any perceived problem of romantic entanglement with herself and the client.

III. <u>Back to the Basics</u>

It goes without saying that facts persuade the jury. Decide which facts are the <u>most</u> persuasive and significant, and return to these facts throughout the closing argument. Refer to facts specifically, and argue them by explaining their significance with explicit references to the issues to which they apply. If you simplify and clearly organize the issues, you can in this way help the jury organize and build a framework for defendant's facts. When arguing the facts, remind the jury what was said by a particular witness and who the witness was. Remind the jury what was demonstrated by a particular exhibit and what the exhibit was. Whenever possible, try to use the testimony of the plaintiff's witnesses to prove an issue. Then, when you refer to the defendant's testimony it will seal the situation. Also, it is important to remember that the defendant should focus on trying its case and not spend its time opposing all the arguments made by the other side.

Finally, in order for jurors to believe your closing argument, you must be yourself. The jury has watched you throughout the trial and it is too late to try to become something that you are not. Indeed, attempting to inject a closing statement with unnecessary drama or emotion may have the unintended effect of overstating the value of plaintiff's claims. In other words, if <u>you</u> get all worked up, the jury may believe that the plaintiff's case is something to get all worked up about! Any displaying of emotion or intensity should be reserved for a fact, issue or policy argument that is strongly in defendant's favor, and if decided against it would create a result the jury can appreciate as unjust. Projecting a calm, matter-of-fact demeanor when arguing that the facts prove defendant's position to be the truth often tends to be the best vehicle for presenting a defendant's closing argument.

Douglas L. Williams

Douglas L. Williams is a partner at Schwartz, Kelm, Warren & Rubenstein in Columbus, Ohio. Mr. Williams also chairs the firm's employment and labor group. He and his group specialize in all facets of employment law, including litigation in the state and federal courts. He is an across the board labor lawyer representing management nationwide.

Mr. Williams was previously an Assistant Professor of Labor and Employment Discrimination Law at The Ohio State University College of Law. Currently, he is an Adjunct Professor with the College of Law where he teaches an employment law litigation seminar.

Mr. Williams is a graduate of the United States Air Force Academy and received his Master of Science from Central Missouri State University. He earned his J.D. with Honors from The Ohio State University.

Mr. Williams lectures often and has published widely on a variety of employment law subjects. He is Vice-Chair for the ABA Committee on Employer-Employee Relations of the Tort and Insurance Practice Section. Mr. Williams practices in state courts of Ohio and California and nationwide in federal courts.

THE PLAINTIFF'S JURY INSTRUCTIONS IN A HOSTILE ENVIRONMENT SEXUAL HARASSMENT CASE

Harriet E. Cooperman
Weinberg and Green
100 South Charles Street
Baltimore, Maryland 21201
410/332-8600

PLAINTIFF'S REQUESTED INSTRUCTION NO. _____

The Plaintiff in this action, Mary Smart, is suing the Defendants, Eager, Angst & Maloney, who is her former employer, and Murray Planet, for sexual harassment. Under the laws of this state and country sexual harassment is unlawful sex discrimination.

If you find that Defendants, or any of them, engaged in the sexual harassment of Plaintiff, in accordance with the instructions that I will give you, then Plaintiff may recover damages.

PLAINTIFF'S REQUESTED INSTRUCTION NO. _____

SEXUAL HARASSMENT-MEANING OF

Sexual harassment is sex discrimination, and is illegal.

Verbal or physical conduct of a sexual nature constitutes sexual harassment when the conduct has the purpose or effect of unreasonably interfering with an individual's work performance or creating an intimidating, hostile or offensive working environment.

Meritor Savings Bank, FSB v. Vinson, 477 U.S. 57 (1986)

PLAINTIFF'S REQUESTED INSTRUCTION NO. _____

SEXUAL HARASSMENT IS EQUIVALENT TO RACIAL HARASSMENT

Sexual harassment which creates a hostile or offensive environment for members of one sex is every bit the arbitrary barrier to sexual equality at the workplace that racial harassment is to racial equality. A requirement that a woman run a gauntlet of sexual abuse in return for the privilege of being allowed to work and make a living can be as demeaning and disconcerting as the harshest racial epithets.

Meritor Saving Bank V. Vinson, 477 U.S. 65 (1986)

Henson v. City of Dundee, 682 F.2d 897 (11th Cir. 1982)

PLAINTIFF'S REQUESTED INSTRUCTION NO. _____

SEXUAL HARASSMENT MUST BE SEVERE OR PERVASIVE

Sexual harassment which is sufficiently severe or pervasive to alter the conditions of the Plaintiff's employment by creating an abusive working environment constitutes sex discrimination, and is illegal.

If you find that defendants permitted a hostile or abusive working environment to exist for Plaintiff, then you must find that defendants engaged in illegal sex discrimination.

Meritor Savings Bank v. Vinson, 477 U.S. 65 (1986)

Henson v. Dundee, 682 F.2d 897, 902 (1982)

PLAINTIFF'S REQUESTED INSTRUCTION NO. _____

HOSTILE WORK ENVIRONMENT-PLAINTIFF'S BURDEN

A hostile work environment exists if it is sufficiently severe or pervasive to alter the conditions of the Plaintiff's employment.

The Plaintiff has the burden of establishing severe or pervasive activity. This burden may be satisfied by evidence of multiple incidents of unwelcome conduct or a particularly egregious incident. The Plaintiff, however, need not establish that the unwelcome conduct took place over an extended period of time.

Carrero v. New York City Housing Authority, 890 F.2d 569 (2d Cir. 1989).

PLAINTIFF'S REQUESTED INSTRUCTION NO. ______

REASONABLE WOMAN STANDARD

In determining whether a hostile environment of sexual harassment existed at Eager, Angst & Maloney, you should apply a reasonable woman standard. This standard requires you to take into account the experiences and perceptions of women. If you find the conduct complained of by Plaintiff sufficiently severe or pervasive to alter the conditions of her employment and create an abusive work environment, then you should find that sexual harassment existed.

In applying the reasonable woman standard you must avoid stereotyped notions of acceptable behavior.

Ellison v. Brady, 924 F.2d 871 (9th Cir. 1991)

Cerillo v. Ward, 770 F.Supp. 815 (S.D.N.Y. 1991)

Austin v. State of Hawaii, 759 F.Supp. 612 (D. Hawaii 1991)

PLAINTIFF'S REQUESTED INSTRUCTION NO. _____

NO "TYPICAL" VICTIM OF SEXUAL HARASSMENT

There is no "typical" victim of sexual harassment. Women are subjected to sexual harassment regardless of age, marital status, education, or profession.

Phillips v. Smalley Maintenance Services, Inc., 711 F.2d 1524 (11th Cir. 1983).

Kyriazi v. Western Electric Co., 461 F.Supp. 894 (D.N.J. 1978).

PLAINTIFF'S REQUESTED INSTRUCTION NO. _____

"UNWELCOME CONDUCT"

Unwelcome conduct means conduct which was not solicited or incited by the Plaintiff and conduct regarded as undesirable by the Plaintiff.

In determining whether the conduct was unwelcome by Plaintiff, you may consider whether Plaintiff's own conduct indicated that it was unwelcome, and you may consider Plaintiff's actions in response to the conduct, including any complaints raised by Plaintiff about such conduct.

<u>Meritor Savings Bank, FSB v. Vinson</u>, 477 U.S. 57 (1986).

<u>EEOC Policy Guidance</u>, pp. 7-8.

PLAINTIFF'S REQUESTED INSTRUCTION NO. _____

VERBAL CONDUCT CONSTITUTES UNWELCOME ACTS

Verbal conduct alone, including derogatory remarks, sexual innuendos and jokes may constitute "unwelcome acts" sufficient to establish sexual harassment.

Katz v. Dole, 709 F.2d 251 (4th Cir. 1983).

Bundy v. Jackson, 641 F.2d 934 (D.C. Cir. 1981).

Hicks v. Gates Rubber Co., 833 F.2d 1406 (10th Cir. 1987).

Hall v. Gus Construction Co., 842 F.2d 1010 (8th Cir. 1988).

PLAINTIFF'S REQUESTED INSTRUCTION NO. _____

PLAINTIFF HAS A RIGHT TO WORK IN AN ENVIRONMENT FREE FROM DISCRIMINATORY INTIMIDATION, RIDICULE AND INSULT

If you find that Plaintiff was forced to work in an environment that was not free from discriminatory intimidation, ridicule, and insult, then you must find defendants guilty of sex discrimination in violation of the law.

<u>Meritor Savings Bank v. Vinson</u>, 477 U.S. 65 (1986).

<u>Rogers v. EEOC</u>, 406 U.S. 957 (1972).

PLAINTIFF'S REQUESTED INSTRUCTION NO. _____

NOT NECESSARY TO FIND INTENT TO DISCRIMINATE
IN ORDER TO FIND LIABILITY FOR
UNLAWFUL EMPLOYMENT PRACTICES, AND SEX DISCRIMINATION

Plaintiff need not prove that defendants had an intent to discriminate against her on the basis of her sex in order to prove her claim of sex discrimination against Defendants.

Northern Inyo Hospital v. Fair Employment Practices Commission, 38 Cal.App. 3d 14 (1974).

PLAINTIFF'S REQUESTED INSTRUCTION NO. _____

EMPLOYER'S LIABILITY FOR ACTS OF SUPERVISORS

An employer is responsible for its own acts of sexual harassment and those of its agents and supervisory employees. This responsibility exists regardless of whether the specific acts complained of were authorized or even prohibited by the employer and regardless of whether the employer knew or should have known of their occurrence.

EEOC Guidelines, Section 1604.11(c)

PLAINTIFF'S REQUESTED INSTRUCTION NO. _____

SUPERVISORY STATUS

I instruct you that Percy Grand, Sam Eggy and Michael Ford were supervisory employees of the Defendant law firm. You must determine whether Murray Planet was a supervisory employee.

In determining whether an individual acts in a supervisory capacity you must look beyond the person's job title and job description, by examining the specific duties, functions and responsibilities performed by the individual at the time of the alleged sexual harassment. If the individual directed the work of other employees, and had authority to recommend, even if not to make, employment decisions affecting others (in such matters as hiring, firing, promotions, evaluations, assignment of work), I instruct you that you should find that individual to be a supervisory employee.

EEOC Guidelines Section 1604.11(c)

PLAINTIFF'S REQUESTED INSTRUCTION NO. _____

EMPLOYER'S LIABILITY FOR SEXUAL HARASSMENT BY CO-WORKERS

An employer is liable for the sexual harassment of its non-supevisory employees if the employer knows and does nothing about the situation.

An employer also is liable for the sexual harassment of its non-supervisory employees if upon a reasonably diligent inquiry the employer should have known of the situation.

An employer is liable for sexual harassment if the employer failed to take preventative measures when it had reason to believe that harassment may have occurred.

Garziano v. E.I. Dupont De Nemours & Co., 818 F.2d 380 (5th Cir. 1987).

Yates v. Avco Corp., 819 F.2d 630 (6th Cir. 1987).

Henson v. City of Dundee, 682 F.2d 897 (11th Cir. 1982).

PLAINTIFF'S REQUESTED INSTRUCTION NO. _____

FACTORS INDICATING EMPLOYER KNEW OR SHOULD HAVE KNOWN OF HARASSMENT

If you determine that Murray Planet was a non-supervisory employee, then you must determine whether the Defendant law firm knew or should have known of the alleged sexual harassment. In reaching this determination you should consider the following:

(1) Whether Plaintiff or any other individual reported or complained of the alleged sexually harassing conduct to the employer, its agent or supervisor,

(2) Whether the employer, its agent, or supervisor observed or was in a position to observe the conduct; or

(3) Whether the employer, its agent or supervisor was or should have been otherwise alerted to the conduct (for example, the conduct was discussed in the presence of such supervisory individual);

(4) Did the employer have a published firm policy against sexual harassment in the workplace;

(5) Did the employer have an established published procedure for receiving, handling and investigating complaints of sexual harassment;

(6) Did the employer conduct an investigation of any complaints of sexual harassment;

(7) Did the employer take any steps to remedy the alleged conduct without adversely affecting the Plaintiff's employment conditions; and, if so, was the harassment remedied.

(8) Did the employer take any adverse action against the alleged harasser.

EEOC Compliance Manual Section 615.4(a)(8)

PLAINTIFF'S REQUESTED INSTRUCTION NO. _____

CONSTRUCTIVE DISCHARGE

Where an employee's working conditions become so intolerable due to actions of the employer or due to harassment by a supervisor and/or co-worker which actions the employer knew of or should have known of, and as a result the employee resigns her employment, the resignation is to be considered a "constructive discharge". A constructive discharge is treated the same as if the employer had terminated the employee's employment. In determining whether a resignation is truly involuntary you should determine whether a reasonable woman in the employee's position would have felt compelled to resign.

<u>Beye v. Bureau of National Affairs, Inc.</u>, 59 Md. App. 642 (1984).

PLAINTIFF'S REQUESTED INSTRUCTION NO. _____

BURDEN TO PROVE DAMAGES ON PLAINTIFF

If you decide for the Plaintiff, then you must consider the damages to which the Plaintiff is entitled. The burden is upon the Plaintiff to prove by a preponderance of the evidence each item of damage that she claims was caused by the Defendants. In considering damages, you must keep in mind that your award must be in accord with the evidence presented in court, and must adequately and fairly compensate that Plaintiff but your award should not be based on guesswork.

For each claim which Defendants are liable, Plaintiff is entitled to recover an amount which will reasonably compensate her for the loss and damage she has suffered as a result of Defendants' unlawful conduct.

PLAINTIFF'S REQUESTED INSTRUCTION NO. _____

BACK PAY AND BENEFITS

If you find that the Defendants are liable for the sexual harassment of the Plaintiff and that the sexual harassment proximately caused her termination of employment, you should award the Plaintiff such amount of money as will reasonably compensate her for the damages resulting from Defendants' sexual harassment and termination of her employment. Plaintiff would be entitled to the back pay that she would have received if Defendants had not sexually harassed Plaintiff and terminated her employment. This amount would consist of the wages and employee benefits Plaintiff would have received from the date of Defendant's termination of Plaintiff to the date of trial. From this amount, you should subtract the total amount Plaintiff has earned during the same period, in wages, earnings or other income and benefits.

3 FJPI Section 104.06

PLAINTIFF'S REQUESTED INSTRUCTION NO. _____

FRONT PAY

If you find that Defendants are liable to Plaintiff for sexual harassment you may also award Plaintiff front pay. Front pay is an award of future lost earnings to make the Plaintiff whole. Front pay is an appropriate award of damages where reinstatement is not feasible because of hositility toward the Plaintiff making a productive and amicable work relationship impossible.

I instruct you that if you find Defendants liable, I have determined that reinstatement is not feasible given the degree of mutual trust and confidence that the nature of a law practice requires.

In determining the period of time for which Plaintiff should be entitled to front pay you should consider such factors as the Plaintiff's skills, the job market, and the nature of the position involved.

Front pay should be calculated in the same manner as backpay. To calculate front pay you should determine the present value of lost earnings that are likely to occur between the date of the trial and the time the Plaintiff should be able to earn the same salary she would be earning at Eager, Angst & Maloney, but for the unlawful discriminatory conduct.

Cassino v. Reichhold Chems., 817 F.2d 1338 (9th Cir. 1987), cert. denied 484 U.S. _______, 47 FEP 1776 (1988).

Brooks v. Woodline Motor Freight, 852 F.2d 1061 (8th Cir. 1988).

Reeder-Baker v. Lincoln Nat'l Corp., 649 F.Supp. 647 (N.D. Inc. 1986).

Snow v. Pillsbury Co., 650 F.Supp. 299 (D. Minn. 1986).

Thompson v. Sawyer, 678 F.2d 257 (D.C. Cir. 1982).

Patterson v. American Tobacco Co., 535 F.2d 257 (4th Cir.) cert. denied 429 U.S. 920 (1976).

PLAINTIFF'S REQUESTED INSTRUCTION NO. _____

PLAINTIFF'S DUTY TO MITIGATE DAMAGES

When an employee is discharged from his or her employment, that employee is under a duty to exercise reasonable diligence in seeking other employment in the same or similar business. What constitutes reasonable diligence is a question of fact depending upon the circumstances of each particular case.

The manner in which a person of ordinary diligence would presumably act under similar circumstances is the standard by which you, the jury, should follow in determining whether this duty was properly performed by the Plaintiff.

The Plaintiff was required to try to diminish any losses resulting from the alleged discharge by making such efforts to secure employment as an average person would make at that particular time and place. The burden of establishing Plaintiff's failure to mitigate damages rests with the Defendants.

PLAINTIFF'S REQUESTED INSTRUCTION NO. _____

COMPENSATORY DAMAGES

Furthermore, in determining damages, you should consider any expenses, mental pain and suffering, fright, nervousness, indignity, humiliation, embarrassment and insult to which the Plaintiff is found by you to have been subjected and which was a direct result of the Defendants' conduct as it relates to the issue of sexual harassment and termination of employment.

PLAINTIFF'S REQUESTED INSTRUCTION NO. ______

PUNITIVE DAMAGES

If you find that Defendants sexually harassed Plaintiff, and that Defendants' actions were willful, and were wantonly, or maliciously done, then you may add to the actual amount of damages such amount of punitive damages as you shall agree is proper. The purpose of such punitive damages is not to compensate Plaintiff, but rather to punish the Defendants, and to deter the Defendants and others from committing such acts in the future.

An act is willfully done if done voluntarily and intentionally and with the specific intent to commit such an act.

An act is wantonly done if done in a reckless disregard of, or indifference to, the rights of the injured party.

An act is maliciously done, if prompted or accompanied by ill-will or such gross indifference to the rights of others as to amount to a willful act done intentionally without just cause or excuse.

3 FJPI Section 86.09

PLAINTIFF'S REQUESTED INSTRUCTION NO. _____

PUNITIVE DAMAGES - FACTORS AFFECTING AMOUNT

In arriving at any award of punitive damages, you are to consider the following:

(1) the reprehensibility of the conduct of the Defendant;

(2) the amount of punitive damages which will have a deterrent effect on the Defendant in the light of Defendant's financial condition;

(3) that the punitive damages must bear a reasonable relation to the actual damages.

However, there is no exact rule by which to determine the amount of punitive damages. You may fix such amounts as in the exercise of your sound judgment and discretion you find will serve to punish the Defendant and to deter others from similar acts.

PLAINTIFF'S REQUESTED INSTRUCTION NO. _____

LIMITATION OF AMOUNT OF PUNITIVE AND COMPENSATORY DAMAGES

The total amount of compensatory and punitive damages that you may award Plaintiff for sexual harassment may be equal to, but may not exceed $200,000.* However, you may award Plaintiff the full amount of her past pecuniary losses, such as medical bills, and these amounts are not to be included in the $200,000 maximum compensatory/punitive damage figure.

*[This is based on assumption that the law firm employed more than 200 but less than 501 employees in each of 20 or more calendar weeks in the current or preceding calendar year.]

Sec. 102, Civil Rights Act of 1991

DEFENDANT'S JURY INSTRUCTIONS

Lisa P. Sullivan
Graham & James
One Maritime Plaza, Suite 300
San Francisco, California 94111
415/954-0385

GRAHAM & JAMES
LISA P. SULLIVAN
One Maritime Plaza, Suite 300
San Francisco, California 94111
Telephone: (415) 954-0200

Attorneys for Defendant
XYZ LAW FIRM

SUPERIOR COURT OF THE STATE OF JUSTICE

COUNTY OF JUSTICE

MARY SMITH, Plaintiff, v. XYZ LAW FIRM, and JOHN DOE, Defendants.	Case No. ABCD 1234 DEFENDANT'S REQUESTED JURY INSTRUCTIONS AND REQUESTS TO THE COURT WITH REFERENCE THERETO

Defendant XYZ Law Firm respectfully requests that the Court:

(1) Give the attached supplemental and special instructions as are identified below and attached hereto and which may be required by developments in the evidence hereinafter presented.

(2) Please advise counsel, pursuant to Rule XX of the State of Justice Code of Civil Procedure (Federal Code of Civil Procedure Rule 51), before the commencement of argument, of the

///

///

content and sequential order of all the instructions which are to be given the jury.

Dated: February 1, 1994

Respectfully submitted,

GRAHAM & JAMES

By______________________
Lisa P. Sullivan

Attorneys for Defendant
XYZ LAW FIRM

Graham & James
One Maritime Plaza
Third Floor
San Francisco
954-0200

PRELIMINARY
INSTRUCTION NO. _____

Duty of Jury

Ladies and gentlemen:

Now that you have been sworn, I will briefly tell you something about your duties as jurors and give you some instructions. At the end of the trial I will give you more detailed instructions, and those instructions will control your deliberations.

It will be your duty to decide from the evidence what the facts are. You, and you alone, are the judges of the facts. You will hear the evidence, decide what the facts are, and then apply those facts to the law which I will give to you. That is how you will reach your verdict. In doing so you must follow that law whether you agree with it or not.

You must not take anything I may say or do during the trial as indicating what your verdict should be. Don't be influenced by my taking notes at times. What I write down may have nothing to do with what you will be concerned with at this trial.

Authority: Manual of Model Jury Instructions for the Ninth Circuit (1985 ed.), 10.01.

GIVEN: __________

REFUSED: __________

MODIFIED: __________

...am & James
...Maritime Plaza
...hird Floor
...n Francisco
...954-0200

PRELIMINARY
INSTRUCTION NO. _____

Evidence

You will decide what the facts are from the evidence which will be presented. That evidence will consist of the testimony of witnesses, documents and other things received into evidence as exhibits and any facts on which the lawyers agree or which I may instruct you to accept.

Authority: Manual of Model Jury Instructions for the Ninth Circuit (1985 ed.), 10.02.

GIVEN: ___________

REFUSED: ___________

MODIFIED: ___________

Graham & James
One Maritime Plaza
Third Floor
San Francisco
954-0200

PRELIMINARY
INSTRUCTION NO. _____

What Is Not Evidence

The following things are not evidence and you must not consider them as evidence in deciding the facts of this case:

1. Statements and arguments of the attorneys.
2. Questions and objections of the attorneys.
3. Testimony that I instruct you to disregard.
4. Anything you may have seen or heard when the court is not in session even if what you see or hear is done or said by one of the parties or by one of the witnesses.

Authority: Manual of Model Jury Instructions for the Ninth Circuit (1985 ed.), 10.03.

GIVEN: __________

REFUSED: __________

MODIFIED: __________

...am & James
Maritime Plaza
Third Floor
...an Francisco
954-0200

PRELIMINARY
INSTRUCTION NO. ______

Direct and Circumstantial Evidence

There are two kinds of evidence: direct and circumstantial. Direct evidence is testimony by a witness about what that witness personally saw or heard or did. Circumstantial evidence is indirect evidence, that is, it is proof of one or more facts from which one can find another fact.

You may consider both direct and circumstantial evidence in deciding this case. The law permits you to give equal weight to both, but it is for you to decide how much weight to give to any evidence.

Authority: Manual of Model Jury Instructions for the Ninth Circuit (1985 ed.), 10.04.

GIVEN: ____________

REFUSED: ____________

MODIFIED: ____________

Graham & James
One Maritime Plaza
Third Floor
San Francisco
954-0200

PRELIMINARY
INSTRUCTION NO. _____

Evidence for Limited Purpose

Some evidence is admitted for a limited purpose only. When I instruct you that an item of evidence has been admitted for a limited purpose, you must consider it only for that limited purpose and for no other.

Authority: Manual of Model Jury Instructions for the Ninth Circuit (1985 ed.), 10.06.

GIVEN: ___________

REFUSED: ___________

MODIFIED: ___________

ıam & James
Maritime Plaza
Third Floor
an Francisco
954-0200

PRELIMINARY
INSTRUCTION NO. _____

Rulings on Objections

There are rules of evidence which control what can be received into evidence. When a lawyer asks a question or offers an exhibit into evidence and a lawyer on the other side thinks that it is not permitted by the rules of evidence, that lawyer may object. If I overrule the objection, the question may be answered or the exhibit received. If I sustain the objection, the question cannot be answered and the exhibit cannot be received. Whenever I sustain an objection to a question, ignore the question and do not guess what the answer would have been.

Sometimes I may order that evidence be stricken from the record and that you disregard or ignore the evidence. That means that when you are deciding the case, you must not consider the evidence which I told you to disregard.

Authority: Manual of Model Jury Instructions for the Ninth Circuit (1985 ed.), 10.05.

GIVEN: __________

REFUSED: __________

MODIFIED: __________

Graham & James
One Maritime Plaza
Third Floor
San Francisco
954-0200

PRELIMINARY
INSTRUCTION NO. _____

Credibility of Witnesses

In deciding the facts of this case, you will have to decide which witnesses to believe and which witnesses not to believe. You may believe everything a witness says or only part of it or none of it.

In deciding what to believe, you may consider a number of factors, including the following: (1) the witness' ability to see or hear or know the things the witness testified to; (2) the quality of the witness' memory; (3) the witness' manner while testifying; (4) whether the witness had an interest in the outcome of the case or any motive, bias or prejudice; (5) whether the witness was contradicted by anything the witness said or wrote before trial or by other evidence; and (6) how reasonable was the witness' testimony when considered in the light of other evidence which you believe.

Authority: Manual of Model Jury Instructions for the Ninth Circuit (1985 ed.), 10.07.

GIVEN: __________

REFUSED: __________

MODIFIED: __________

ham & James
e Maritime Plaza
Third Floor
San Francisco
954-0200

PRELIMINARY
INSTRUCTION NO. _____

Credibility of Witnesses - Discrepancies in Testimony

You, as jurors, are the sole judges of the credibility of the witnesses and the weight their testimony deserves. You may be guided by the appearance and conduct of the witness, or by the manner in which the witness testifies, or by the character of the testimony given, or by evidence to the contrary of the testimony given.

You should carefully scrutinize all the testimony given, the circumstances under which each witness has testified, and every matter in evidence which tends to show whether a witness is worthy of belief. Consider each witness' intelligence, motive and state of mind, and demeanor or manner while on the stand. Consider the witness' ability to observe the matters as to which he has testified, and whether he impresses you as having an accurate recollection of these matters. Consider also any relation each witness may bear to either side of the case; the manner in which each witness might be affected by the verdict; and the extent to which, if at all, each witness is either supported or contradicted by other evidence in the case.

Inconsistencies or discrepancies in the testimony of a witness, or between the testimony of different witnesses, may or may not cause the jury to discredit such testimony. Two or more persons witnessing an incident or a transaction may see or hear it differently; and innocent misrecollection, like failure of recollection, is not an uncommon experience. In weighing the effect of a discrepancy, always consider whether it pertains to a

Graham & James
One Maritime Plaza
Third Floor
San Francisco
954-0200

matter of importance or an unimportant detail, and whether the discrepancy results from innocent error or intentional falsehood.

After making your own judgment, you will give the testimony of each witness such weight, if any, as you may think it deserves.

You may, in short, accept or reject the testimony of any witness in whole or in part.

Also, the weight of the evidence is not necessarily determined by the number of witnesses testifying to the existence or nonexistence of any fact. You may find that the testimony of a small number of witnesses as to any fact is more credible than the testimony of a larger number of witnesses to the contrary.

Authority: Manual of Model Jury Instructions for the Ninth Circuit (1985 ed.), 73.01.

GIVEN: __________

REFUSED: __________

MODIFIED: __________

ham & James
Maritime Plaza
Third Floor
San Francisco
954-0200

PRELIMINARY
INSTRUCTION NO. _____

Burden of Proof

This is a civil case. Mary Smith has the burden of proving the case by what is called the preponderance of the evidence. That means that Mary Smith has to produce evidence which, considered in the light of all the facts, leads you to believe that what she claims is more likely true than not. To put it differently, if you were to put Mary Smith's and XYZ Law Firm's evidence on opposite sides of the scales, Mary Smith would have to make the scales tip slightly on that side. If Mary Smith fails to meet this burden, the verdict must be for XYZ Law Firm.

Authority: Manual of Model Jury Instructions for the Ninth Circuit (1985 ed.), 10.08. [as modified]

GIVEN: __________

REFUSED: __________

MODIFIED: __________

Graham & James
One Maritime Plaza
Third Floor
San Francisco
954-0200

PRELIMINARY
INSTRUCTION NO. _____

<u>Multiple Defendants</u>

Although there are two defendants in this action, XYZ Law Firm and John Doe, it does not follow from that fact alone that if one is liable, both are liable. Each defendant is entitled to a fair consideration of its or his own defense, and is not to be prejudiced by the fact, if it should become a fact, that you find against the other. Unless otherwise stated, all instructions given you govern the case as to each defendant.

Authority: Manual of Model Jury Instructions for the Ninth Circuit (1985 ed.), 71.06.

GIVEN: ___________

REFUSED: ___________

MODIFIED: ___________

PRELIMINARY
INSTRUCTION NO. _____

Province of Court and Jury

After the evidence has been heard and arguments and instructions are concluded, you will retire to consider your verdict. You will determine the facts from all the testimony that you hear and the other evidence that is submitted. You are the sole and exclusive judges of the facts, and in that field neither I nor anyone else may invade your province.

On the other hand, and with equal emphasis, I instruct you that you are bound to accept the rules of law that I give you whether you agree with them or not.

The law of the United States permits the judge to comment on the evidence in the case during the trial or in instructing the jury. Such comments are only expressions of the judge's opinion as to the facts; and the jury may disregard them entirely, since the jurors are the sole judges of the facts.

Authority: Manual of Model Jury Instructions for the Ninth Circuit (1985 ed.), 70.06.

GIVEN: __________

REFUSED: __________

MODIFIED: __________

Graham & James
One Maritime Plaza
Third Floor
San Francisco
954-0200

PRELIMINARY
INSTRUCTION NO. _____

Conduct of the Jury

I will now say a few words about your conduct as jurors.

First, do not talk to each other about this case or about anyone who has anything to do with it until the end of the case when you go to the jury room to decide on your verdict.

Second, do not talk with anyone else about this case or about anyone who has anything to do with it until the trial has ended and you have been discharged as jurors. "Anyone else" includes members of your family and your friends. You may tell them that you are a juror in a case but do not tell them anything else about it until after you have been discharged by me.

Third, do not let anyone talk to you about the case or about anyone who has anything to do with it. If someone should try to talk to you, please report it to me immediately.

Fourth, do not read any news stories or articles or listen to any radio or television reports about the case or about anyone who has anything to do with it.

Fifth, do not do any research or make any investigation about the case on your own.

///
///
///
///
///
///
///

...am & James
Maritime Plaza
Third Floor
...an Francisco
954-0200

Sixth, do not make up your mind about what the verdict should be until after you have gone to the jury room to decide the case and you and your fellow jurors have discussed the evidence. Keep an open mind until then.

Authority: Manual of Model Jury Instructions for the Ninth Circuit (1985 ed.), 10.10.

GIVEN: ___________

REFUSED: ___________

MODIFIED: ___________

Graham & James
One Maritime Plaza
Third Floor
San Francisco
954-0200

PRELIMINARY
INSTRUCTION NO. _____

Outline of Trial

The trial will now begin. First, each side may make an opening statement. An opening statement is neither evidence nor argument; it is an outline of what that party intends to prove, offered to help you follow the evidence.

Next, the plaintiff will present witnesses and defendant may cross-examine them. Then defendant will present witnesses and plaintiff may cross-examine.

After that, the attorneys will make their closing arguments to summarize and interpret the evidence for you, and I will give you instructions on the law.

You will then retire to deliberate on the verdict.

Authority: Manual of Model Jury Instructions for the Ninth Circuit (1985 ed.), 10.13.

GIVEN: __________

REFUSED: __________

MODIFIED: __________

am & James
Maritime Plaza
Third Floor
an Francisco
954-0200

POST TRIAL
INSTRUCTION NO. ______

Duties of Jury to Find Facts and Follow Law

Members of the jury, now that you have heard all the evidence [and the arguments of the lawyers], it is my duty to instruct you on the law which applies to this case. These instructions will be in three parts: first, the instructions on general rules that define and control the jury's duties; second, the instructions that state the rules of law you must apply, i.e., what Mary Smith must prove to make the case; and third, some rules for your deliberations. A copy of these instructions will be available for you in the jury room to consult if you find it necessary.

It is your duty to find the facts from all the evidence in the case. To those facts you must apply the law as I give it to you. You must follow the law as I give it to you whether you agree with it or not. And you must not be influenced by any personal likes or dislikes, opinions, prejudices or sympathy. That means that you must decide the case solely on the evidence before you and according to the law. You will recall that you took an oath promising to do so at the beginning of the case.

In following my instructions, you must follow all of them and not single out some and ignore others; they are all equally important. And you must not read into these instructions

///

///

///

///

Graham & James
One Maritime Plaza
Third Floor
San Francisco
954-0200

or into anything I may have said or done any suggestion as to what verdict you should return - that is a matter entirely for you to decide.

Authority: Manual of Model Jury Instructions for the Ninth Circuit (1985 ed.), 12.01.

GIVEN: __________

REFUSED: __________

MODIFIED: __________

am & James
Maritime Plaza
hird Floor
n Francisco
954-0200

POST TRIAL
INSTRUCTION NO. _____

Burden of Proof

At the beginning of the case, I told you that plaintiff has the burden of proving the case by a preponderance of the evidence. That means that Mary Smith has to produce evidence which, considered in the light of all the facts, leads you to believe that what Mary Smith claims is more likely true than not. To put it differently, if you were to put Mary Smith's and XYZ Law Firm's evidence on opposite sides of the scales, Mary Smith would have to make the scales tip slightly on that side. If Mary Smith fails to meet this burden, the verdict must be for XYZ Law Firm.

Authority: Manual of Model Jury Instructions for the Ninth Circuit (1985 ed.), 12.02. [as modified]

GIVEN: __________

REFUSED: __________

MODIFIED: __________

Graham & James
One Maritime Plaza
Third Floor
San Francisco
954-0200

POST TRIAL
INSTRUCTION NO. _____

Opinion Evidence, Expert Witness

You have heard testimony from persons described as experts. Persons who, by education and experience, have become expert in some field may state their opinion on matters in that field and may also state their reasons for the opinion.

Expert opinion testimony should be judged just as any other testimony. You may accept it or reject it, and give it as much weight as you think it deserves, considering the witness' education and experience, the reasons given for the opinion, and all the other evidence in the case.

Authority: Manual of Model Jury Instructions for the Ninth Circuit (1985 ed.), 12.07.

GIVEN: ___________

REFUSED: ___________

MODIFIED: ___________

am & James
Maritime Plaza
Third Floor
an Francisco
954-0200

POST TRIAL
INSTRUCTION NO. ______

Nature of Plaintiff's Claims - Sexual Discrimination and Harassment

In this case, Mary Smith claims that she has experienced two different types of sexual discrimination. First, she claims that she was fired because of her sex. Second, she claims she has experienced sexual harassment in her employment.

Because different things must be proved to establish these different claims, I will first instruct you on what Mary Smith needs to prove in order to prevail on her claim for sexual discrimination in employment. I will then provide instructions on the elements Mary Smith must show to establish a claim for sexual harassment.

Authority: Meritor Savings Bank, FSB v. Vinson, 477 U.S. 57, 64-65 (1986).

GIVEN: ____________

REFUSED: ____________

MODIFIED: ____________

Graham & James
One Maritime Plaza
Third Floor
San Francisco
954-0200

POST TRIAL
INSTRUCTION NO. _____

<u>Burden of Proof in Claims of Sexual Discrimination in Employment</u>

The law does not require an employer to justify a decision to discharge an employee. Rather, it is Mary Smith who must show that XYZ Law Firm fired her because of her sex. In order for Mary Smith to prevail on her claim, she must prove by a preponderance of the evidence all of the following:

(1) That she belongs in a protected class;

(2) That her job performance was satisfactory;

(3) That she was discharged; and

(4) That similarly-situated men were retained.

If Mary Smith proves all these things, XYZ Law Firm may nonetheless show that it had a reason other than sex for its actions.

If XYZ Law Firm shows that Mary Smith was fired for a reason other than sex, Mary Smith may still show that this reason was only a pretext for sex discrimination.

///
///
///
///
///
///
///
///
///

In order to find for Mary Smith on her claim for sexual discrimination, you must find that she has proved by a preponderance of the evidence that XYZ Law Firm was motivated by an intent to discriminate and fired her because of her sex.

Authority: <u>St. Mary's Honor Center v. Hicks</u>, 113 S.Ct. 2742, 2747-8 (1993); <u>McDonnell Douglas Corp. v. Green</u>, 411 U.S. 792, 802 (1973); <u>Texas Dept. of Community Affairs v. Burdine</u>, 450 U.S. 248, 252-53 (1981); <u>Levy v. Regents Univ. of Cal.</u>, 199 Cal.App.3d 1334, 1343, 245 Cal.Rptr. 576, 581 (1988), <u>cert</u>. <u>denied</u> 102 L.Ed.2d 221, 109 S.Ct. 231 (1988).

GIVEN: ____________

REFUSED: ____________

MODIFIED: ____________

Graham & James
One Maritime Plaza
Third Floor
San Francisco
954-0200

POST TRIAL
INSTRUCTION NO. _____

Sexual Discrimination in Employment - Pretext

In order to prove that XYZ Law Firm's stated reasons for her discharge are pretextual, Mary Smith must show by a preponderance of evidence that the decision-maker responsible for firing her acted with a discriminatory purpose.

The relevant inquiry is into the decision-maker's motivation. To prevail, Mary Smith must show that this individual decided to fire her because of her sex.

Authority: DeHorney v. Bank of America National Trust & Savings Assoc., 879 F.2d 459, 467-68 (9th Cir. 1989); La Montagne American Convenience Products, Inc., 750 F.2d 1405, 1412 (7th Cir. 1984).

GIVEN: ____________

REFUSED: ____________

MODIFIED: ____________

am & James
Maritime Plaza
Third Floor
an Francisco
954-0200

POST TRIAL
INSTRUCTION NO. _____

<u>Sexual Harassment Claim</u>

Mary Smith also claims that she has been sexually harassed in her employment with XYZ Law Firm, and by a partner, John Doe. To prevail on this claim, Mary Smith must prove by a preponderance of the evidence that she was sexually harassed by John Doe and that both defendants are liable for such harassment. Under certain circumstances, XYZ Law Firm can be held liable for harassment perpetrated by John Doe in his capacity as a co-worker.

I will first instruct you on the elements Mary Smith needs to prove in order to establish that she was sexually harassed. I will then instruct you on the requirements for holding the firm liable for John Doe's actions.

Authority: <u>Meritor Savings Bank v. Vinson</u>, 477 U.S. 57, (1968).

GIVEN: __________

REFUSED: __________

MODIFIED: __________

Graham & James
One Maritime Plaza
Third Floor
San Francisco
954-0200

POST TRIAL
INSTRUCTION NO. _____

Sexual Harassment Elements

To establish that there was sexual harassment, Mary Smith must prove by a preponderance of the evidence all of the following elements:

(1) That she was directly subjected to or personally witnessed unwelcome verbal or physical conduct of a sexual nature;

(2) That she indicated that such conduct was unwelcome; and

(3) That such conduct was pervasive and destructive to such a degree that it changed the conditions of her employment and created an abusive work environment.

In evaluating whether the harassing conduct was severe enough to create an abusive work environment, you are to consider whether a reasonable woman viewing the conduct objectively would find it to be so. Sexual innuendo or vulgar language that is trivial or only annoying is not enough to establish sexual harassment; instead, the plaintiff must show a concerted pattern of harassment of a repeated or routine nature which unreasonably interfered with plaintiff's work performance or created a work environment a reasonable woman would find abusive. In applying this standard, you should also consider all the circumstances under which the conduct took place, including the nature of the unwelcome acts (i.e., whether they included physical touching or only verbal remarks), how often there were offensive encounters, the total number of days over which all of the offensive conduct occurred, the situations in which the sexually-harassing conduct

ıam & James
Maritime Plaza
Third Floor
ıan Francisco
954-0200

occurred, and whether the plaintiff actually was adversely affected by the conduct. Additionally, you should consider whether a reasonable woman would find the conduct to be of a sexual nature.

If you find that a reasonable woman's work environment would not be substantially affected by the conduct, or that the conduct was not sexual in nature, then Mary Smith has failed to prove that she was sexually harassed.

Authority: *Meritor Savings Bank v. Vinson*, 477 U.S. 57, 67-68 (1986); *Jordan v. Clark*, 847 F.2d 1368, 1373 (9th Cir. 1988), *cert. denied*, 109 S.Ct. 186 (1989). *Brooms v. Regal Tube Co.*, (7th Cir. 1989); *Rabidue v. Osceola Refining Co.*, 805 F.2d 611, 620 (6th Cir. 1986), *cert. denied* 107 S.Ct. 1983 (1987); *Ellison v. Brady*, 924 F.2d 872, 879 (9th Cir. 1991).

GIVEN: __________

REFUSED: __________

MODIFIED: __________

Graham & James
One Maritime Plaza
Third Floor
San Francisco
954-0200

POST TRIAL
INSTRUCTION NO. _____

<u>XYZ Law Firm's Liability for Sexual Harassment by John Doe</u>

Even if you find that Mary Smith provided evidence of sexual harassment by John Doe which was sufficiently pervasive or severe to create an abusive work environment, in order to prevail on this claim against XYZ Law Firm, Mary Smith must also prove that XYZ Law Firm knew or should have known of the harassment, and failed to take prompt corrective measures.

Authority: <u>Rabidue v. Osceola Ref. Co.</u>, 805 F.2d 611, 621 (1986); <u>Katz v. Dole</u>, 709 F.2d 251 (1983).

GIVEN: ___________

REFUSED: ___________

MODIFIED: ___________

ham & James
Maritime Plaza
Third Floor
an Francisco
954-0200

POST TRIAL
INSTRUCTION NO. _____

Damages - Sexual Discrimination or Harassment

If you find XYZ Law Firm discriminated against Mary Smith because of her sex, you may give to Mary Smith such damages as you find were caused her by such discrimination. Such damages may include:

(1) The value of plaintiff's loss of compensation and benefits, if any;

(2) The emotional distress, if any, suffered by plaintiff; and

(3) Punitive damages

Authority: Civil Rights Act of 1991

GIVEN: ___________

REFUSED: ___________

MODIFIED: ___________

Graham & James
One Maritime Plaza
Third Floor
San Francisco
954-0200

POST TRIAL
INSTRUCTION NO. _____

<u>Punitive Damages - Sexual Harassment</u>

If you should find that XYZ Law Firm is liable for Mary Smith's injuries, then you have the discretion to award, in addition to compensatory damages, punitive damages. You may award punitive damages if Mary Smith proves that the firm's conduct was wanton and reckless, not merely unreasonable. An act is wanton and reckless if it is done in such a manner, and under such circumstances, as to reflect utter disregard for the potential consequences of the act on the safety and rights of others. The purposes of punitive damages is to punish a defendant for shocking conduct and to set an example in order to deter him and others from committing similar acts in the future. Punitive damages are intended to protect the community and to be an expression of the jury's indignation at the misconduct.

The awarding of punitive damages is within your discretion - you are not required to award them. Punitive damages are appropriate only for especially shocking and offensive misconduct. If you decide to award punitive damages, you must use sound reason in setting the amount - it must not reflect bias, prejudice, or sympathy toward any party. The amount can be no more than is necessary to fulfill the purpose of punitive damages, and in no event can exceed $100,000. In this regard, you may

///

///

///

///

consider the financial resources of XYZ Law Firm in fixing the amount of punitive damages.

Authority: United States Supreme Court: <u>City of Newport v. Fact Concerts, Inc.</u>, 453 U.S. 247, 266-67, 101 S.Ct. 2748, 69 L.Ed.2d 616 (1981). Civil Rights Act of 1991.

GIVEN: ____________

REFUSED: ____________

MODIFIED: ____________

Graham & James
One Maritime Plaza
Third Floor
San Francisco
954-0200

POST TRIAL
INSTRUCTION NO. _____

Mitigation of Back Pay Damages

The law requires Mary Smith to take reasonable steps to minimize the damage she suffers, or have her award of damages cut down if she does not.

XYZ Law Firm has the burden of showing that Mary Smith did not make reasonable efforts to seek other employment and that there was a chance she might have found comparable employment if she had done so.

If you find that Mary Smith did not make reasonable efforts to seek comparable employment, then the amount she might have earned must be deducted from any damages awarded to plaintiff.

If you find that the evidence shows a willful loss of earnings, you may not award back pay. Examples of willful conduct include failure to remain in the labor market, refusal to accept substantially similar employment, failure to diligently search for alternative work, or voluntarily quitting alternative employment without good reason.

Authority: Sangster v. United Air Lines, 633 F.2d 864, 867-68 (9th Cir. 1980), cert. denied, 451 U.S. 971 (1981).

GIVEN: __________

REFUSED: __________

MODIFIED: __________

ham & James
e Maritime Plaza
Third Floor
San Francisco
954-0200

POST TRIAL
INSTRUCTION NO. _____

Intentional Infliction of Emotional Distress

Mary Smith's second theory of recovery is against defendants John Doe and the firm for intentional infliction of emotional distress. Mary Smith is entitled to recover damages for severe emotional distress if a cause of such emotional distress was the outrageous unprivileged conduct of the defendants done either with the intent to cause emotional distress or with reckless disregard of the probability of causing such emotional distress.

The elements of a cause of action for intentional infliction of severe emotional distress are:

1. The defendants engaged in outrageous, unprivileged conduct;

2. With the intent to cause, or with reckless disregard of the probability of causing, emotional distress;

3. The plaintiff suffered severe emotional distress; and

4. Such outrageous, unprivileged conduct of the defendants was a cause of the emotional distress suffered by the plaintiff.

Authority:

GIVEN: __________

REFUSED: __________

MODIFIED: __________

Graham & James
One Maritime Plaza
Third Floor
San Francisco
954-0200

POST TRIAL
INSTRUCTION NO. _____

Emotional Distress - Defined

The term "emotional distress" means mental distress, mental suffering or mental anguish. It includes all highly unpleasant mental reactions, such as fright, horror, grief, shame, humiliation, embarrassment, anger, chagrin, disappointment and worry.

Authority:

GIVEN: __________

REFUSED: __________

MODIFIED: __________

ham & James
e Maritime Plaza
Third Floor
San Francisco
954-0200

POST TRIAL
INSTRUCTION NO. ______

Severe - Defined

The word "severe," in the phrase "severe emotional distress," means substantial or enduring as distinguished from trivial or transitory. Severe emotional distress is emotional distress of such substantial quantity or enduring quality that no reasonable person in a civilized society should be expected to endure it.

In determining the severity of emotional distress you should consider its intensity and duration.

Authority:

GIVEN: ____________

REFUSED: ____________

MODIFIED: ____________

Graham & James
One Maritime Plaza
Third Floor
San Francisco
954-0200

POST TRIAL
INSTRUCTION NO. _____

Extreme and Outrageous Conduct - Defined

Extreme and outrageous conduct is conduct which goes beyond all possible bounds of decency so as to be regarded as atrocious and utterly intolerable in a civilized community.

Extreme and outrageous conduct is not mere insults, indignities, threats, annoyances, petty oppressions or other trivialities. All persons must necessarily be expected and required to be hardened to a certain amount of rough language and to occasional acts that are definitely inconsiderate and unkind.

Extreme and outrageous conduct, however, is conduct which would cause an average member of the community to immediately react in outrage.

Authority:

GIVEN: ___________

REFUSED: ___________

MODIFIED: ___________

aham & James
e Maritime Plaza
Third Floor
San Francisco
954-0200

POST TRIAL
INSTRUCTION NO. ______

<u>Intentional and Reckless - Defined</u>

A defendant intended to inflict emotional distress if it is established that he or she desired to cause such distress or knew that such distress was substantially certain to result from his or her conduct.

A defendant's conduct is in reckless disregard of the probability of causing emotional distress if he or she has knowledge of a high degree of probability that emotional distress will result and acts with deliberate disregard of that probability or with a wanton disregard of the probable results.

Authority:

GIVEN: ____________

REFUSED: ____________

MODIFIED: ____________

Graham & James
One Maritime Plaza
Third Floor
San Francisco
954-0200

POST TRIAL
INSTRUCTION NO. _____

Intentional or Negligent

If conduct is negligent, it is not willful; if it is willful, it is not negligent. You may not find that defendants both intentionally and negligently caused emotional distress. If you find that defendants negligently caused severe emotional distress, you cannot find that defendants intentionally caused emotional distress.

Authority: [G.D. Searle & Co. v. Superior Court, 49 Cal.App.3d 22, 122 Cal.Rptr. 218 (1975).]

GIVEN: __________

REFUSED: __________

MODIFIED: __________

…ham & James
…e Maritime Plaza
Third Floor
San Francisco
954-0200

POST TRIAL
INSTRUCTION NO. _____

<u>Negligent Infliction of Emotional Distress</u>

Mary Smith's third theory of recovery is against defendants John Doe and the firm for negligent infliction of emotional distress. Smith is entitled to recover damages for severe emotional distress if a cause of such serious emotional distress was the negligent conduct of the defendants.

The elements of a cause of action for negligent infliction of severe emotional distress are:

1. The defendants engaged in negligent conduct.
2. The plaintiff suffered severe emotional distress.
3. Such negligent conduct of the defendants was a cause of the severe emotional distress suffered by the plaintiff.

Authority: [BAJI 12.80]

GIVEN: __________

REFUSED: __________

MODIFIED: __________

Graham & James
One Maritime Plaza
Third Floor
San Francisco
954-0200

POST TRIAL
INSTRUCTION NO. _____

Damages - Negligent Infliction of Emotional Distress

If you find that Mary Smith has proven by a preponderance of the evidence that defendants acted negligently and caused her to suffer severe emotional distress, then you must decide the amount of money damages necessary to reasonably compensate her. In making any award of money damages for negligent infliction of emotional distress, you may not award punitive damages.

Authority: [BAJI 12.80 (as modified)]

GIVEN: ___________

REFUSED: ___________

MODIFIED: ___________

ham & James
e Maritime Plaza
Third Floor
San Francisco
954-0200

POST TRIAL
INSTRUCTION NO. _____

Damages - Intentional Infliction of Emotional Distress

If you find Mary Smith has proven that the actions of the defendants were "extreme and outrageous" and were done for the purpose of inflicting severe emotional distress on her, then you must decide the amount of money damages necessary to reasonably compensate her for the emotional harm she suffered. In so doing, you must determine whether she actually suffered the emotional harm and whether it was caused by the actions of defendants, as opposed to a prior experience or pre-existing mental condition. In making any award of money damages for intentional infliction of emotional distress, you must exercise your authority with calm and reasonable judgment, and the damages, if any, which you fix are to be just and reasonable in light of the evidence concerning the nature of the act committed and the extent of the injury which that action caused.

Authority: [BAJI 12.88 (as modified)]

GIVEN: __________

REFUSED: __________

MODIFIED: __________

Graham & James
One Maritime Plaza
Third Floor
San Francisco
954-0200

POST TRIAL
INSTRUCTION NO. _____

Speculative Damages Not Permitted

Damages must be reasonable. If you should find that the plaintiff is entitled to a verdict, you may award her only such damages as will reasonably compensate her for such injury and damage as you find, from a preponderance of the evidence in the case, that she has sustained as a proximate result of the accident.

You are not permitted to award speculative damages. So, you are not to include in any verdict compensation for any prospective loss which, although possible, is not reasonably certain to occur in the future.

Authority: Manual of Model Jury Instructions for the Ninth Circuit (1985 ed.) 85.14.

GIVEN: __________

REFUSED: __________

MODIFIED: __________

...ham & James
...e Maritime Plaza
Third Floor
San Francisco
954-0200

POST TRIAL
INSTRUCTION NO. _____

No Double Recovery

The general theory of damages bars double recovery for the same wrong. Only one complete satisfaction is permissible.

Authority:

GIVEN: ____________

REFUSED: ____________

MODIFIED: ____________

Graham & James
One Maritime Plaza
Third Floor
San Francisco
954-0200

POST TRIAL
INSTRUCTION NO. _____

Instructions on Damages Not Indicative of Court's View of the Merits

The fact that I have instructed you as to the proper measure of damages should not be considered as intimating any view of mine as to which party is entitled to your verdict in this case. Instructions as to the measure of damages are given in the interest of completeness and for your guidance in the event you should find in favor of Mary Smith from a preponderance of the evidence in the case in accordance with the other instructions.

Authority: 2 Fed. Jury Prac. and Instruc., 3 Ed. No. 74.02.

GIVEN: ___________

REFUSED: ___________

MODIFIED: ___________

ham & James
Maritime Plaza
Third Floor
San Francisco
954-0200

POST TRIAL
INSTRUCTION NO. ______

Entity Not to Be Prejudiced as Such

The fact that a law firm is a party must not prejudice you in your deliberations or in your verdict.

You may not discriminate between a business and natural individuals. Each is a person in the eyes of the law. Each is entitled to the same fair and impartial consideration and to justice by the same legal standards.

Authority: [BAJI 1.03 (as modified)]

GIVEN: ____________

REFUSED: ____________

MODIFIED: ____________

Graham & James
One Maritime Plaza
Third Floor
San Francisco
954-0200

POST TRIAL
INSTRUCTION NO. _____

Chance or Quotient Verdict Prohibited

The law forbids you to determine any issue in this case by chance such as the flip of a coin, the drawing of lots or by any other chance determination. For example, if you determine that a party is entitled to recover, you must not arrive at the amount of damages to be awarded by agreeing in advance to determine an average and to make that your verdict, without further exercise of your independent consideration, judgment and decision.

Authority: [BAJI 15.33 (as modified)]

GIVEN: __________

REFUSED: __________

MODIFIED: __________

am & James
Maritime Plaza
Third Floor
an Francisco
954-0200

POST TRIAL
INSTRUCTION NO. _____

Reaching Agreement

Each of you must decide the case for yourself, but you should do so only after considering all the evidence, discussing it fully with the other jurors, and listening to the views of your fellow jurors.

Do not be afraid to change your opinion if you think you are wrong. But do not come to a decision simply because other jurors think it is right.

This case has taken a great deal of time and effort to prepare and try. There is no reason to think that it could be better tried or that another jury is better qualified to decide it. It is important therefore that you reach a verdict if you can do so conscientiously. Therefore, if it looks at some point as if you may have difficulty in reaching a unanimous verdict, and if the greater number of you are agreed on a verdict, the other jurors may want to ask themselves about the basis for their feelings when a substantial number have reached a different conclusion. You should not hesitate to reconsider your views from time to time and to change them if you are persuaded that this is appropriate.

///

///

///

///

///

///

Graham & James
One Maritime Plaza
Third Floor
San Francisco
954-0200

It is important that you attempt to return a verdict, but, of course, only if each of you can do so after having made his or her own conscientious determination. Do not surrender an honest conviction as to the weight and effect of the evidence simply to reach a verdict.

Authority: Manual of Model Jury Instructions for the Ninth Circuit (1985 ed.), 13.03.

GIVEN: ____________

REFUSED: ____________

MODIFIED: ____________

POST TRIAL
INSTRUCTION NO. _____

Communication with Court

If it becomes necessary during your deliberations to communicate with me, you may send a note through the marshal [or bailiff], signed by your foreperson or by one or more members of the jury. No member of the jury should ever attempt to communicate with me except by a signed writing; and I will communicate with any member of the jury on anything concerning the case only in writing, or orally here in open court. Remember that you are not to tell anyone - including me - how the jury stands, numerically or otherwise, until after you have reached a unanimous verdict or have been discharged.

Authority: Manual of Model Jury Instructions for the Ninth Circuit (1985 ed.), 13.05.

GIVEN: __________

REFUSED: __________

MODIFIED: __________

LISA P. SULLIVAN
Associate, San Francisco Office

AREA OF PRACTICE:	Employment Advice and Litigation
EDUCATION:	B.A., Georgetown University (1981) J.D., University of Santa Clara School of Law (1987)
ADMITTED:	California

Ms. Sullivan joined Graham & James in 1987. Ms. Sullivan specializes in representing clients in the areas of labor and employment law, including litigation, advice directed towards preventing wrongful termination and employment discrimination claims, drafting of employment contracts and personnel policies, termination letters and consulting agreements. Ms. Sullivan has represented clients in federal and state courts on wrongful termination lawsuits and employment discrimination claims.

Ms. Sullivan is a member of the American Bar Association, California State Bar Association, and the Bar Association of San Francisco, Labor and Litigation Sections.

Ms. Sullivan has spoken before employer and management groups on employment-related issues, most recently on "Employee Policies for Intellectual Property Protection" for Corporate Counsel Seminar Series; on "Emerging Personnel Practices in U.S.-Japan Ventures" for Intercultural Communication Specialists and NeoConcepts; and on "Women's Issues in Working with the Japanese" for the California State Bar. She most recently wrote "Representing the Individual Co-Defendant in Employment Cases" for the American Bar Association; "Defending the Alleged Sexual Harasser" for The Brief; and "Two Courts Adopt New Standard to Determine Sexual Harassment" for The National Law Journal.